THE RECONSTRUCTION OF THE REPUBLIC

Twofold thesis: p. 70

THE RECONSTRUCTION OF THE REPUBLIC

HAROLD O. J. BROWN

Mott Media, Inc., Publishers
Milford, MI 48042

Leonard George Goss, Editor   A.G. Smith, Designer

Manufactured in the United States of America

Library of Congress Cataloging in Publication Data

Brown, Harold O.J.   1933-
    The Reconstruction of the Republic

    Includes index.
    1. Christianity—United States. 2. Christianity and politics. I. Title
BR515.B76   209'.73   76-57954
ISBN 0-915134-86-1

Contents

Foreword

From time to time a book appears which promises a truly seminal influence on a generation. My prediction is that in time to come, Harold O. J. Brown's *The Reconstruction of the Republic* will be recognized as such a book. Written first against a backdrop of the celebration of the bicentennial of American independence, and now updated, it focuses upon the dual and often antithetical political traditions in the United States: one, broad, comprising the great bulk of the American people; the other, narrow, comprising a specialist intellectual elite.

Since its beginnings, the United States has been the latter-day embodiment of the values of the Christian West, the inner dynamism of which in the 17th and 18th centuries was still sufficient to civilize a wilderness.

The Western political tradition is wide and deep, encompassing thousands of years of human history. It draws its vitality from the profound insights of the Judeo-Christian Scriptures and from the accumulated experience of nations and eras from classical Greece to the present. The other tradition is an alien graft, embedded in our national history at a very early date, which now seeks to supplant the original rootstock.

It is commonly assumed that these two branches of our culture may be termed the right and the left. But these divisions are properly termed the conservative, because it sums up and seeks to preserve the authentic deposit of our cultural heritage in all of its transcendental and historical aspects, and the liberal, or preferably, rationalist. Rationalism derives from an 18th century movement that denies our spiritual origins and sets up man and human reason as the sole rule of a purely material universe. It is historically and semantically incorrect to describe these divisions as "the right" and "the left."

Politics is pre-eminently a rationalist science. Rationalists not only invented modern politics, they also invented the terms upon which politics is based. Through their eyes, politics is the instrument of choice for achieving the goal of all rationalists, namely, permanent and ongoing revolution. The terms right and left refer to a narrow spectrum of individuals who differ only on how far and how fast this revolution should proceed. Although commentators habitually refer to conservatives in the U.S. as "right wing," usually with the pejorative "ultra" or "extreme," they are making the mistake of using rationalist terminology to describe non-rationalists.

Until the early 1960s there existed in the U.S. a fairly stable consensus on the underlying values of our society. The foremost social institution was the family. Church or synagogue attendance and membership were, by the standards of any nation, extraordinarily high. The country had serious social problems, but resolving them did not seem beyond the powers of men of good will.

But it was at this point that a number of seismic shocks were administered to the body politic by a rationalist-dominated Supreme Court. Religious values were summarily barred from public schools when the Court decided that prayer and Bible reading were a violation of the First Amendment. After setting in motion the forces that would deny millions of American public school children the most perfunctory contact with the spiritual, moral and ethical foundations of their culture, the Court then delved deeper into the same First Amendment and found that it sanctioned broad new freedoms for pornographers to ply their trade, and an avalanche of obscenity and violence descended on the news stands and theaters of the United States.

The social results were predictable. One could only say, with the farmer in the Scriptures who saw his field bring forth a crop of weeds and tares, "An enemy hath done this." As the seventies further declined into a maelstrom of riots, inflation, political scandal, drug addiction, crime, perversion and abdication from responsibility, the Supreme Court accelerated the process of social dismemberment with its decrees that for all practical purposes legalized abortion on demand.

It was this violent break with our tradition of preserving human life that profoundly disturbed millions of hitherto complacent people who over the years had formed the habit of accepting as Divine Revelation the rationalist dicta of the Supreme Court. Many devout believers of all faiths found themselves unable to accept the moral relativism that made a disposable commodity of human life.

So it was with great uneasiness that this nation began to prepare to celebrate its bicentennial. To many it seemed that the country was setting out on its third century by severing its ties with religion, morality, and virtue. It was a time characterized not by confidence, but by apprehension and unease.

People were looking for guidance, but it was not forthcoming. The so-called main line churches had long since made their peace with ra-

4

tionalism and revolution. Thus it fell to a coalition of pro-family activists and evangelical churchmen to provide the leadership in the battle with the so-called "Liberal establishment" — the government, the media, the schools, the foundations — in order to preserve this country's transcendent spiritual and moral values.

The Reconstruction of the Republic was one of the blueprints on which the amazing turnabout in American politics in 1980 was based. Many Christians who had been diffident about their values and their identity, cowed by the secular humanism they saw enshrined on every side, began to see the necessity of participating in the political discourse. They filed out of the pews and into the polling places and on November 4, 1980, they made history.

It remains to be seen whether the republic will be reconstructed along the lines advocated by Dr. Brown, but Christian political activism is now a powerful force in American public life. The disfranchised Christians, of whom Dr. Brown writes with such conviction, have taken it upon themselves to let their light shine before men, and I for one welcome their illuminating presence.

Jesse Helms
U.S. Senate

Author's Preface to the Second Edition

Every author would like to be able to report that from the day it appeared, his book was an instant success. Unfortunately, when the *Reconstruction of the Republic* first appeared early in 1977, its success was "modest." Jimmy Carter had just assumed the presidency, and even then it was clear that he was not going to move the country or the government in the direction of biblical and spiritual values. There were no effective challenges to the "imperial judiciary" that gave us one-man, one-vote, bussing and abortion on demand.

But during Carter's presidency, much happened to shake Americans from their Watergate-induced political stupor. First the regime of the Shah of Iran collapsed, hardly a year after President Carter had hailed him as one of America's loyalest friends. The price of gasoline, already double that of 1973, was doubled again. The summer of 1979 was a dry one, as far as gasoline was concerned, with long lines, longer waits, odd-even day sales, and rapidly rising prices. But the greatest blow to American pride came in the take-over of the U.S. Embassy in Teheran by "student militants." For over a year this atrocity lasted, revealing the United States as vacillating, weak, and bumbling. Finally the Soviet Union invaded Afghanistan and our President, unable to take effective counter-measures against the Soviet government, contented himself with telling America's Olympic athletes to stay home from Moscow.

In 1979 a new force burst onto the political scene. Dubbed the "religious New Right," it united conservative Christians in opposition to what was finally perceived as a secularist destruction of virtually all of the

7

traditional values of American life. The Moral Majority, the Religious Round Table, and pro-family groups rallied evangelical Protestants, conservative Catholics and many others to a defense of the old values. Ridiculed at first, the religious Right came into its own in the 1980 elections. No longer an object of ridicule, it is now the target of opposition and criticism by people as diverse as George McGovern and Billy Graham. During the 1980 campaign and since it, I have often heard the themes of *The Reconstruction of the Republic* expounded from political platforms — sometimes by speakers who have read it, sometimes by those who probably have never heard of it. If its ideas were ahead of their time in 1976, they are up-to-date today.

America had reached a turning-point by 1976, when the first edition of *The Reconstruction* was written. I predicted that year that not much time remained to our nation to check our disastrous decline and to change our course. The years 1976–1980 were wasted as far as constructive change was concerned — but they did accomplish one vital thing — they persuaded the American people in record numbers that the nation was headed for disaster — and finally the people reacted.

As Jacques Ellul warns in *The Political Illusion,* people today have a tendency to crown political figures with religious glory and to look upon them as new Messiahs. It would be wrong to ape Christians of the past in proclaiming our new president, Ronald Reagan, as though he were a sort of new Messiah. Fortunately, Mr. Reagan seems very little inclined to messianic illusions. Perhaps as our oldest president he is too well experienced in the fickleness of fame and of worldly homage to be susceptible to the flattery and adulation that have turned the heads of many leaders of the past. Nevertheless, while it would be wrong to give Mr. Reagan — or any mortal — a quasi-religious "savior" title, it is only fair to recognize that he not merely symbolizes America's new mood of hopefulness, but has done more than any other individual to make it possible.

America still needs a reconstruction — more desperately than in 1976, when the need was already desperate enough. To achieve that goal, we still need to have our people understand the problems, the threats, the challenges, and the opportunities before us. It is to help create this understanding that this new edition of *The Reconstruction of the Republic* is sent forth. And it is to two of the men who have done more than any others in our time to bring such understanding within reach that this present volume is dedicated — to President Ronald W. Reagan and Senator Jesse Helms.

8

1

How Many Days?

And Jonah began to enter into the city a day's journey, and he cried, and said, Yet forty days, and Nineveh shall be overthrown.

Jonah 3:4

We do not know enough about the historical setting of Jonah's remarkable mission to know whether his message of imminent disaster came as a shock to the people of Nineveh, or whether they were already prepared for it as a result of a crisis situation in which they found themselves. Whether it came as a surprise or not, the reaction of the government and people was immediate — and effective. The king called for public repentance and fasting. And God spared the city — somewhat to the prophet's chagrin, according to the story, for he had apparently been looking forward to seeing his predictions of doom fulfilled.

It would take someone with a supernatural gift of prophecy to tell us the number of days or weeks or years that the American commonwealth can be expected to endure without, to borrow Jonah's expression, being overthrown. No one would want to give us only forty days. But it does not take a prophetic gift to see that, if present developments are prolonged, disaster on a national scale is inevitable.

Being able to predict judgment within forty days has a great advantage: the warning produces a prompt and decisive reaction. there was clearly no time to be lost. In consequence, king and people acted immediately, and the catastrophe Jonah had predicted was averted. But suppose he had predicted judgment not in forty days but in forty years? In a way, that would have been a greater prophetic accomplishment, for it is

9

clearly easier to see things shaping up for an imminent disaster than to read the future four decades hence. But forty years is a long time; much can happen, conditions change, new people come into power, and so on. If Jonah had predicted a forty-year margin before judgment overcame Nineveh, he and most of his hearers would have grown old or perhaps died before the time ran out. As the limit approached, those who remembered the prophet and his warning forty years earlier would probably have been few and isolated.

Unfortunately, in the United States, as we enter the last fifth of the twentieth century, there is no one with the authority of an Old Testament prophet to spell out for us the timetable of our national decline. There seems to be no imminent danger that it will be achieved within forty days. But is there any guarantee that the nation will last forty years? In the first fifteen years after World War II, from 1945 to 1960, the United States rose to a position of apparently unchallengeable preeminence in political, industrial, scientific, and economic power. Then followed the decade of the sixties, in which it appeared that we could allow ourselves the luxury of almost limitless disruption and division both internally and in the sphere of foreign policy without paying a significant price in our standard of living or way of life. In fact, it was not until 1971, with the first of a series of formal and informal devaluations of the United States dollar, that the bills for the sixties began to come due. Even so, the 1972 presidential election campaign was carried on—in contrast to the previous election of 1968—in an atmosphere of comparative tranquility and without any sense of urgency, and the same held true in 1976 and 1980.

Several things began to happen early in 1973; the second inauguration of Richard Nixon was followed, two days later, by the decision of the United States Supreme Court in *Roe* v. *Wade,* in effect legalizing abortion on demand—a move that might appear to have little bearing on our international and internal situation, unless we stop to think that as a result of *Roe* v. *Wade,* there are perhaps nine million fewer Americans alive today, in 1981, than there would have been without it.* The proto-

*Although the number of legal abortions performed in the United States from 1973 to 1981 appears closer to 10,000,000 than 9,000,000, we should bear in mind that abortion was already available virtually on demand in some jurisdictions, illegal abortions were widespread, and it is probable that birth control measures would be more carefully practiced if abortion were not easily available to take care of "mistakes." Nevertheless, it is undeniable that unrestricted abortion is having a very marked effect on the United States birth rate, and therefore, from a long-range perspective, on the nature of our population, the relative distribution of age groups, and on economic life in general. The long-range implications of the precipitate decline in live births for defense, education, industry, and social security in the years ahead are already making themselves felt.

cols providing for the withdrawal of American military forces from Vietnam did not seem, early in 1973, to mean that our efforts there had to be regarded as an ignominious failure. Before long, however, it became all too evident that that was the case: South Vietnam suffered its debacle in 1975, we failed to check the Soviet-Cuban action in Angola in 1976, we stood by—or perhaps even facilitated it—as the Shah of Iran was overthrown in the winter of 1978–79, suffered the second doubling of oil prices, the fearfully humiliating take-over of our embassy in Iran, and finally the Soviet invasion of Afghanistan, all before Christmas of 1979.

Although it has recovered a bit since the victory of Ronald Reagan, the U.S. dollar today is worth only about half, in terms of major foreign currencies, of what it was worth until 1971. It will buy about one-twelfth as much gold or oil as in 1971, and sometimes even less. The United States and the other wealthy, industrialized nations seem to have no recourse against constant, extortionate increases in oil prices. Many of the underdeveloped nations have been brought to the edge of bankruptcy by those same oil prices. Almost as though it had been planned in advance, some of the measures taken in the United States for the protection of the environment have done their bit to increase the cost of living and of doing business, to worsen our competitive position, and to add to the growing economic problems. We seem to be in the process of losing all rail passenger service, and major urban mass-transit systems, such as that of metropolitan Chicago, are in or facing catastrophic conditions. The continuing decline in the birth rate, only partly offset by immigration, legal and illegal, is going to make the United States a continent-sized old folks' home by the year 2000.

The disastrous collapse of our efforts in Indochina, whatever the reasons for it may be and whether or not we could have done anything to avert it, has spelled decline for our influence throughout Asia and indeed throughout the world. Richard Nixon seems to have sought to buy support for his ventures in Vietnam by ending the military draft, and in consequence, only a few years later, our military forces are showing signs of terrible inadequacies. The dismal failure of President Carter's attempted rescue of the U.S. hostages in Iran in 1980 may not have been a good example of the best that the United States can do today, but it was widely perceived as such around the world—particularly when contrasted with similarly daring, but thoroughly successful, attempts by Israelis, West Germans, and British. The only asset that we seem to have gained in the years since 1971 is a tenuous tacit alliance with Communist China. It is a sad commentary on America's decline to reflect that while in 1953, or even as late as 1968, the United States felt strong enough to stand up to both the Soviet Union and China together, we are now dependent on the hope of support by China in order to face down the Soviet Union.

Britain: A Precedent for America

In 1945, Great Britain, one of the three principal victors of World War II, enjoyed a tremendous triumph. Although it had paid a higher cost, proportionally speaking, in lives and treasure than the United States, it still stood at the head of a worldwide empire and had not suffered anything like the devastation and loss of life of the Soviet Union, or of Germany, its principal enemy. Yet within a few years the British Empire was in the process of rapid disintegration, and the industrial power that had done so much to crush Nazi Germany found itself lacking in energy to compete successfully in the postwar world. As early as the 1940s and early 1950s many predicted the impending eclipse of Britain as a great power, although to most this seemed unthinkable. It became increasingly unavoidable, particularly after the United States joined the Soviet Union in imposing on Britain and France a humiliating withdrawal from their Suez intervention of 1956. Yet somehow many of those who already saw, in the 1950s, what lay ahead for Britain find it hard to grasp that nation's low estate today.

In 1981, after the humiliating end of twenty years of American involvement in Vietnam, America is in some ways in a position similar to that of Britain thirty years earlier. Resources are still there, people are still there, the power base is still there. And yet somehow there seems to be a widespread opinion, even among patriotic Americans, that nothing will be done, that nothing can be done, even that nothing *ought* to be done, to prevent the continuation and acceleration of our national decline. Almost as in a dream, we debate the future of social security and the prospects for national health insurance when we ought to be asking whether we will long have an independent national existence or whether our social structure can survive for many years into the future.

Perhaps the situation that faces us today is something like that which faced Germany early in 1944. If we look at the situation objectively, we ought to recognize that to continue along the course we are now following will, in the long run, be disastrous. But because we have no long-range vision and no mechanism for changing course, we prefer not to think about it, and to go on trying to solve immediate problems without recognition of the fact that all our short-term improvements will

12

rapidly become meaningless in the light of the progressive deterioration of our total situation. Americans like to think of themselves as progressive and open to new ideas, but in fact our system of government is one of the most innately conservative in the world. It takes America a long time to become aware of problems, and still longer to react to them. We are very slow to come to grips even with the oil-energy problem; therefore it is not surprising that we are nearly oblivious to the much larger complex of problems of which energy is only one aspect. The victory of Ronald Reagan in November, 1980, seems to augur a change in the nation's spirit. But our problems are so great that no mere change of mood will resolve them. In fact, there is some danger that the new breath of optimism will blind us to their continuing seriousness.

Jonah gave the people of Nineveh forty days, and they reacted: the king ordered a nationwide change of attitude (repentance), and the people responded. Fortunately, the American people have more than forty days; in fact, four years have passed since the first edition of this book was published, and while our situation has not improved, except in spirit, it has not been dramatically worsened. But do we have forty years? Or even ten? Can we be certain that the United States, in independent, recognizable form, will still exist in 2021? Or even in 1991?

Perhaps it would be good if there were someone with the authority and conviction of an Old Testament prophet to tell us that if we do not change drastically, and at once, the course we are following, our nation will not survive the next forty years. Jerry Falwell and a few others have taken up this cry, but despite their successes, so far they have not won the hearing across America that Jonah won in Nineveh. And alongside of Jerry Falwell, at least some other Christian leaders, who ought to know better, are crying, "False alarm!"

On the other hand, perhaps it is just as well that no one, so far, has really succeeded in making us recognize the seriousness of our situation, for it is not at all clear that there is one simple solution, such as repentance for the people of Nineveh. As long as we do not have a clear vision of what our society is and of what it should be, getting frantic about our present situation and our probable future problems will not help us much. Panic is not the cure for anything. Our national situation is difficult, but disaster is not yet inevitable. In order to avoid it, we must do more than simply see it coming. We must have a vision of the alternative, and a plan for attaining it. It is to a recovery of national vision that this essay is dedicated.

Because its author is a convinced Christian, readers of the present work will not be surprised to find Christian answers proposed to present national problems. "But," some may object, "this is not a Christian nation. Only a minority of Americans are committed Christians. How can Christian proposals, even if they might work, be accepted by non-Christian Americans?" It will be our endeavor in these pages to show the degree to which Chistian proposals can and will appeal even to non-Christians, because all human beings are made in God's image and to some extent, as St. Paul writes, know the judgment of God upon their moral actions (Romans 1:32). If men and women really are made in the image of God, as the Bible teaches, then these proposals may hope for a fair hearing, at least to the extent that they conform to what God teaches and to what He has implanted in the human heart. But if men are not made in the image of God, then not only is Christianity false, but democracy and the theory of responsible self-government are illusions. In such a case there would be no point in talking about a reconstruction of the republic; we should instead be prepared to come to terms with the world that B.F. Skinner envisages, a world "beyond freedom and dignity."

2

Double Vision

Where there is no vision, the people perish.

Proverbs 29:18

What the Old Testament puts rather abstractly, the New Testament makes very explicit: "If the blind lead the blind, both shall fall into the ditch" (Matthew 15:14). To lack vision is to be blind. The lack of a comprehensive vision for society is not as self-evident a handicap as the total lack of sight, but its implications for a society and its citizens are equally if not so immediately disastrous.

Do we have a vision in late twentieth-century America? Herbert Marcuse, the hostile but often bitingly accurate critic of America and its affluence, speaks of our society's "supreme promise" as an ever-increasing comfort for an ever-increasing number of people. Is this in fact our vision? If so, it would seem that we are on the road to failure. In the first place, we are no longer making progress towards it, as we were when Marcuse published *One-Dimensional Man* and *An Essay on Liberation*. We still enjoy relative affluence on a national scale, but our comforts are being somewhat reduced, and the number of those who have access to them, instead of continuing to grow, is declining.

Whatever faults the American system had and has, in the areas of justice, economics, morals, education, or any other, there can be no doubt that no other society has ever produced so lavishly for so many of its citizens as did the United States in the 1950s, 1960s, and into the 1970s. The dissatisfaction that exists on every hand does not lie, objectively speaking, in the lack of material goods and comforts. We cannot, of course, pretend that there is no hardship, no privation, no suffering in America today. But we can make several observations about our situation: (1) those who are most alienated from America and the American "way of life" are frequently *not* those who lack material assets—or, if they do lack them, it is because they have voluntarily given them up, not because they were denied them; (2) with the exception of a relatively small number of extreme cases, whose plight is often caused by physical or mental conditions which no amount of material help can really remedy, even the poorest and least privileged citizens of the United States today are relatively well-off by comparison with the vast majority of human beings during most of man's history, and even by comparison with the vast majority of people alive today; (3) those who "enjoy" the benefits of American affluence are not for that reason satisfied with the system. Among its most vehement detractors are journalists and entertainers who relish its luxuries. Their uneasiness reflects more than simply fear that they may lose what they now have. It represents not merely hatred of society, but self-hatred, based on unacknowledged, unresolved guilt. Self-hatred leads to self-destruction. There may be something naive about "I Love America" days and campaigns and certainly no responsible, biblical Christian should make the mistake of identifying the United States with the Promised Land. But at the very least, God in his Providence has entrusted this land and its resources to us (Acts 17:26), and it is very poor stewardship to hate it. It becomes ridiculous and irresponsible if we allow our feelings of guilt—or others'—to cause us to abandon and ruin the rich and bountiful land that God has given us. A false sense of national guilt is no substitute for individual repentance, and it is a dangerous guide for national policy.

American "Guilt" and Americans' Guilt Feelings

Probably one of the most fundamental elements in America's lack of vision—or what we might better call her double vision—lies in the widespread American ambivalence towards national guilt and righteousness.

Is it possible for a whole nation to be guilty? One of the most controversial clauses in the Treaty of Versailles was the one requiring Germany to accept the guilt for starting World War I. In addition to being historically false—for all students of history now acknowledge that the causes of World War I were too complex to lay the exclusive "guilt" at the feet of a single nation—this forced admission of collective guilt on

16

Germany's part was one of the majory factors contributing to the outbreak of World War II. World War II was followed by the War Crimes Trials, in which many leading figures of defeated Germany and Japan were convicted of having plotted and waged aggressive war, but this time, whole nations were not branded as collectively guilty. This is not the place to take up the legality or justifiability of the War Crimes Trials. What is interesting about them, at this point, is that while individuals, and in some cases whole organizations, such as the Nazi party and the SS, were declared criminal, not even Germany was declared, as a nation, to be guilty.

If it was impossible to state with any confidence that "Germany," as opposed to individual German leaders, was collectively guilty in World War II, how is it possible for us today to feel that "America" or "all Americans" are collectively guilty for the national prosperity that, despite all setbacks, we still enjoy? The late Martin Luther King, Jr. lost all sense of perspective in comparing the United States in the 1960s with Nazi Germany during World War II. Few Americans really accepted such a fantastic comparison, yet many were disturbed and unsettled by it. Indeed, we do have many things on our conscience as a nation: how are we to handle them? Because we have been far less than perfect in the past, must we defer to all our adversaries, however outrageous, in the present and in the future? Some important opinion-makers seem to think that we should. And while such sentiment originated among left-wingers who actually did hate America, they are beginning to find a hearing among conservative and evangelical Christians, especially the more sensitive. This often leaves the Christian attempt to influence public policy to those who while well-intentioned are naive, sometimes too naive to be taken seriously by secular society.

American guilt feelings over America's continuing if tarnished affluence are paradoxical. When the other nations of the world want to equal us in what we have and enjoy, it seems contradictory for us to beat our breasts and echo their condemnation of us for already having what they are trying to get—in some cases by taking it from us. Even more ironic is the fact that those who are loudest in condemning America for her selfishness, greed, and exploitation of Third World countries and her own minorities are people who themselves luxuriate in American affluence and would never think of modifying their own appetites or consumption. Journalists, legislators, and movies actors are prominent among those who denounce America's exploitation of the poor, but few indeed are those who have followed Jesus' advice to the rich young ruler to "go, sell what you have, and give to the poor."

In addition to guilt feelings about America's relative affluence, there is also a great deal of self-criticism about our military establishment and our "aggressive, imperialistic" intervention in the affairs of other nations. It is not necessary to write out a blanket justification for all America's military and diplomatic policies — indeed, such a thing would be impossible — to see that, by comparison with those of the countries that condemn us, they are not outstandingly perverse.

Anyone who has attended an international conference can probably verify the observation that has been made at recent meetings of the World Council of Churches and other international religious bodies. Delegate after delegate from other countries will rise to condemn one or another aspect of American behavior, policy, or life. And Americans rise, almost without exception, to echo, "Indeed, we are guilty. When may we be punished?" Yet most of those same Americans will return, after the international conference, to a comfortable post at WCC headquarters in Geneva, or to an executive or university position in America, where they will continue to live in luxury even by comparison with the majority of their fellow Americans, not to mention the internationals to whom they confessed our national guilt.

How are we to explain this paradox? What has happened is this: the underlying spiritual heritage of America is basically Puritan-Protestant. Even those whose religious commitments were not Calvinist or even Protestant, such as Roman Catholics, Jews, and mere Deists, were to a large extent subscribers to what Max Weber called the "Protestant ethic." One of the fundamental features of this "Protestant ethic" — which is not very compatible with the essential teachings of Protestantism, but that is another matter — is the feeling that material prosperity is a sign of God's blessings, earned, at least in part, by our obedience to him. This is the famous "gospel of wealth," which says, in effect, "One is rich if one is good." Americans were using two incompatible principles for evaluating goodness: the popular consciousness measured goodness in terms of what we might call traditional moral values: honesty, thrift, moderation, sexual self-restraint, fidelity in marriage, and the like, and the "gospel of wealth" — wealth is the reward for goodness. Those traditional values often, although not always, led to economic advancement. Thus to a limited extent it may have been correct to say, "Those who are morally good will prosper." Gerald Ford put it this way in 1976: "America is great because it is good."

By the mid-1960s, however, as the hedonistic revolution and the Playboy philosophy came into their own, America was no longer practising the traditional virtues. "If it feels good, do it." "Grab all the gusto you can get." Even while abandoning traditional biblical and moral restraints, Americans could not free themselves from the old awareness that such restraints are necessary and good and that disregarding them is culpable and brings trouble. Hence, despite our advertising slogans and the popularity of the hedonistic Playboy philosophy, we feel uneasy, even guilty, about the self-indulgent way our personal lives and our national life are shaping up. Nevertheless, our affluence remains—although it is beginning to get a bit shabby. Because of our Christian-biblical-Puritan heritage, we cannot be comfortable in the hedonistic self-indulgence we love, and we instinctively feel that we must somehow pay for it. But our new, modern, me-oriented philosophy forbids us to call self-indulgence wrong. Since *something* has to be wrong in order to account for our feelings of guilt, we attribute them not to our conduct but to our wealth, our power, and our influence. Instead of repenting of wrong actions, we blame the "system"—this time, not for producing economic privation, but for producing prosperity. This is an absurd situation. But is there a better way to explain the fact that our intellectual leaders will feel no guilt at all over the destruction of millions of unborn American children, while engaging in loud laments over the commercial interests that try to sell artificial milk to African mothers?

What has been said about Americans and our guilt feelings does not apply across the board, of course. It applies only to the more modern, enlightened, and liberated. A great percentage of Americans are still persuaded of the desirability of honesty, thrift, modesty, self-restraint, and fidelity. And a very large percentage of us do not have the financial means to engage in such conspicuous consumption of luxuries that we would make ourselves feel guiltily self-indulgent. Such Americans—and they surely make up a very large portion of the population, if not necessarily the majority—resent being called guilty for the enjoyment of things they feel they have earned.

Unfortunately, as the development of American society in the direction of ever-greater self-indulgence continues, more and more Americans who still have strong Judeo-Christian ethical sensitivities are accommodating themselves to patterns of living that they intuitively feel or consciously know to be wrong. Hence they too begin to feel guilty, and become susceptible to the mentality that confesses guilt for things that are not in themselves wrong in order to avoid acknowledging that which is really wrong.

The American way of life is plunging more and more of us into real guilt in areas that are plainly defined by our religious teachings and where we have strong built-in convictions. However often we may tell ourselves that these things are "hangups," there is no way for the average product of a Judeo-Christian background to spend his life indulging himself in things he knows or subconsciously feels to be wrong—especially in the area of personal indulgence and sexual morality, where biblical teaching is so rigorous—without developing a great load of guilt. However, if we repudiate or are unwilling to follow the religious teachings that would tell us to acknowledge, confess and repent of, and refrain from such misdoing, we need to have some way to explain to ourselves the deep feeling of uneasiness at the way things are going and the very widespread foreboding that we have something very unpleasant coming to us.

This pervasive, largely unrecognized sense of guilt for the wrong things produces a double vision that is morally paralyzing to individuals, and on a large scale becomes confusing and paralyzing for national policy as well. We cannot run either a rational domestic or foreign policy on what R. J. Rushdoony calls "the politics of guilt and pity," particularly false or misapplied guilt and unwarranted self-pity. The answer to this is an individual and national stock-taking: a recognition of the source of our problems. We are indeed guilty of many things, and have many problems. But in general it is not the news and entertainment media that can identify them for us. The *Washington Post* and the *New York Times* may be great metropolitan dailies, but they are not very satisfactory as spiritual guides or manuals of ethics.

As the French Protestant theologian Paul Ricoeur points out in *Finitude and Culpability,* all people have a generalized sense of culpability, of *malaise,* but a knowledge of the Law of God is required to bring this sense of culpability to a focus and to deal with it. This is precisely what our society does not want to hear; consequently, in increasing numbers we cannot deal with our sense of culpability, and resort to subterfuges such as confessing the whole nation guilty because of our affluence in an effort to escape guilt.

Bread Is Not Enough

All this goes back to a maxim clearly spelled out in the Bible, first in the Old Testament and then in the new: "Man shall not live by bread alone" (Deuteronomy 8:3, Matthew 4:4). At the time that those words were first set down, and again in Roman-ruled Palestine when Jesus recalled them, bread alone was a tremendous problem for many if not most of the world's people. And, although they were not sure of always having enough bread, even then they frequently realized that there is much more to life than bread alone. It was only the very rich, however, who had the experience of the emptiness that comes when, after having lived for material goods, "bread alone," one has all or more than one can consume. It was only a small minority that was rich enough to recognize the truth that material things alone cannot satisfy men and women and enable them to "live" in the full sense of the word. For the others—the majority of the world's people throughout history—the maxim must have served more as a consolation for not having enough food and other material goods than as a warning that those goods, alone, are not enough to make us happy.

In the late twentieth-century America more people than ever before at any time in the world's history are experiencing the truth of that biblical "Man shall not live by bread alone." Particularly since the Second World War, America has reaped the benefits of a remarkable combination of natural resources, hard work, military triumph, and the relative absence of serious competition. While America has never officially made bread, or money, its supreme value, precisely when bread was becoming universally available, not merely in sufficiency, but really in a sickening abundance, our society unfortunately began to tell people, in effect, that there is nothing better for which to live. In other words, just as those goals turned out not to satisfy, they were proclaimed to be all that there is. As long as human beings lack food, shelter, a measure of security and of opportunity, they can always think that if they only get a bit more, they will be happy. But when vast numbers of people have not merely enough but more than enough, so much that it is no longer interesting, then, if they have not already learned of something more important than bread to give content to their lives, there is no alternative to disillusionment, indifference, and lassitude.

If we look back at America's early history, we will recognize that people have never come to this country, either in the colonial period, after independence, or during the great waves of immigration during the latter nineteenth and early twentieth centuries, looking for bread alone. Of course people did come to the New World looking for economic opportunities they could not find in the Old. But the magnetic attraction that America held for so many of the people of the world, right up to the point when we began to indulge in our national orgy of self-deprecation and self-condemnation, has to be explained by something more than the promise of bread alone, or of what Marcuse called "ever-increasing comfort." People came to America because it meant something to them spiritually, not just economically. But today, for the most part, all that our

21

leaders have to offer us is a somewhat better distribution of a diminishing loaf of bread . . . "by bread alone."

A Double Source

The vision that inspired the birth of our nation, beginning with the establishment of colonies in an uncharted wilderness, then of an independent nation, and finally of a worldwide industrial, economic, and military empire, was certainly more than "bread alone." Can our worldwide standing be preserved if we now think of nothing more than bread alone?

What is the vision that created America? It is self-evident that it had tremendous power. Is there anything about it that is still valid, that can inspire us anew today? Is there any part of it that we still possess, or that we can recover? In order to answer the questions, we must look at the source of the American vision. When we do so, we immediately see that we cannot isolate a single source, or even a single vision.

America is a land of contrasts. We all know that our racial heritage is mixed: there is "a little bit of everything." Within this very mixed racial heritage, two racial stocks stand out: Caucasian or "white" and Afro-American or "black." Something similar may be said about America's spiritual heritage. There too there is a little bit of everything: but two basic forces stand out: we may call them biblical Christian and secular humanistic.

America's Biblical Heritage

It may seem strange to speak of a "biblical heritage" as opposed to a Christian one. Perhaps the expression *biblical*, being unfamiliar in this context, is not entirely suitable. But there are two good reasons for using it here instead of "Christian." First and most obviously, although the majority of Americans, from the Colonial period to the present, have been Christians by conviction or at least by association, America's small Jewish minority has made a very substantial contribution to our national life and culture, much greater than its relative size would lead us to expect. By saying "biblical" rather than "Christian" heritage we specifically include the Jews in it. Some Jews may feel uncomfortable at such Chris-

22

tian inclusiveness, but undeniably most of the ethical, legal, and social content of our Christian heritage is also part of the Jewish heritage. In the area of faith and salvation — "soteriology," to use the technical term — there is considerable difference between Jewish and Christian beliefs. But politics and the doctrine of the state are not concerned with salvation, but rather with ethics. And Jewish and Christian ethics are very similar, almost identical. Hence it is proper, in talking about a recovery of vision for American political life, to speak of our "biblical" rather than "Christian" heritage. Some groups, those who have no particular regard for the Bible, will still feel left out, but it is fair to say that the great majority of America's people are at home in the ethics of our biblical tradition. Indeed, the Bible itself says, and history shows, that even the nations that do not have the Law (the Old Testament) have a measure of God's Law written in their hearts (Romans 2:14–15). The civil and criminal codes of every nation in the world correspond to a remarkable degree with basic principles of biblical law, as indeed they must, if God has made man in his own image and if man, even though fallen, continues to possess a measure of natural understanding of the principles of God's justice.

There is a second reason for speaking of a "biblical" rather than a Christian heritage. The word Christian implies, or at least ought to imply, a conscious personal, religious commitment. One has a heritage whether or not one is consciously committed to it. Thus even Nikita Khrushchev quoted the "old Russian proverb" that says, "Whatever a man soweth, that shall he also reap." (This proverb, of course, is Galatians 6:7.) From our perspective, it makes better sense to use the designation "Christian" only for people and institutions that are personally, explicitly, and consciously committed to Christian beliefs and ethics. In this sense America is not and never was a "Christian" nation. No doubt throughout our nation's entire history, a majority of her people have always identified themselves to some extent with the Christian faith, but at least since Independence, our official institutions have never been formally Christian. (Several of the colonies did have established churches, and two retained them into the nineteenth century.) But the Bible and its teachings have had a tremendous formative influence on our people and our institutions even when they have not been accepted as authoritative, as the Word of God. It is unquestionably correct to state that American culture, American attitudes, even our literary style, our language, our laws and our political institutions are largely biblical in origin and inspiration.

The Bible as the Source

What does it mean in practice to say that our institutions are largely biblical in origin? It means something very simple and tremendously important: the basic source of values in American society is the Bible. Eliminate the Bible — as our courts, schools, and other social institutions have done and continue to do — and you cut values off from their principal source. The Bible, of course, is not the *only* source, for there is a second source of major importance: we may call it philosophical humanism. Non-biblical in origin, it is sometimes neutral towards Christianity, sometimes hostile; its contemporary manifestation, usually called secular humanism, is actively hostile to biblical religion, indeed to all religion. It is important to note that while philosophical humanism has contributed many valuable things to the development of American society and life, it has never been the primary source; indeed, it has always relied to a large extent for its framework on the explicitly Christian value-system out of which it emerged. In its militant contemporary form as secular humanism, humanism might conceivably succeed in driving out America's biblical heritage: that is certainly its determined goal today. But although it might conceivably eject it, it can never replace it. The heritage of secular humanism, like that of Stoic philosophy, really can appeal only to the elite. It is too ephemeral to motivate the masses, despite its claim to be, as it were, the religion of man. A society with secular humanism as its value structure will be one in which only a certain "elite" have vision — the rest will have to be manipulated and controlled. This is precisely what has happened in Communist nations, and it is what secular thinkers such as B. F. Skinner have called for in modern America: once we are *Beyond Freedom and Dignity,* in other words, have rid ourselves of the "delusion" that man, as man, is free and has dignity, then we will be ready to submit to the control of our scientific elite.

We have noted that there are two fundamental sources of values in American life — the primary, rich, and broad source of the Bible and biblical religion, and the secondary, derivative, but powerful source of philosophical humanism. The thing that we have not mentioned, however, is the very instrument that is so often cited as the source of America's values — and in this citing lies a fateful error. We speak, of course, of the United States Constitution. It is of crucial importance to recognize that the United States Constitution does not contain either biblical or humanistic values. Strictly speaking, it does not contain values at all: it is an instrument of government, not a source of values. To treat the

United States Constitution as the source of values—as the United States Supreme Court regularly does—is in effect to say that there is no real source of values, that values are perfectly arbitrary, that a Court may impose whatever values it wishes. This is certainly what has been happening in the United States for at least several decades: the question with which the present book is concerned is whether this is acceptable to America and to her people.

The Constitution: Its Nature and Its Limitations

The United States Constitution is not a *source* of fundamental values. It is an *instrument* whereby fundamental values can be protected, defining the procedures, principles, and methods whereby government can function to allow the people to give content to their lives. The Constitution itself cannot give that content. In the early days, no one supposed that it would. There was a sufficiently clear value-consensus among Americans so that, while degrees of commitment or differences of emphasis existed, there was little doubt as to the fundamental nature of good and evil, of virtue and vice. These things were not defined in the Constitution because Americans of the federal era generally knew and agreed about what they are. Today, if there is disagreement or ignorance—as increasingly there is—fundamental values cannot be found in the Constitution. *They simply are not there.*

To choose a simple example: the idea that all human beings should be free is not in the United States Constitution. It was not put there when the Constitution was adopted, for the obvious reason that human slavery was legal in several states. In fact, Article I makes specific provision for the institution of slavery. When Americans later came to the conclusion that human slavery is intolerable, they did not find this principle in the Constitution. Quite the contrary: they had to put it in. Thus we had the War between the States, and ultimately the Thirteenth Amendment. Where did they get the conviction that slavery was intolerable? Very largely from our biblical heritage, strongly influenced by the moral fervor inspired by nineteenth-century revivalism, and secondarily from rationalism and a philosophical, natural-law view of the rights of man. Even the nineteenth-century Unitarianism that contributed so strongly to abolitionist sentiment in New England was, at the time, strongly biblical in origin, although perhaps more akin to Jewish religiosity than to that of Christian trinitariansim.

25

Now, of course, it can be argued—as for example in the various school desegregation cases—that the Constitution requires integration, and ultimately bussing and other developments. But if the Constitution, by implication since it does not do so expressly, requires these things today, it is because people decided that they are in an ultimate sense, *just,* and hence put them into the Constitution via the Thirteenth and Fourteenth Amendments.* If the Constitution itself is the ultimate source of values, then we would in effect be saying that right is what two-thirds of each house of Congress and three-quarters of the states, at any one time, define to be right. And neither the Christians, nor the Unitarians, nor the rationalistic Deists among the Founding Fathers would have accepted such a notion. The purpose of the Constitution was to create a framework for the preservation of values that the people acknowledge to be right and good, not to create those values.

The role of the Bible and its values in American life is of course not constitutionally founded. This is a true statement, but its significance should not be misunderstood. Where various people live in an American city may be determined by consulting the local telephone directory, but that does not mean that the telephone directory determines where they shall live, ought to live, or would choose to live. It only records, more or less correctly, where they happen to reside at the time of publication. The United States Constitution does not tell us what is right, or what our chosen values were at the time the Constitution was adopted. The Constitution, for example, does not expressly grant people the right to life—as the post-World War II West German constitution, by contrast, does. It merely establishes governmental forms that are intended to permit people to live and to exercise and enjoy fundamental rights that are acknowledged as ordained, in the words of the Declaration of Independence, by "Nature and Nature's God," not by the people and their representatives. If the Constitution, that small document of hardly twenty pages (depending on the format and edition), were the real source of our fundamental values, those values would be few indeed and our culture and civilization unthinkably barren.

Perhaps the fundamental, although not *constitutional,* importance of the biblical heritage to American life can be illustrated by reference to the Homeric heritage of Greece. Homer wrote in a period before our reli-

---

* It can of course be cogently argued, as former Watergate Special Prosecutor Archibald Cox does in *The Role of the Supreme Court in American Government* (New York: Oxford, 1976), that the amendments do not logically require these things, but that is not the point here. The point is that the ultimate reason for requiring specific things such as integration and bussing, if they are to be required, cannot be that they are in the Constitution, but that they are morally right, and hence have been or will be put into it.

able history of Greece begins. By the classical period with its famous dramatists, poets, philosophers, and lawgivers, it is unlikely many people really believed literally in Homer's world of gods and goddesses who took part in the public and private life of human beings. Certainly few if any "believed" in Homer as authoritative or literally true in the way that traditional Christians believe the Bible. Nevertheless, the imagery and ideals that Homer evoked had a powerful influence on later Greek life. Even today, despite the fact that the Greeks went over virtually *en masse* to Christianity, considerable traces of his influence remain. Take the *Iliad* and the *Odyssey* out of Greek life and civilization, and the results would be startling. The comparison is weak, because the Homeric contribution to modern Greece is nowhere near as pervasive as the biblical contribution to modern America. We cannot even say that to remove the Bible and biblical values from our system would leave us with "bare bones"; indeed the bare bones of our laws, of our society, and its values come directly from biblical authority. To remove from public law, for example, all laws that have a biblical origin would be an absurdity: we would have to repeal the laws against, murder, theft, and rape.

In the Christian world, and especially in America, which was a Bible-reading and Bible-quoting country, large numbers of people accepted and still accept the Bible and its message as authoritative and reliable. It means far more to them than Homer ever did to the Greek. Add to that number the even greater number of those who learned its stories in childhood, who read it as literature, who quote it for rhetorical purposes, and who take comfort from its passages in distress or adversity even if they do not really believe them to be true, and we recognize that the Bible, its images, ideas, and values had and still have a very marked effect on American culture. If there was any room for doubt about this, the Watergate affair, including the hearings, trials, and public reaction should have removed it. The Bible was quoted by both the accused and their investigators; there was much talk of guilt, and there were several spectacular conversions, some more explicitly Christian than others.

Perhaps only a minority of Americans today know the Bible and its teachings well, and only a minority accept them as a true and authoritative standard for faith and life. But more Americans know the Bible well than anything else. It is undoubtedly correct to say that modern America is probably still more biblical in its values and images than the Soviet Union is Marxist. How many average Russians know in any detail the specific tenets of Marxist-Leninist doctrine? How many of those who had to memorize selections from the Marxist classics in school still remember them, or are now convinced that they are true? Soviet literature dealing with the "problem" of the persistent influence of Christianity in the USSR frequently refers to the average Russian's ignorance of the Marxist-Leninist principles that should enable him, according to the official view, to refute all religious arguments and reject all religious influences. It is probably fair to say that even today, after almost sixty years of Marxist dominance, the Christian heritage in Russia enjoys more general acceptance than Marxist-Leninist doctrine. Even Khrushchev, on occasion, quoted Scripture.

Of course it is incorrect to speak of America as a "Christian" nation if by such an expression we mean (1) that all or a large majority of Americans are consciously committed to Christ and to Christian teaching; (2) that the Founding Fathers were largely inspired by Christian beliefs; (3) that our constitutional documents and government institutions were deliberately based on Christian patterns; (4) that our official government conduct, in foreign and domestic policy, is in any sense consciously patterned on Christian principles. None of these things is true. But if by "Christian" nation we mean that the most persuasive religious, cultural, and ethical influence in the country is and has been that of Christianity, or that Christianity affects the hearts and minds of Americans at least as much as Marxism does that of Russians, then it is clearly correct to think of America as "Christian" and to speak of a "Christian heritage." However, even if we try to make it clear that by calling our country "Christian" all we mean is that its culture is colored by, not committed to, Christianity, misunderstandings will probably still persist. Non-Christian Americans will think that we are trying to place them outside the heritage of our country, and serious Christians may think that it debases the name Christian to apply it to a whole society that is at best tinted with Christian colors but by no means corresponds to Christian ideals. Therefore it seems to make better sense to speak of America's biblical heritage. This is one of the two main sources of our national vision, and historically speaking it is the broader, stronger, and more valuable source. As a result of a slow but continuous development, it is in danger of being largely eliminated. What will remain is the weaker, shallower secular source.

Secular Humanism

If the American Revolution had occurred in the late seventeenth century rather than in the late eighteenth, there is a good chance that the new nation would have been strongly Puritan in orientation. As a matter of fact, during the seventeenth century, much of the religious and intellectual life in the American colonies was much more distinctively Puritan and Bible-centered than in England after the restoration of the monarchy. But by the last quarter of the eighteenth century, when the movement for independence from Britain burst forth, much of American intellectual life had been profoundly influenced by rationalism and the Enlightenment. Turning away from the Bible and the concept of an authoritative divine revelation, eighteenth-century humanistic thinkers sought religious truth from reason alone. They wanted to leave behind the limited world of the Bible, tied to the history of a small, peculiar people, the Jews, and to the life and teachings of one Jew in particular, Jesus of Nazareth. For them, all that is true in Christianity can be found more satisfactorily and in a more universally valid form by philosophical inquiry and common sense. Of course it was not a question of rejecting God or the idea of God; the eighteenth-century mind was sufficiently logical to see great merit in the idea of God as First Cause, Unmoved Mover, Great Architect, or Supreme Being. But the God of the eighteenth-century philosophers shared little more than the name and some of the more abstract titles (such as "Supreme Being") with the God of the Bible, of the great Fathers, Doctors, and Reformers of church history. Nevertheless, while not "establishing" Christianity, the new nation was far from repudiating it.

Many of the partisans of American independence were committed Christians. At the same time, several of the foremost leaders were far more inclined to a kind of philosophical rationalism, deism, or even nonreligious freethinking than to biblical religion. Of the first six presidents, four were from Virginia, two from Massachusetts. John Adams and John Quincy Adams were Unitarians, and while the Unitarians of that period gave a place of singular respect to Jesus Christ, they had definitely broken with the traditional Christian belief concerning him. George Washington and James Monroe were Episcopalians of a rather watery variety; in his various addresses, Washington makes frequent references to "that Almighty Being," "the Great Author of every public and private good," "the Invisible Hand which conducts the affairs of men," and similar constructions that are much more in line with philosophical deism or Freemasonry than with orthodox Christianity. Thomas Jefferson was the only one of the six who professed no religious affiliation. Together with Episcopalian James Madison, he put through the Virginia Statute of Religious Liberty, a law disestablishing the Anglican or Episcopal Church in Virginia. Except in the case of Jefferson, whose dislike for revelation and the Christian faith are rather plain, we do not need to think that these men were themselves indifferent to the Christian faith, but merely that they wanted to establish the principle of religious toleration. Yet even a modest familiarity with their lives and works indicates that they were more deistic than Christian. In light of the fact that people of non-Christian background, i.e., Jews, were a miniscule minority in the original Colonies and the new States, we have to recognize in the Founding Fathers' scrupulous avoidance of reference to Christ something more than a mere expression of tact towards non-Christians. Between the early colonial charters and compacts that explicitly mention the Christian faith and speak of Jesus Christ as the Lord and Saviour of the world, and the Declaration of Independence, there is a marked difference. The Declaration speaks only of "Nature and of Nature's God," and of "Divine Providence." Believing Christians among the signers and among the colonists may have seen no reason to object to such formulations, for they also occur in orthodox Christian writings, alongside of more clearly Christian expressions. But it is no accident that in the Declaration of Independence they stand alone, without more explicit reference.

A book of documentation was produced in 1966 by a leading conservative Protestant publishing house to demonstrate the contention that America has a distinctively and consciously Christian heritage and origin: Benjamin Weiss, *God in American History: A Documentation*.[1] Senator Mark O. Hatfield and President Gerald R. Ford (at that time House Minority Leader), both leading Christian laymen, wrote favorable comments on the book and expressed gratitude for the evidence it presented concerning the religious foundations of our nation. Even a cursory reading of *God in American History* reveals two things: first, the United States Constitution is not among the documents cited. The reason is simple: the federal Constitution nowhere mentions God. Second, the constitution of each state, from Delaware, the first to join the Union in 1787, to Hawaii, the last to be admitted, 170 years later, makes at least some reference to God. Hawaii's is a rather vague reference to "divine guidance," while Massachusetts with its Puritan heritage refers more explicitly to him as the great Legislator of the universe, speaks of his providence, and implores his direction (a somewhat stronger word than "guidance"). Virginia's constitution makes reference to "Christian forbearance, love and charity" as "the mutual duty of all," and Vermont's even more explicitly states: "Every sect or denomination of Christians ought to observe the sabbath or Lord's day, and

[1]Benjamin Weiss, *God in American History: A Documentation* (Grand Rapids: Zondervan, 1966).

30

keep up some sort of religious worship, which to them shall seem most agreeable to the revealed will of God."[2]

Why is the federal Constitution absolutely silent about God when every state constitution makes at least some reference to him? There are two reasons for this. The first was undoubtedly the real historical reason. The second has a greater influence today. First, at the time the Constitution was adopted the majority of Americans took it for granted that God should be acknowledged, honored, and worshipped. There were statewide established churches in Virginia until 1786, in Connecticut until 1818, and in Massachusetts until 1832. What the States wished to avoid, in adopting the First Amendment to the Constitution, was the establishment of a *national* as opposed to a merely statewide church. Clearly the Constitution could not have been intended to prohibit the existence of an established church in individual states, inasmuch as two states kept established churches until well into the nineteenth century.

The second reason behind the federal Constitution's "neutrality" towards God lay, of course, in the rationalistic spirit of men such as Thomas Jefferson, who were at most philosophical Deists. They were willing to acknowledge a Supreme Being in some general way, but were very much opposed to accepting any particular revelation as authoritative or any particular religion as true. But even so, they could hardly have succeeded in promoting a Constitution that turned its back on the God of the Bible. For most Americans, the purpose of the First Amendment was to insure that no particular variety of Christianity be given the upper hand in the country as a whole. For Jefferson and people who thought like him an underlying idea may have been to go beyond the influence of "narrow" Christianity in the name of a universal toleration. However, the Constitution does not mention any "wall of separation" between church and state. This concept first appears in Jefferson's presidential correspondence. Individual Christians or other religious groups were often enthusiastic about the principle of Jefferson's "wall of separation" when it seemed to them that the state or federal government was promoting the interests of another Christian denomination. Now more and more of us are realizing that this "wall" has been used to isolate all religious and Christian elements from every aspect of daily life that is touched by government at any level, and of course most strikingly from education. What began as a barrier to any state church now serves as a barrier to all religion. When public school education appeared, in the eyes of many Roman Catholics, to be a kind of indoctrination in Protestantism, it was

[2]*Ibid.*, pp. 166, 176, 200–201.

31

the Catholics who called for greater separation of church and state to get rid of the unwanted Protestantism. Protestants, fearing that Catholics with their vast structure of educational, medical, and charitable institutions might obtain public tax funds for their religious activities, also clamored for increasing the height and thickness of the "wall of separation."

In the early 1960s, in the Supreme Court's school prayer and Bible-reading decisions,[3] the "wall of separation" was, figuratively speaking, extended up to heaven, leaving the children in government public schools on one side, and not merely the churches but God in isolation on the other. We have now reached a paradoxical situation for a country with a Christian heritage where the majority of the people still profess adherence to one form or another of Christianity. Although sessions of Congress and the Supreme Court are opened with a form of prayer, it is "unconstitutional" to have any recognition of God in government schools. In most school districts, it is easier to offer a course in the occult or in transcendental meditation, a westernized derivation of Hinduism often masquerading as "science," than in the teachings of the Bible. Although the Bible is the greatest single literary influence on English language and literature, most public school boards now shy away from offering any instruction in it because of the well-founded fear that to offer such a course would probably result in court action and eventual prohibition. "No establishment" has come to mean "no expression."

What remains when all biblical or Christian elements are deliberately removed from our educational system? The answer is secular humanism. But American humanism, which is largely a sophisticated reaction to Christianity, is too weak to stand alone. At the time of American independence, any existing town that might have been chosen as permanent capital—for example, New York, Philadelphia, or Boston—would have been dominated, architecturally speaking, by its churches, just like the towns of Europe. By creating a new town as the center of the "new order of ages" (*Novus Ordo Seclorum* [or *Saeculorum*], one of the mottoes on the Great Seal of the United States), the young nation was able to place at its center not the house of God but the residence of a man, the White House. The great churches of various communions—the National Cathedral, the Basilica of the Immaculate Conception, the National Presbyterian Church, to name three of the most impressive—are all on the periphery of the nation's capital. At the center are the White House, the residence of the Chief Executive, and the Capitol, where laws for the "new order

---

[3]*Engel* v. *Vitale*, 1961, and *Schempp* v. *Abingdon Township School Board*, 1963.

of the ages" are made. In prominent view are the impressive monuments to three men, Washington, Jefferson, and Lincoln. The most striking is the Washington Monument, an obelisk of Egyptian inspiration, originally associated with pagan sun worship. Inscriptions on both the Jefferson and the Lincoln memorials actually refer to "this temple." The symbols of Washington may tend to an "establishment of religion," but it is not biblical religion.

All of us who grew up in America are familiar with these buildings and monuments and do not, in all likelihood, think of them as *religious* nor suspect that they take the place of buildings erected for the worship of God. It would be too much to claim that the capital was laid out and these monuments built in a conscious effort to place man and his glory at the center and to drive God and his worship to the fringes of national life. Yet undoubtedly there was some such motivation, at least on the subconscious level, just as there was when King Louis XIV of France, the "sun king," built his magnificent capital at Versailles and put his own bedchamber (from which he conducted his affairs of state) at the center. It was not the French Revolution with its attacks on religion and its temporary establishment of a cult of Reason that first removed God, symbolically speaking, from the center of French national life. The absolute monarchy had already done it.

The United States was the first nation of European heritage to eliminate Christian symbolism from the national insignia. We may doubt that the cross seen on the Swiss, Swedish, Norwegian, Danish, and Finnish flags means much today, or that many Britons ever think about the fact that the Union Jack is made up of three superimposed crosses. Nevertheless, it is rather suggestive that the new North American republic did away with the cross in its national symbolism, despite the fact that the Colonies, in 1776, were certainly no less Christian than the mother country.

If some of America's leaders in 1776 would gladly have cut themselves off from the specifically Christian element in their background, most would have been horrified at such a thought. Indifference to organized Christianity certainly characterized Thomas Jefferson, as well as Benjamin Franklin, whom sociologist Max Weber called a "colorless Deist." Nevertheless the majority of those who fought the War of Independence and built the new nation gave a Christian interpretation to their leaders' vague remarks about "Divine Providence" and the "great Sovereign of the Universe." In the rebellious Colonies, there were two different spiritual reasons for rejecting the King: those of Puritan sentiments wanted to exalt only God as king, while the philosophically inclined Deists wanted to put Man rather than a particular man, the king, at the center. The interests of these two groups coincided enough to enable them to make common cause against King George III, but when they came to build a new commonwealth, this spiritual ambivalence became a handicap. It is no accident that the personal, biblical tone of many of the public pronouncements of the Revolutionary War period was lost during the writing and adoption of the Constitution after the war was over. No longer in immediate peril, American politicians felt much more self-sufficient.

Let us not read too much into America's early rejection of Christian symbols. Even Nazi Germany retained the cross for some purposes, such as the insignia for its warplanes, but did not preserve many Christian values. On the other hand, symbols are nothing if not symbolic, and it is fair to say that the elimination of Christian elements from the symbolism of the new republic foreshadowed the subsequent removal of Christian content from its educational and legal systems.

The Clash of Symbols

During World War II, Americans often joked about the fact that Hitler's symbol, the swastika, was a double cross. To those who know more about Indo-Aryan symbolism, it is evident that while he thought he was adopting an ancient symbol for prosperity and good luck, in fact he reversed it and produced the symbol for death and decay. The two most characteristic symbols of European Christendom have been the cross, which figures in the heraldry of most of the non-Communist countries, and the eagle—the old symbol of Rome, picked up by the Holy Roman, Austro-Hungarian, Napoleonic, German, and Russian empires, as well as by the United States, Nazi Germany, and the Bundesrepublik. What symbols did America choose to indicate its values and its goals?

The Messiah and the Pharaohs

A great deal of American literature in the colonial and federal periods and beyond reflects an identification of the New World or the new country with Zion, with God's chosen people or nation. Much of the American dream is frankly messianic, and suggests the hope of achieving something like a kingdom of God in America. This messianism was and continues to be a strong part of our national heritage, even of our political heritage, and expresses itself in future-oriented, almost eschatological platforms and slogans, ranging from the Founders' *Novus Ordo Seclorum* ("new order of the ages") through Franklin D. Roosevelt's New Deal and Lyndon B. Johnson's Great Society to Richard M. Nixon's abortive New American Revolution. But a curious feature of it all is this: although the messianic hope may have been borrowed from the Bible and its imagery of the earthly Kingdom of God, much of the symbolism is taken from precisely those this-worldly empires that were most in conflict with the God of the Bible.

For example, some American symbolism is Egyptian in origin, such as the Washington Monument. Egypt would not seem a likely source of symbols for a new republic founded largely by Christians. Egypt, the land of the pharaohs where tens of thousands of slaves were sacrificed to the glory of a single ruler in building the pyramids, appears in the Bible as the archetype of opposition to Israel, the people of God. Egyptian wisdom is worldly wisdom, the opposite of revealed knowledge, and the later Islamic conquest of Egypt allows things Egyptian to appear—for example in Milton's *Paradise Lost*—as symbolic of rebellion against God himself. Yet the Great Seal of the United States bears a pyramid, quintessential symbol of Egyptian lore. This pyramid is surmounted by an eye, intended to represent the all-seeing Eye of God, but such symbolism is more deistic than biblical. Both the obelisk and pyramid are architectural symbols, and the architect and his creative work were favorite symbols of eighteenth-century rationalism and of Freemasonry, to which society Washington as well as many other eighteenth-century leaders belonged.

Since a direct resort to Egypt as the source of America's symbols is absurd, it is clear that their presence is more to be attributed to the influence of Freemasonry. Although there are various streams of Freemasonry, and for many Masons the society is supportive of rather than hostile to Christianity, there is within the movement an element of religious universalism that precedes, and surpasses, "sectarian" Christianity. The fact that Masonic symbols were picked up by the new republic when Christian ones were ignored probably suggests that for some of the Founders, at least, the revolt against the monarchy of George III was also a revolt against the specific authority of biblical revelation. Since the majority of the committed Christians in the Colonies were of Calvinist background, and by tradition very uninterested in religious symbolism, it is not at all surprising that they made no effort to place the cross or anything else specifically Christian alongside the pyramid and the eagle. The symbols of the state, except in times of great national crisis, were less significant than the familiar things: home, farm, shop, family, church. Indeed, in times of crisis, leaders and people alike resorted even more strongly to biblical symbolism and ideals for inspiration: *The Battle Hymn of the Republic,* used in the nation's greatest crisis to date, the Civil War, speaks of death on the Union, antislavery side of the war as a parallel to the death of Christ: "As He died to make men holy, let us die to make men free." Whether this parallel is theologically justifiable is not the point, but rather the fact that the sacrificial death of Christ on the Cross eighteen centuries earlier was still so vividly perceived that it could be used with great effect to encourage Union soldiers to risk their own lives. The clash with Nazism from 1941 to 1945 clearly confronted the United States with a more obvious rejection of Christianity, biblical values, and Christian civilization by far than did the conflict of the North with the South. Yet no comparable "Battle Hymn" came out of World War II. In the continuing American rivalry with contemporary Communism, while individual Christian leaders frequently speak of the defense of Christianity against "godless Communism," the nation as a whole, far from stirring up religious sentiments in support of a conflict with a basically antireligious system, relies almost exclusively on secularistic motivation and hence produces at best a watery enthusiasm for national defense and American self-interest.

The Humanist Vision

The second element in America's "double vision," which was in a less prominent place prior to the 1930s, but is gradually coming to dominate today, is a man-centered religion called humanism. Unfortunately, it is also a grievously disoriented, rootless humanism, and as such it is not capable of effectively taking the place of the religious values it is successfully driving from the scene. It would probably be desirable to try to confine ourselves to the term "secular humanism," for there is a kind of humanism that takes its cue from the biblical doctrine of man made in the image of God and which is essentially compatible with Christianity—Erasmus of Rotterdam, a contemporary of Martin Luther, exemplified such "Christian humanism." But since the publication of the two *Humanist Manifestoes,* "humanism" has come to mean secular humanism, and we shall use the term accordingly.

Church historians know that there is a type of Unitarianism that really exists only as a reaction to Calvinist Puritanism. When Calvinism is strong, it evokes a flourishing Unitarian reaction. But when Calvinism pales, the Unitarian opposition also fades out. In the same way, there is a kind of humanism that really exists only as a mild alternative to the Christian view of man. The biblical doctrine of man as made in the image of God endows the human race with a great dignity, but also with momentous responsibility and great duties. There is a moment in nontheistic humanism, for example during the Italian Renaissance, when people seem to be able to preserve the concept of human dignity apart from the majesty and sovereignty of God. Another such moment occurred early in American history. The hopes placed in what Americans could make of their country were so magnificent that they could hardly be expected to come true apart from the aid of God. And his aid was continually requested, genuinely and sometimes just for the sake of the form, by generations of Americans from our earliest days to the present. But for the humanist element in America, this "divine succor" was really much more of a formality than something they genuinely thought they needed. Man, it was felt, was good enough to do it on his own.

Unfortunately, as the kind of vigorous Christian faith that kept people, in dependence on God, to a certain level of human performance and virtue faded, the ability of unaided human beings to attain that same standard appears to have dropped precipitously. Thus while many of us thought that we were good enough to accomplish all that is necessary without God, it soon became evident that apart from faith in God and fear in him, we are by no means likely to stay good enough long enough to achieve much of the good that we hope.

It is no doubt theoretically possible to develop a completely nontheistic humanism that is not conceived as a movement of rebellion against the sovereignty of the God of the Bible. But optimistic, value and virtue-oriented humanism in America, indeed in the whole of Christendom, has always appeared as a kind of reaction to the Christian view, and, like all reactions, derived much of its direction and sense of purpose from what it was opposing. At the point that it succeeds in weakening the Christian ethos enough to be truly free of it, however, it also loses its own direction and its own power.

To return to our symbols, we may say that as long as the eagle and the pyramid were only symbols of government as a little sphere in which man exercised a careful and prudent autonomy under the watchful eye of God, they were relatively harmless. In the Civil War era, men who believed that they would be rewarded by Christ did not object to the presence of the secular symbols. But once the Christian consciousness has been thoroughly banished, very few indeed will be willing to fight for the sake of the eagle, the pyramid, or even the Stars and Stripes. Both

Christianity and Communism (as well as Hinduism, Islam, and certain other religious and quasi-religious movements) are world-historical forces: they can inspire allegiance (and opposition), loyalty, and sacrifice. But the secular mythology of post-Christian America, with its flag and eagle symbols and a twenty-page contract, the Constitution, as its fundamental source of values, is simply not on the same scale.

America is entering what will undoubtedly be the most crucial century of her national existence to date. We cannot last out the century with no vision, or with double vision; nor with the kind of contentless bicentennial patriotism that is the modern equivalent of ancient Roman emperor-worship—officially sanctioned and quite correct, but hardly something one would die for.

3

Facing the Facts

Carthage and Corinth, two great cities of the ancient world, crashed to their ruin amid smoke and flame in 146 B.C., destroyed and sacked by Roman troops. Thirteen years later a Roman tribune, Tiberius Gracchus, was clubbed to death in a fracas led by an exconsul. These tragic episodes showed clearly that Rome's power throughout the Mediterranean world was dominant and unchallengeable, but that her internal stability was weakened and threatened. She was gaining the whole world: must she at the same time lose her own soul?

H. H. Scullard
From the Gracchi to Nero

In 1945 Berlin and Tokyo, two great cities of the modern world, crashed to their ruin amid smoke and flame. Eighteen years later an American President, John F. Kennedy, was shot to death in a bizarre incident which has not yet been convincingly and thoroughly explained. In the years since Kennedy's murder, America may well seem to be in the same situation of turmoil and unrest that beset Rome after her overwhelming triumphs in the Third Punic War.

But there is one tremendous difference between republican Rome after the Third Punic War and republican America after the Second World War. In the Third Punic War, Rome had effectively demolished every other power strong enough to challenge her seriously. In the east, the Parthian kingdom (Persia) was strong enough to prevent Rome from expanding further in its direction, but not powerful enough to invade and imperil Rome. As a result, Rome could afford to be racked by internal turmoil and civil war for over a century—from the assassination of Tiberius Gracchus in 133 B.C. to the victory of Octavian (Augustus Caesar) over Mark Antony in 30 B.C.—without ever coming into serious danger of losing her worldwide hegemony.

America in the late twentieth century is not in the same comfortable situation as Rome in the second and first centuries before Christ. Far from being alone in the world, we are not even the most powerful nation. There are two other "great powers," each of them larger in population, the two of them, at least to some extent, allied against us, and between them controlling or influencing a substantial portion of the rest of the world, including the sources of raw materials essential to our economy, without which we would be hard put to defend ourselves against them. While both Russia and China have numerous satellites and allies on whose support they can unquestionably count, we have several nominal allies of moderate size and strength, inlcuding two great industrial powers, Japan and West Germany. Unfortunately Japan is demilitarized and West Germany is somewhat stalemated by the fact that East Germany is firmly in the Soviet orbit. Japan and West Germany are far from us and right on the borders, so to speak, of the Soviet Union and China: West Germany is separated from the USSR only by the Soviet satellites, Poland and East Germany, and Japan has only a small inland sea separating it from the Asian mainland dominated by China and Russia. In addition, while the totalitarian governmental system in power in Russian and China means that those nations inevitably present a solid front against us, our own allies, Japan and West Germany, have a pluralistic, democratic system and they are seldom of one mind about their relations with us. Needless to say, our dismal record in supporting our South Vietnamese allies has already given other nations cause to reflect on the wisdom of casting their lot irrevocably with us in a serious international conflict.

To return to our parallel from ancient history, Rome could afford, for a century or more, the luxury of being a "house divided against itself," without succumbing as a result, for the simple reason that there was no other power on the outside with the determination or the ability to attack her. The United States owes its national independence to the fact that during the Revolutionary War, Britain was involved in fighting more dangerous adversaries all over the globe; in addition France, the greatest European power of the era, intervened directly on America's behalf. The War of 1812 occupies a prominent place in our own history, but we are seldom made fully aware of the fact that, as far as the British were concerned, it was only a minor diversion in their twenty years' war with revolutionary and Napoleonic France. After defeating France, Britain might well have gone on to reconquer her former colonies in North America, but thought better of making the attempt. Having the United States as a cobelligerent did not materially help Napoleon, who was ultimately overwhelmed by the coalition fighting against him, but there can be no doubt that the long British struggle with Napoleon helped America by keeping Britain fully occupied and making the British unwilling to go on fighting us once their principal adversary, France, had been defeated.

America's momentous internal struggle, the War between the States of 1861-65, was waged without interference on the part of the powerful European states. Had either Britain or France intervened on the side of the Confederacy, the South would have probably become independent, and of course the subsequent history of North America and of the world would have been quite different. But the Europeans were otherwise occupied and had little interest in involving thelmselves in North America, and as a result the United States was able to afford the dubious luxury of a profound and bloody internal conflict without being seriously threatened from abroad. As a matter of fact, once the North had defeated the South, it emerged from the war so strong militarily and industrially that it rather quickly persuaded Napoleon III to drop his Mexican adventure and leave the hapless "emperor" he had installed there, Maximilian, to be overthrown.

During the first century and a half of American independence, the United States enjoyed a relatively secure situation with no serious dangers of foreign invasion. Three factors contributed to this security: first, of course, there was the fact that the colonist — and then the newly independent Americans — had shown themselves capable of fighting off some of Europe's best forces, especially when the Europeans were hampered by commitments elsewhere and by the logistics of transatlantic campaigning. Second, there was the comparative isolation of the United States, separated from Europe by three thousand miles of ocean. Third, there was the always uneasy balance of power in Europe: none of the major powers was in a position to risk exposing itself to the hostility of a European neighbor by committing the majority of its military strength to intervention in North America.

Today, each of America's three great bulwarks has been eroded. The European balance of power, which kept the highly industrialized, well-armed European powers preoccupied with each other and away from us, has been shattered, not least by America' own decisive intervention in the two World Wars. World War I eliminated one great power, Austria-Hungary, from the international scene, and World War II eliminated

41

several more: Germany and Japan were crushed, while Britain and France were sufficiently weakened so that they find it virtually impossible to have an independent foreign and military policy of any real international impact.

In addition, we are no longer on the outside, watching the interplay of other, greater powers, but we have become one of the principal actors. As things have turned out, all of the other powers that might have been strong enough to challenge us—and hence to balance each other—were eliminated, except for one, the Soviet Union. Since 1950, it has become evident that Communist China is or will shortly be a third "superpower." Unfortunately, the prospects of balancing China and Russia against one another to insure our own tranquility are not very good, because despite elements of rivalry, they have a joint commitment to world revolution and can generally cooperate with one another to the disadvantage of the United States. Although America has tried, with some success, to play off China against Russia, it should be evident that the ideological hostility of both those powers to us is so great, and their common interest in the "liberation" of the rest of the world is so strong, that we cannot take much comfort from the friction that frequently arises between them. In every significant conflict of interests, even though it has appeared for a time that we have been able to draw one or the other over to our side, in the long run we have lost, and when they have quarreled, it has only been over the division of the spoils they succeeded in taking from us.

The comparative isolation of the United States from the other major power centers thanks to our two oceans, instead of being a source of strength, is now really a weakness. Oceans no longer protect a nation from intercontinental missiles, and so no longer provide any security whatsoever against a devastating nuclear attack. On the other hand, because the United States is a maritime power, confronting two great land powers dominating the Eurasian land mass, the seas pose a tremendous logistical problem for us. Whenever the Soviet Union or Communist China challenge us, they take pains to make sure that it will be at the end of our strategic reach and quite close in for them. Thus in attempting to sustain South Vietnam, we were at a tremendous logistic disadvantage, and the same is of course true of any efforts we might now make to intervene in the Middle East, particularly after the dismantling of our base and supply system in the Mediterranean and, more recently, in Portugal and the Portuguese Azores. The one time that the Soviet Union ignored the principle of challenging us only at the end of our reach was in the attempt to convert Castro's Cuba into what looked like an aggressive forward base for the USSR. That attempt, as we know, was a qualified setback for the Soviet Union, even though by no means a total victory for us. Soviet successes in Central America may now challenge us again right in our own backyard.

Thus two of the trumps that we held in the past are no longer in the hand: there is no longer a balance of great world powers preoccupied with each other and thus willing to leave us alone, but only two other great powers, allied in many respects, not least in hostility to us and to the whole economic-political-social system we represent. The oceans no longer protect us; instead of hampering our enemies, they make it difficult for us to support our friends. But what about the third trump, which so far our potential opponents have respected, or else disregarded to their undoing: the strength and effectiveness of America's own military forces?

Here two things must be said: first, there can be no doubt that the United States still possesses tremendous military strength. However, it must be recognized that in absolute terms our strength is now inferior to that of at least one of our potential adversaries alone, namely the USSR, to say nothing of the USSR and Communist China combined. Very significantly, especially in view of our traditional role as a maritime power, our naval strength is already inferior to that of the Soviet Union. And the Soviet preponderance will continue to grow.

This creates a new situation in recent world history: both land and sea superiority are in the hands of a single power. During the nineteenth century, when France appeared to be the greatest land power, Britain had the mastery of the sea. After the Franco-Prussian War, military superiority passed to Germany, but Britain remained supreme at sea. During World War II, one of the two major Axis powers, Japan, was primarily a naval power, and for a time it appeared to be mounting an effective challenge to the two English-speaking Allied powers who shared control of the seas, the United States and Britain. The destruction of the Japanese navy preceded the ultimate defeat of Japan and left the American navy as the unchallenged mistress of the world's oceans.

Since World War II, American naval strength has not been maintained in the face of the challengingly rapid increase in Soviet naval power. We have never had an army to rival that of either the Soviet Union or Communist China; in this respect, we are like Britain in the nineteenth century vis-à-vis France and Germany. Thus, although we are by tradition and situation a maritime power rather than a land power, we find ourselves in a position of inferiority at sea as well as on land.

Figures and estimates comparing American naval and military power

43

with that of our principal potential adversaries vary, depending on the way the relative superiorities and inferiorities in the different arms and classes of weapons are weighted. What is in many ways even more disturbing than the decline in the relative strength of American forces on paper is the undeniable evidence of a widespread deterioration in morale and effectiveness. It is no secret that inability to agree on goals, strategy, and acceptable tactics undermined the effectiveness of our military operations in Indochina, with the disastrous results that are now history. More than this, there is no doubt that the fighting personnel of all the different arms have suffered a marked decline in morale and combat readiness. This is due in part to the prolonged frustrations resulting from the nature of the Vietnamese conflict, in large measure to the rise in drug abuse (deliberately fostered by our adversaries), and to the outbreak of racial and other social conflicts in the air, land, and naval services.

From a purely military perspective, then, it must be admitted that the United States are no longer in a position to face with any degree of confidence the prospect of a serious foreign assault by one or both of our principal rivals. We have our nuclear arsenal, it is true. This arsenal is now inferior to that of the Soviet Union but is still sufficient, we are told, to destroy both the Soviet Union and the rest of the world. Unfortunately, instead of guaranteeing that the Soviet Union will not launch a nuclear attack on us, the chief effect of the present nuclear stand-off is to make it certain that we cannot use our nuclear weapons against the USSR, even in an extreme situation, because what they would do to us by way of retaliation would be even worse than what we could possibly do to them.

Pointing to a Debacle?

Does all this mean that the United States are in imminent danger of sudden collapse, such as happened to France in May and June of 1940 when the Germans finally launched their blitzkrieg in the West? Certainly the speed and the totality of the disaster that befell the French came as a surprise to almost everyone, including the Germans. There is a recent parallel. In early March 1975, no one in South Vietnam or the United States expected the total collapse of South Vietnam within six weeks. The history of the world is full of situations in which a government or a nation that had appeared relatively secure suddenly was overwhelmed and obliterated. If we are going to face the facts as they exist at the two hundredth anniversary of American independence, must we therefore reckon with the possibility that we will not reach 210 or 220?

At the very least, it is instructive to note how quickly an apparently stable situation can be transformed into total catastrophe. Of course, in France in 1940 there were many clues to what might happen if and when Germany attacked in force. The French and British armies were numerically superior to the German, and had the advantage of immensely well-fortified positions—the ill-fated Maginot Line—in some sectors of the front. The French were even superior to the Germans in the quality and number of their tanks. They were inferior in the air, and more important, in the organization and tactical ability of their ground units. And there was a singular lack of enthusiasm and inspiration on the French side. But no one really thought that those disadvantages were so great that they would lead to an abrupt collapse of the whole French army.

The United States suffers today from many disadvantages similar to those that prevailed in France in 1940. Of course, we are not at war. However, that is not necessarily a great advantage, because today nations can pass from being officially at peace to being invaded and overwhelmed in a matter of days if not hours. The fact that we are not now at war certainly is no guarantee of a long breathing-space. We cannot count on having years or even months between the flashing of unmistakable danger signals and the ultimate test of strength and will. Certainly it would be unwise to assume that American public opinion is more united or American internal morale better than that of France in 1940. America's resolve seems to be recovering, but it has yet to be tested.

Some of the Differences

The similarity between the United States after World War II and Rome after the Third Punic War lies in the fact that total victory in a far-flung overseas war was followed by tremendous social unrest at home. The difference between the situation of the Roman and the North American republics lies in the fact that Rome had no powerful foreign enemies to threaten her while she was trying to resolve her internal social problems. America does. The similarity between the United States of today and the France of 1940 lies in the fact that the military forces of both, while apparently strong and in good order, may be far weaker where it counts than appearances indicate, and also in the fact that in America today, as in France then, leadership in the face of a threatening situation is divided and confused. Even today, even after the tremendous victory of Ronald Reagan in the 1980 presidential election, there are substantial elements among America's political leadership, both Democratic and Republican, who seem determined to prevent him from consolidating our strength and to keep our country divided and indecisive. Indeed, many of our leaders seem to feel guilty about our present standing and to want to reduce it. The difference, of course, is that in 1940 France was at war with a powerful adversary and knew it. We are not at war, at least not formally, and there is certainly no general feeling that our national existence is in immediate and great danger. The period from the fall of Poland to the blitzkrieg in France was called the *drôle de guerre* — funny war. Are we now in a "drôle de paix"?

World history is full of the story of nations whose decline and fall was provoked not by any underlying and irremediable weakness, but by the simple failure to recognize warning signals and take corrective action while there is yet time. Will the fate of the United States in the last quarter of the twentieth century add one more name to the melancholy list?

4

The Years Ahead

> The loss in physical force is not the only one which the two sides suffer in the course of the combat; the moral forces also are shaken, broken, and go to ruin. It is not only the loss of men, horses and guns, but in order, courage, confidence, cohesion and plan, which come into consideration when it is a question whether the fight can be still continued or not. It is principally the moral forces which decide here, and in all cases in which the conqueror has lost as heavily as the conquered, it is these alone.
>
> Karl von Clausewitz
> *On War*

What lies ahead for the great North American republic, conceived by some as the successor to ancient Rome, and for perhaps twenty years the architect of a modern "pax Americana" like the ancient *pax Romana?* As we try to forget our disastrous Vietnam war, many have pointed out that the total casualties suffered by the United States in Vietnam only equal one year's automobile traffic deaths, while the $150 billion spent in the futile struggle was less than the budget of the Department of Health, Education, and Welfare for two years.

Unfortunately, as Clausewitz pointed out in 1832, it is not only the loss in "men, horses and guns" that is important. What has happened to order, courage, confidence, cohesion, and plan? Is it still possible for a fight to be carried on, or not? When President Ford ordered American forces to intervene and free the captured United States merchant ship *Mayaguez* on May 14, 1975, the reaction throughout America and even a large part of the world was overwhelmingly enthusiastic. Although Senator Henry Jackson at first uttered fears that we might be once again involving ourselves in a Gulf of Tonkin-type quagmire, he quickly changed his opinion as he saw the reaction to Ford's "precipitous" action.

In several respects, the freeing of the *Mayaguez* was a costly operation—several United States personnel lost, as well as considerable American military equipment, all for the sake of securing the immediate release of forty American seamen and a ship that would probably have been released ultimately anyway. Why, then, the overwhelmingly enthusiastic response? Clausewitz' observation gives us the answer. The *Mayaguez* incident, for a second at least, showed the world—but particularly Americans themselves—that our "moral forces" are not altogether at an end. We can still take effective and decisive action, given sufficient provocation. It is, of course, altogether likely that the Cambodian seizure of an unarmed United States merchant vessel was a deliberate provocation, intended to find out whether the humiliations suffered in Cambodia, Vietnam, and Laos had so undermined our national willpower that nothing would make us react. And it is instructive that there has so far been no further similar direct provocation. Such an incident certainly does not win security for us, but it at least ought to postpone another frontal challenge. It did not, of course, forestall the indirect challenge in Angola.

If the *Mayaguez* incident was a kind of shot in the arm to America's national self-esteem, the storming of the U.S. embassy in Teheran and the subsequent fifteen months' ordeal for our hostages was a blow. President Carter's ill-fated rescue attempt would have been an even greater morale-builder had it succeeded, but as it ended in a debacle, it only made us look more ridiculous and impotent than ever.

Quick Action versus the War of Attrition

The United States has been involved in two major military undertakings since World War II; the Soviet Union has now been involved in three. The United States fought a "police action" in Korea. The conflict in Vietnam was not so euphemistically named. In the two affairs, U.S. forces had been actively involved, with varying degrees of intensity, for at least thirteen of the thirty years between the end of World War II and the loss of Indochina in 1975. The Soviet Union's two active military adventures since World War II were close to its own borders, in Hungary (1956) and Czechoslovakia (1968). Although there was no direct conflict between the United States and the Soviet Union, clearly the interests and wishes of each were at stake. Where the Russians made an effort, they did it promptly, determined to use all the force necessary and more, and totally successfully. There was grumbling, complaining, critical comment from "world opinion," but generally, after the fact, more or less grudging acceptance. In addition, the Soviet Union participated directly in the Cuban expedition to Angola. This was also direct, speedy, and effective. There was a certain amount of international distress, but it has subsided. The United States, in the last analysis, could take comfort only from pious remarks by the Cubans to the effect that, for the moment, they are planning no further adventures. During the Christmas season of 1979, with the U.S. embassy in Iran in the hands of "student militants," the Soviet Union embarked on a military adventure in Afghanistan. It was not as neat as the previous actions in Hungary and Czechoslovakia, and it is not over yet, but it seems to have been much more efficacious than our intervention in Vietnam.

American intervention in Korea was extensive, speedy, and limited. All Americans will be familiar with the dramatic way in which American forces, under the leadership of General Douglas MacArthur, first liberated South Korea, then overran most of the north, only to be thrown back by the intervention of a massive army of Chinese "volunteers." The ultimate result was a kind of stalemate, preserving the independence of South Korea but with no clear victory for the United States. We allowed ourselves to be drawn into extensive "peace talks" while the fighting went on, with the effect that more American casualties were suffered after the talks began than before. It is generally believed that even this relative success was achieved only thanks to the apparently well-founded Communist apprehension that the United States might use its immense nuclear superiority against them.

In South Vietnam, as all the world knows, the situation was reversed. According to the maxim of the ancient Chinese military theoretician Sun Tzu, "Where the war is protracted, the resources of the state will not suffice." At the beginning of the Vietnam intervention, Lyndon Johnson felt that our wealth and resources were so great that we could not only allow the war to be protracted almost without limit, but could also embark on hitherto unprecedented domestic spending programs. The consequences are now history: defeat in Vietnam, humiliation in the diplomatic arena, and economic disarray at home.

Quick action comes easily to a dictatorship. Hitler successfully and almost bloodlessly launched *coups de main* in Austria and Czechoslovakia. His whirlwind campaign in Poland was much bloodier, but Germany's losses were light. Similarly, the blitzkrieg in Western Europe paid Germany immediate and handsome dividends. The Soviet Union acted speedily and with great force in Hungary and in Czechoslovakia. Casualties were relatively light in both cases—although international indignation was shrill—and the consequences, from the Soviet perspective, altogether satisfactory. Sometimes even a democracy can act with tremendous energy, as Israel did in launching the Six Days' War. Democracies, however, are more sensitive to public opinion than dictatorships, even when they are acutely conscious of their own national danger. Thus Israel hesitated to launch preventive action in 1973, and was itself surprised and badly mauled in the Yom Kippur War. The United States suffers from a twofold disability. Unlike Israel, we are not acutely conscious of national peril. We do not have the feeling that one serious mistake could destroy us. In addition, we are divided internally, not only about how to defend our interests, but about whether our interests deserve defending. As a result, it is very unlikely that we will ever be able to imitate Russia or even Israel in taking sudden, decisive action when we think it to be necessary. We require a long buildup of tension, considerable provocation, and—under the strange concept of "graduated response" or "escalation"—a number of weak measures before we are prepared to take strong ones.

At the present time, the military situation vis-à-vis the Soviet Union is not developing clearly. Alarmed by the Soviet measures in Afghanistan, President Carter began taking steps in 1980 to arrest the decline of America's military strength. Unfortunately, he himself had already done much to worsen the decline by cancelling plans for the B-1 bomber, a nuclear aircraft carrier, and the neutron bomb, as well as reducing the range and effectiveness of the much-touted "cruise missile." Since his election in 1980, President Reagan has made the strengthening of our defense forces a top priority, and Congress has largely supported him. Nevertheless, the situation is now so bad that it will require great efforts to recover a measure of equality vis-à-vis the Soviet Union—not to mention vis-à-vis a renewed Soviet-Chinese alliance—and there is always some danger that our attempts to restore our military preparedness may provoke the Soviet Union into a preventive attack. Perhaps our decline is now in the process of being reversed, but it is too early to be sure.

Until we see clear evidence that the trend has been reversed, it is fair to repeat the generalization made in 1977: There can be no doubt, however that our possible adversaries are growing continually stronger while we and our probable friends grow weaker. The history of mankind is such that we can easily predict the outcome of such a trend if it continues long enough: the attack and conquest of the weaker by the stronger. It may comfort us to imagine that our nuclear "sufficiency" makes direct attack by the Soviet Union unthinkable. But there are many alternatives to direct confrontation, as Vietnam and Angola illustrate. What will we do if the USSR, without resorting to nuclear attack, suddenly does something that appears to threaten our continuing existence: for example, by creating a situation in which we can no longer receive the supply of Middle Eastern oil on which we have become dependent? Are we going to attack a weaker, non-nuclear oil-producing state such as Canada or Venezuela in order to supply our needs? Or will we simply accept the further decline in power and national wealth, the economic crisis and attendant dislocations, that a newer and more serious embargo would bring?

At some point, present trends will have to be reversed, if the decline of America is not going to result in America's fall. We still have an abundant, though not excessive, supply of weapons of war. But more and more of those who will have to use them are not convinced of the rightness of their country's cause nor of their ability to win. "It is," as Clausewitz said, "principally the moral forces which decide here."

Will the United States be able, in the years ahead, to rebuild the foundations of our traditional moral strength, to recapture the high morale that never failed us even during the difficult early years of World War II? Of course, moral strength alone is of little value if the physical means of modern technological warfare are not available. It is unlikely, though, that we will entirely denude ourselves of the weapons of modern war. There are too many skeptics in Congress and in any administration ever to allow the United States to place its national security totally at the mercy of another great power's benevolence and good intentions.

Unfortunately, weapons development and manufacture, difficult though it can be, is easier to achieve than a recovery or moral strength. The years ahead will not be bright and easy ones for the United States, even under the most favorable of circumstances. But they do not need to be hopeless and defeated ones. The key to a recovery of world respect is a recovery of self-respect. And ultimately our self-respect or lack of it depends not only on the mass-media-promoted self-image that we have, but even more on what we really are. In the last analysis, it will come back to our vision. Where there is no vision, the people perish. The American people are not yet at the point of perishing, but they are at the point of having lost their vision. After that, it may take a longer or a shorter period of time, but unless there is a recovery of vision, there is no alternative but prolonged decline and ultimate disaster on a national and personal level.

5

An Unequal Contest

In other words, economic life naturally does not go on in a moral vacuum. It is constantly in danger of straying from the ethical middle unless it is buttressed by strong moral supports. These must simply be there, and, what is more, must constantly be impregnated against rot. Otherwise our free economic system, and with it any free state and society, must ultimately collapse.

Wilhelm Röpke
A Humane Economy

What are the marks that distinguish a free man from a bondservant or slave? According to ancient Roman law, there were four freedoms that characterized the free man: he could represent himself in court; he could choose his employment; he could choose his place of residence; he could choose his citizenship or allegiance. Each of these freedoms may be guaranteed by law. But none of them can be exercised without a certain amount of economic or financial freedom.

The United States, and to varying degrees most of the other countries of the democratic West, is in a paradoxical situation in the late twentieth century. More and more laws and regulations are being enacted to protect the individual's freedom. At the same time economic developments are taking place that threaten to deny him the ability to exercise that freedom. Some of these developments are determined by political decisions of the government. For example, a schoolteacher employed on the New York side of the Hudson River will find it legal but very expensive to give up his New York post and accept one on the other side of the river in New Jersey, for he will stand to lose accumulated retirement benefits. Here economic decisions on the part of the government restrict, in effect, the individual's freedom to choose his work and the place where he wants to live, even though the laws allow it.

Personal liberty, then, depends in a real sense on personal economic freedom. It is possible to conceive of a society in which the average economic level is high but where little personal political freedom is enjoyed, although usually such a situation does not last long. As people develop economic freedom of action, they come to demand political freedom as well, and either achieve it or are repressed, in which case their economic situation is usually worsened as a result. It is also possible to conceive of a society that enjoys considerable political freedom but where everyone is terribly poor. Such conditions prevailed, at least until recently, in India. But there the social problems accompanying poverty were so great that they seemed, at least to India's ruler, Mrs. Gandhi, to be incompatible with personal and political freedom, which she has abolished for a time at least.

A democratic society with a high level of personal freedom depends on a reasonably high level of personal economic freedom. A highly regulated economy, such as that of socialist Sweden, may give lip service to the ideal of the citizens' freedom. But as the recent ordeal of film director Ingmar Bergman illustrates, increasing economic controls bring with them the loss of personal and even artistic freedom.

Political freedom can be—and frequently is—abolished with a stroke of the pen, backed up by military and police power. Economic freedom usually erodes slowly. Hence threats to it are less obvious. But when economic freedom falls to a sufficiently low level, whatever political freedom remains becomes practically meaningless or will be abolished.

Political freedom thus depends on a sound economy. But a sound economy is not self-maintaining. It depends on moral values. Moral values, in turn, are not self-perpetuating. Indeed, in the atmosphere of a productive free economy, based on competition, the quest for personal gain, and ever-increasing consumption—which certainly promotes self-indulgence—moral values tend to decline or, to use Röpke's expression, to rot. When they are rotten enough, they can no longer support the weight of the structure of a free economy, but collapse and bring it down with them. The economy *needs* moral values, but cannot itself produce them. Another source is required for that. What can that source be?

54

America is now experiencing what we might call the debauchery of the free-market economy. As Austrian economist Joseph Schumpeter pointed out long ago, if capitalism falls, it will not be because of its failures, but because of its successes. In showering necessities, optional goods, and luxuries upon virtually everyone living under it, capitalism stimulates self-interest, selfishness, and self-indulgence to a degree that it destroys the self-discipline and personal integrity without which a viable free economy cannot exist. As America has become wealthier and wealthier, Americans have come first to disregard, and finally to repudiate, the very values upon which their wealth was based. They are like the Roman soldiers of the Emperor Valens, so used to the power and tranquility that Roman arms had won and maintained over the centuries that they were unwilling to wear their heavy armor or train with heavy weapons. Then, when suddenly threatened by an invasion, they found that they were no longer in condition to use them. A Roman army was destroyed and the emperor lost his life.

Sources of Moral Values

Are there governments that can generate moral and spiritual values? Indeed there are. Unfortunately, the praiseworthy activity of generating moral and spiritual values, when taken over by a government, becomes suddenly sinister. For the governments that generate their own autonomous value systems are those we designate as totalitarian.

A totalitarian government does not confine its activities to such traditional functions as "providing for the common defense" and "promoting the general welfare." When a government owns the means of production, it produces the material values of society, i.e., its goods, to the extent that they are produced at all. Totalitarianism, however, does not confine itself to producing goods, but claims the right to define the Good, i.e., to define values.

A nation needs moral strength, moral values, to survive. A government may undermine and destroy them—as our government to some extent has done. Or it can attempt to create them. But government-created values smack of totalitarianism and thought control. Clearly what we need is a strong source of values other than the government. This Christianity and the churches once provided. Will they be able to do it again? Will they dare?

Totalitarianism and Authoritarianism

It is important to recognize the difference between *totalitarianism* on the one hand and mere *despotism* or authoritarian dictatorship on the other. Authoritarianism, dictatorship, and tyranny of various forms have been with us as long as mankind has been civilized enough to have government. Authority, from the Latin *auctoritas*, means the right or the ability to command voluntary assent to one's wishes and instructions. Authority in this sense is a necessary attribute of every good leader. According to Roman theory (although not Roman practice), the Senate's authority rested on the moral worth of the Senators, who were obeyed because they were respected. Later, under the principate or Empire, the *princeps* or Caesar was, in theory at least, obeyed because of the respect he enjoyed as "first" in the Senate and in the state. In fact, Augustus Caesar merely voted first in the Senate, and the majority of other Senators voted in agreement with him. Authority, in theory at least, attaches to the individual, not to his office. Unfortunately, many of those who have the power to command others lack the moral authority to win their voluntary consent, and therefore impose their will by force. This perversion of true authority is called authoritarianism. An authoritarian system is one in which the individual ruler always asserts his will. It is objectionable because it suppresses individual freedom, but it is not the same thing as totalitarianism.

The characteristic feature of totalitarianism is this: in a totalitarian system, the ruling power — not necessarily an individual autocrat — seeks to control everything, to direct the whole society, right down to the individual citizen's desires and even tastes. The ancient Roman Empire was not totalitarian: the emperors demanded *obedience,* but they did not seek to tell their subjects all that they should do, want, and think. Indeed, totalitarianism is a modern phenomenon, made possible only by modern technology. Until the advent of modern means of communication and surveillance, it was not possible for a ruler to know in detail what his subjects were doing. Only when they refused to pay their taxes, to obey orders, or actively revolted, did they come to his attention. And he did not have at his disposal the means to instruct them on the details of their lives. The way they lived the greater part of their lives was determined by tradition, custom, and individual preference. Modern technology has presented the government, whether run by an autocratic individual or by a democratically chosen body of representatives, with the power to communicate in detail with everyone, and to prescribe the details of daily life. At the same time, it has provided the government with much better means for observing and recording the degree to which individuals comply with its wishes. The means to impose totalitarianism are technological and bureaucratic; the means to resist it are moral and spiritual.

The Destruction of Intermediate Structures

As Hannah Arendt has demonstrated in her classic work, *The Origins of Totalitarianism,*[1] one of the basic features of totalitarianism is the abolition of all the intermediate structures and institutions within society—the church, labor unions, social clubs, fraternal associations, independent schools, even family solidarity. Its goal in so doing, conscious or not, is the creation of an "atomistic mass" of isolated individuals. In the "atomistic mass," it is every man for himself and every woman for herself. Individual ties, personal loyalties, friendship, ties of blood, business and religious associations and the like fade in insignificance. The individual exists in only one important relation, to the state power.

The difference between totalitarian and pretotalitarian society may be likened to that between a modern conscripted army and a medieval army on the feudal pattern. In a modern conscript army, the individual soldier is summoned directly by the central government, sent to a training camp with people drawn from all over his nation, most of them complete strangers, and assigned to a unit according to central planning. In the medieval feudal army, the king or ruler—we cannot speak of a medieval king as a "central power"—summons his chief vassals to arms. Each of them goes in turn to his own vassals, the lesser lords who depend on him, and calls them to arms. Finally, at the local level, each local ruler assembles his own men-at-arms. The individual foot soldier is responsible to his immediate superior; he serves with relatives, neighbors, and friends from his own district; the king's orders to him are transmitted through someone he knows, and it is his immediate commander to whom he owes personal loyalty. The modern national army is thus "totalitarian" almost by definition. Citizens in a free society may well agree to relinquish their individual rights to serve in such an army as a necessity for national survival, but they cannot fail to be aware that they are in fact surrendering rights. The fact that a modern army is a model of the totalitarian state explains much of the resentment of ordinary free citizens against compulsory military service. It also explains the remarkable militarism, military organization, and high degree of military

[1]Hannah Arendt, *The Origins of Totalitarianism* (Cleveland: World, 1951; 2nd edition, 1958).

preoccupation in the supposedly "peace-loving" totalitarian states, past and present.

Just as there are no feudal structures in a modern army, totalitarianism will not permit intermediate structures to exist in its modern form of the state. It destroys all existing structures and their values and substitutes its own structure and its own values. Because totalitarian systems seek to control the thinking and the desires of their subjects, they necessarily have to be preoccupied with "education" and "re-education." The totalitarian state is not interested in teaching the "three Rs," or even the type of thing that is taught in American civics courses: how to fit in, how to adjust. It wants to teach its citizens *everything*—not merely what they must do to meet their obligations, but what they must *want,* and even why they must want it. Totalitarian states often boast a high level of literacy. In societies that were once backward, there is great emphasis on teaching reading, so that all the people can read and absorb the leader's viewpoints.

During the early days of the Protestant Reformation, the Reformers stressed the need to teach ordinary people to read, so that they could read and study the Bible. This had a liberating effect on them, and increasing literacy went hand in hand with the rise of civic freedom. But that is because the Bible is basically a liberating book: "If ye continue in my word . . . ye shall know the truth, and the truth shall make you free" (John 8:31–32). In early America, the Bible and texts such as the old McGuffey's Readers formed the fundamental part of children's early reading experience, and both promoted moral values, a sense of responsibility, and an awareness of duty to one's neighbor and to society. But what the Bible can do positively, other texts can accomplish negatively. As Jacques Ellul points out in his book *Propaganda,* literacy can be a tool for the imposition of totalitarian doctrines:

> Mao simplified the script in his battle with illiteracy, and in some places in China new alphabets are being created. This would have no particular significance except that the texts used to teach the adult students how to read—and which are the only texts to which they have access—are *exclusively* propaganda texts. . . . Thus, we see here a wonderful shaping tool: The illiterate are taught to read only the new script; nothing is published in that script except propaganda texts; therefore, the illiterates cannot possibly read—or know—anything else.[2]

---

[2]Jacques Ellul, *Propaganda: The Formation of Men's Attitudes* (New York: Knopf, 1965), p. 110.

The fundamental feature of totalitarianism, then, is that the state determines everything. Totalitarianism may also involve an authoritiarian dictatorship, but it need not. Modern Sweden, for example, has a representative government, freely elected. Yet modern Sweden has moved very far in the totalitarian direction, for its freely elected government has gone a long way towards determining everything that the Swedish people may have, want, do, or even think.[3]

This is the reason why it is important to distinguish between authoritarianism and totalitarianism. Both are bad, but authoritarianism is less sweeping and easier to overthrow than totalitarianism. In the United States, we have had more than one president who has acted in an authoritarian fashion. But it is not the "imperial presidency" in America that confronts us with the danger of totalitarianism, but rather the all-embracing bureaucracy. For it is the impersonal, immense bureaucracy, not a single, power-hungry political leader, that threatens to tell Americans every single thing that they may or may not have, want, do and think.

The American Civil Liberties Union launched a fund drive late in May, 1981, using the "threat" of the Moral Majority and other religiously-oriented groups as a scare tactic to prod potential donors into giving. What the leaders of the ACLU and similar groups may not recognize is the fact that there is a fundamental difference between what the Moral Majority would do, if it had the power to accomplish all it desires, and what a totalitarian political system such as communism would do. Both would impose a measure of censorship, it is true, and hence the ACLU opposes both (although it seems to be more worried about the Moral Majority than about Communism). But while the Moral Majority would censor pornography and encourage people to read the Bible, even in schools, Communism would censor pornography and *require* people to study Marxism-Leninism; then it would demand that they live accordingly. There is a parallel in the fact that both would censor pornography, but there is a world of difference in what they would do positively. Even if people were required to read the Bible, it simply does not provide either the justification or a program for totalitarian control. Marxism-Leninism does. If Jerry Falwell were to become, like Oliver Cromwell, a Puritan "Lord Protector" of the United States, the doctrines he espouses, based on the Bible, would not compel or even encourage him to suppress the ACLU. But we can be certain that if Communism ever takes over the nation, the ACLU and similar civil rights and civil liberties groups will

[3]Roland Huntford, *The New Totalitarians* (New York: Stein and Day, 1972), describes this situation.

be among the first to go—despite the fact that they may have contributed to the Communist takeover by weakening the spiritual forces that could have resisted it. That is the difference between totalitarianism and authority. Authority demands a measure of respect and obedience; of course it can demand too much, and become authoritarian. But totalitarianism by its very nature demands total control, and even when it is more or less benevolent in spirit, like Swedish socialism, it intends to see that everything in the society is done in accordance with its wishes.

The difference between a free society and a totalitarian one is fundamentally a moral-spiritual difference, just as the difference between the Bible and *Das Kapital* is fundamentally a moral-spiritual difference. Unfortunately, American society tends to concentrate on the economic advantages of a free society when contrasting it with a totalitarian one; economic advantages are there, but to draw attention to them as though they were of fundamental importance is rather like comparing Moses to Karl Marx on the basis of Moses' greater readability and more elevated style.

The Free Market vs. the Directed Economy; Marxism vs. the "American Way of Life"

If the struggle for the hearts, minds, and lives of men in society today were fought out solely on the relative productive efficiency of competing economic systems, there is no doubt that the free-market economy would win hands down. Unfortunately, it is very seldom indeed that people have the opportunity to choose between a free and a state-directed economy solely on their respective economic merits. The free-market economy is a by-product as well as a requirement of a free society. Where freedom goes, the free economy is not likely to survive. Similarly, it is impossible to choose only a state-directed *economy*, if one were to prefer that to a free one, because the state cannot direct the economy unless it also directs a great deal more, as the Swedish experience shows and Britain is also learning.

To make the problem clear, we might say that a "capitalist economy" cannot defend itself against Communism any more than a great capitalist corporation, such as IBM, can effectively defend itself against the United States government. The reason is evident: IBM has only financial resources; the government has the authority to legislate, and the police and ultimately the military power to enforce its decisions. A capitalist economy may produce better than a Communist one, but it cannot defend itself against *Communism*, because Communism is more than an economic system; it is also a political system and includes military power. Logically, then, the capitalist or free economy, if it comes to an all-out conflict with a Communist system, needs the support of noncapitalistic, noneconomic institutions, namely military forces.

The same thing is true in the spiritual and ideological realm where values clash. The fact that a free-market economy may produce more efficiently than a state-controlled one by no means assures that people will invariably choose it in preference to state control. A free-market economy is only an economy: it does not provide the values, the moral and spiritual reasons for preferring, and if necessary struggling to keep, the free form of economic organization. Communism, by contrast, is not only an economic system: it also is an ideology, and provides the philosophical, "spiritual" values to justify its own existence.

One of the reasons that liberal groups such as the ACLU and George McGovern's "People for the American Way" appear to fear traditional morality more than totalitarian doctrine is a virtually total indifference to spiritual realities. They see our society's basic problems as economic and political in nature and look on the preoccupation with moral questions as a distraction if not a subterfuge to keep people from adopting the "correct" political solutions. Unfortunately many Christians and many defenders of the free market fall into the same trap and defend the free market basically with economic arguments. These may be valid; indeed, they generally are, but they are not enough to carry the day for freedom, for freedom is basically a spiritual issue, not an economic one.

Fragmentation vs. Centralization

One of the fundamental features of a nontotalitarian society is its complexity. No one agency or authority determines and provides everything. Material goods are provided by a free-market relation between industry, commerce, and finance. Education is provided by a complex of public and private schools. Information and entertainment are provided by a variety of media conglomerates and independent producers. Values are supposed to be generated by religious groups, philosophical schools, and other rival voices. It is this very complexity that gives us freedom, but it is also this complexity that makes us vulnerable to assault by a centralized, systematically coordinated force such as Communism.

America, or the "American way of life," is at a disadvantage in the spiritual or ideological struggle with the totalitarian systems of this world. We can only present partial visions to rival their total solutions. "Democracy" or "representative government" is not an equal match for the Communist vision, because democracy, like the free market, is only a partial thing: a mechanism for doing one thing, namely choosing a government and making laws. Democracy, like the free market, is fundamentally a method, not an idea or a philosophy. It is a better method, in this imperfect world, than the rival methods, but it cannot justify itself. It will only be adopted, and can only be defended, if we have reasons for adopting and defending it that come from outside the method itself.

Everyone recognizes that capitalism achieves greater productivity and profit than the various socialist or communist alternatives. In fact, opponents of capitalism now make this into an accusation, stating that capitalism only satisfies people's materials needs (or "false needs," according to the famous critique of radical leftist Herbert Marcuse). The old Communist charge, that capitalism needs the support of religion, promising people "pie in the sky by and by" to trick them into enduring their misery today, has been replaced. Religion is no longer "opium for the people," at least not in capitalist society. (Strangely, both traditionalist and pentecostal-revivalist Christianity are gaining strength in Communist countries, perhaps because the people *there* need that kind of "opium" to take their mind off the realities of life in "socialist society.") Today the charge is that capitalism reaches its greatest accomplishment in the "consumer society," supplying the material needs of people but starving them spiritually. And it is true, as refugee Russian novelist Aleksandr Solzhenitsyn has charged, that people in the West have by and large lost their spiritual values. We luxuriate in "freedom," which has really become only license to "do your own thing," or, put more elegantly, to have one's "individual lifestyle." Yet we are losing or have lost the strength of purpose and self-discipline necessary to preserve freedom. In fact, by and large, we hardly think of freedom as a value. Evidence for this is the constant favorable comment, at times verging on adoration, in the media, among political leaders, and less frequently in the general public, for countries such as Communist China where freedom is totally nonexistent.

In the absence of widespread commitment to deeply held values, and where there is no inner discipline, the great accomplishments of a liberal capitalistic society are more show than substance. Freedom of expression, easy travel, "free sex," underground newspapers, and all the attractive and less attractive expressions of liberty in a free society will not provide the power of resistance or endurance in the face of oppression. To expect "free enterprise" to withstand a determined assault from the coordinated, highly organized forces of Communism is a pathetic illusion. We need not think of a *military* assault: even a concentrated economic offensive could quickly prove irresistible. How much vigor did the West show in opposing the Arab oil boycott? And how well did the West react to the politicization of the Olympic Games in 1972 and 1976? How effective was President Carter's grain embargo and boycott of the 1980 Summer Olympics as a response to the Soviet intervention in Afghanistan? In the long run, after they have tasted defeat, humiliation, conquest, and oppression, a once-free people may bestir themselves to throw off the oppressor. But to expect a "free society," in which "freedom" means only the ability to seek one's own comforts, to resist a sustained and determined attack, whether psychological, economic, or military, is foolish. It would be no more reasonable than to have expected France to withstand Nazi Germany because of the superiority of French culture to Nazi cultural politics. French culture had not organized anything; Nazi propaganda, however perverted, had thoroughly organized German power to crush the French.

The contest between the United States and the other more or less free countries of the world on one side and world Communism on the other is and has always been an unequal one. Paradoxically, right up to the present time it has always been in the military arena that the free world has stood the best chance of success against the Communist powers. It is for this reason that the Communists have scrupulously avoided provoking an all-out military confrontation with the West. We might win militarily, but we are losing spiritually.

Neither democracy as a form of government nor capitalism as a means of economic organization can stand up to Marxism in the intellectual and spiritual arena because neither is really a moral force. Calling Marxism a system of morality does not mean that it is a system of *good* morality, but simply that it deals with moral issues and offers answers to them, something that neither democracy nor capitalism per se does. Nor does the American way of life.

The only way that America and the free world can resist the sort of challenge that Communism and the world revolution represent is by recovering what Röpke says is lacking in life that is *merely* economic: strong moral supports. The capitalistic system that produces material abundance does not produce moral values, but rather consumes them. To return to the biblical theme, "Not by bread alone," we can say that the capitalist system has gone a long way toward poisoning itself. For decades it has produced bread in such abundance that its beneficiaries (not

63

those it has exploited) have forgotten that there is such a thing as the Word that "proceeds from the mouth of God," by which they and their lives will be judged.

American society has become increasingly, and ever more openly, *hedonistic*. In other words, the pursuit of pleasure has become our highest goal. The philosophers, teachers, and spiritual leaders of mankind have known from the dawn of civilization that the unchecked pursuit of pleasure destroys the vitality of an individual or a civilization. But capitalistic economics offers no barrier to hedonism, even though prolonged hedonism will destroy the kind of individual self-discipline capitalism requires. Nor can democracy provide the basis for checking hedonism. After all, democracy is only a system for giving people what they want, and if they are hedonists, pleasure is what they want. A barrier to hedonism can only be created from a source that transcends both capitalism and economic methods on the one hand and democracy and political methods on the other.

Conclusions

The free world, with its more or less free governmental and economic institutions, is challenged on every level by totalitarian Marxism. This is abundantly evident. That most of us who live in the relatively free nations prefer life in them to life under totalitarian rule is also evident. Whether we have the willpower and the persistence to continue a long struggle, long enough for our present challengers to drop out, or perhaps be replaced by others, is not so evident.

As long as we pit a partial answer against a total system, we are doomed to defeat. We may win the struggle in one area, but we will lose it everywhere else, and in consequence lose overall.

Capitalism cannot stand against Marxism. Neither can democracy. Nor can capitalism and democracy, even together, stand against Marxism. Marxism is bigger than both combined, because it has a moral and a philosophical dimension that they lack. Capitalism and democracy are techniques; Marxism is a spiritual force. Even with inferior techniques, a spiritual force can win, as America discovered to her chagrin in Vietnam. Only if we can recover a moral vision that goes beyond the capitalist promise of more goods for more people and the democratic offer of free elections will we be able to stand successfully against the total vision that is Marxism. We have to know what to produce, and what to choose, and neither capitalism nor democracy, which are only methods, can tell us that.

Who or what will provide the answer? Government can try to do it. And in fact that is precisely what is happening in American society at the present time. Government in America is not consciously in the business of creating values, at least not in the heavy-handed way that the Soviet government is. But as the traditional moral sources fade out, or are pushed into the background, government begins to fill the vacuum. Unfortunately, as had already been said, if government ever begins to give us our values—to tell us what to want and what to think—then we will indeed already have totalitarianism.

Hitler's Germany put up a very good fight against Soviet Communism. In fact, without American assistance, it is quite likely that the Russians would have lost to Germany. But there is hardly anyone who would be willing to accept Nazi ideology in order to be able to stand up to Marxism. One totalitarian system can stand up to another. But can a complex, nontotalitarian society stand up to a totalitarian one? Indeed it can, provided it is *complete.* It is not necessary for it to be totalitarian, with one central governmental authority providing all the elements necessary for a world-historical conflict: economic production, governmental organization, motivation and morale. But it is necessary that all those elements be provided.

America has now experienced the first really lost war in her history, the Vietnam War. We may try to put it out of our minds, and some may say that it was not really we who lost the war, but the "militarist Thieu clique." But that is just self-deception. Whether or not we were in it legally, or wholeheartedly, or put forth our best effort, the fact is that we lost it. We had production, we had organization, but we lacked motivation and morale. As a result "the world's most powerful nation," to cite our own propaganda, or at the very least the world's foremost industrial power was defeated by a small, underdeveloped nation a tenth its size. As an Indian commentator observed, Nazi Germany or imperial Japan would not have lost a war under such circumstances.

If we did so badly in a small war, a limited war, what hope do we have in a major conflict, one that threatens our national existence? Very little, unless we can provide the motivation and the morale that were lacking during the Vietnam years. There *is* a way to do it short of adopting a totalitarian mentality to rival the Russians', but it will not happen by itself. We have to discover it, understand it, and implement it.

6

Preliminary Balance

And his servant said unto him, Alas, my master! how shall we do? And he
answered, Fear not: for they that be with us are more than they that be
with them.

II Kings 6:15-16

These preliminary observations concerning the state of the American
Republic at the beginning of its third century certainly make one wonder
about the fate of the Republic, not merely in the next century, but in the
immediate future. In medicine, proper diagnosis is a prerequisite for successful treatment. In business, an adequate analysis of all the relevant
factors is necessary for effective planning. With so momentous a thing
as choosing a course for the third century of the Republic, correct diagnosis and adequate analysis are no less necessary.

In the preceding chapters, we have observed that America has only
a limited time left to go on making mistakes affecting her own internal
health. We noted that America's vision of herself and of her goals for
the future, always a little fuzzy due to our "double vision"—our traditional mixture of biblical and humanistic elements, is now being virtually
extinguished by the loss of the biblical element and the concomitant
weakening of the humanistic component. The facts are that America is
rich, divided, morally disoriented, and militarily weak. We confront a
world that is poorer, where there are at least two powers each of which
is larger and far more united than we, and we have declining military
resources and morale. Our projection for the years ahead indicates that
even more important than the losses and the decline in military capacity

is the frightening deterioration of our moral strength, of our morale (*morale*, indeed, is only a variant form of *moral*). This deterioration places us in an unequal contest, one in which we have no reasonable prospect of success, because we are attempting to match an opponent who is at full strength while we are at partial strength and not even altogether clear about whether we want to try to win.

If these factors were the only factors, it would appear futile indeed to talk about preserving, let alone restoring, the Republic. It would appear to be necessary only to try to find the least expensive and disgraceful way out. Indeed, many observers of American foreign policy think that that is more or less what we are now trying to; that the Vietnam-era slogan, "Peace with honor," is only a euphemism for what now seems our highest hope, defeat without total disgrace.

If this were the complete picture, it would be pointless to discuss the future of the Republic. However, the negative factors—all of which are very real—are not the only ones. The quotation at the head of the chapter, an exchange between the prophet Elisha and his servant when they were surrounded by troops of the Syrian king at Dothan, may serve as an appropriate moto for the second part of our analysis of the condition of the Republic: the assessment of our strengths. We are indeed —even quite literally—surrounded. But if we still have the chance to say, They that be with us are more than they that be with them.

What are some of the positive factors on our side? First, some of the material ones. We still have a vast nation. The continental United States, despite our supposedly excessive population (at least according to the devotees of Zero Population Growth) still appears almost empty by comparison with the crowded regions of Europe and Asia. We have tremendous agricultural capacity, vast natural resources, and an impressive industrial plant. And we have a diverse, vigorous population. Vast areas of the American landscape are still totally unspoiled. And anyone observing our population in large groups, particularly outside a few congested urban areas, cannot fail to notice that it still appears vigorous, active, enthusiastic. Americans are a well-educated people, with a higher percentage of university graduates than any other country (although there is some distressing doubt as to how valuable some American "higher education" may be). Despite the recession, Americans remain a generous people. And Christian churches (as well as Jewish communities and a number of smaller religious groups) are far stronger and better attended in the United States than anywhere else in the world.

Our nation still has tremendous reserves in human strength, despite what often seems a concentrated effort to dissipate them.

Since we have the resources, the people, and the knowledge necessary to withstand the adversities that threaten us, why should we be apprehensive? What is lacking? The answer, of course, is the will. The United States, in the late 1970s, faces a crisis of the will unprecedented in our history. When France of the Third Republic confronted Nazi Germany in the later 1930s, she was militarily superior to her adversary. But—as became evident during the period of French vacillation over the remilitarization of the Rhineland, the Austrian *Anschluss*, and the takeover of Czechoslovakia—the French lacked the determination to use their resources. This French weakness was, of course, assiduously cultivated and fostered by the Nazis, and it paid handsome dividends in 1940, when Hitler was able to conquer France in hardly longer than it had taken him to crush Poland. In some ways, America's position in the late 1970s is better than that of France in the late 1930s. we have never had a tremendous bloodletting, a loss of human resources, such as France suffered in World War I. On the other hand, we are not, as France was in the 1930s, militarily stronger than our possible enemies. And we do suffer, as France did, from a defeatist mentality. We have had no clear victories since 1945, over thirty years ago. No one under forty can remember the days when the American armed forces were covered with glory and earned the grateful admiration of most of the world's people. After 1975, our military appears rather like that of Nazi Germany at the end of World War II, defeated and despised.

Yet, despite all this, it is still possible to echo Elisha's words. The United States, whatever our failings—and they are many—still, for the moment at least, stand for freedom, for justice, for compassion. Indeed, and we should not hesitate to say it, we even stand for Christianity and the right to honor and worship the God of Abraham. If world history is a blind whirl of events, dictated by chance constellations of forces, there could be little hope for a nation that has squandered so many of its resources and faces enemies as numerous and as powerful as the United States have and do. But if the God revealed in the Bible, in the history of the Jews and of the Christian church, is indeed alive, real, and the Lord of Time, and if America in any significant way seeks to align itself with His Law and His purposes, then there is much hope. There can even be confident assurance.

But how can the United States, as a "secular, pluralistic" nation, in any sense seek to align itself with the Law of YHWH, with the God of the Bible, with the cause of Christ? A secular, pluralistic nation indeed could hardly do such a thing. But need America consider itself secularistic? We are, from our independence, a country without an established

69

church. That is well and good. But are we, or need we be, a nation without God? It would be odd to think that, if the First Amendment made America wholly and totally secular, we have continued for two hundred years to use the motto, In God We Trust. This book, dedicated to the reconstruction of the American republic, has a twofold thesis: First, that a recovery is possible if we consciously seek it under the guidance of the God of the Bible, and second, that such a quest, far from being a repudiation of our national spiritual heritage, is precisely a recovery and fulfillment of it.

7

Government Goodness

> Now some thinkers hold that goodness comes by nature, others that we acquire it by habit, others that we are made good by teaching.
>
> Aristotle
> *Ethics*

Human beings, wherever they may be found in the world, and at whatever period of history you care to consider, have always been very concerned about the education of their children. In a primitive, tribal society, education may take place chiefly as *initiation*, the hunters and warriors introducing the boys to their lore, subjecting them to increasingly difficult tests, and frequently marking the boys' transition to manhood by initiatory ceremonies, while the women do the same thing for the girls in their growth to womanhood. In a more highly developed society, there are institutions and even whole systems of education.

The reason for this is simple enough. Nothing that human beings have, make, or cherish can endure for more than one generation—traditionally, thirty years—unless the present generation can impart its knowledge, skills, and above all, values to the next generation.

The preoccupation with the transmission of values is common to every culture. Even people whose theory of education falls into Aristotle's first category—thinking that goodness comes by nature—make an effort to create an educational environment that will enable the growing child to develop the goodness that is supposed to be inherent in him.

America, a country of tremendously diverse cultural heritage, could not place great confidence in habit—traditional ways of doing things

71

—as a means of imparting "goodness," or a sense of values, to the young. Traditions are too diverse in America; they vary from place to place, even from family to family.

In a way, it would seem as though American educational philosophy corresponded to Aristotle's third category—to the view that "goodness" comes by teaching. No other country in the world spends so much money, time, and effort in the educational process. We start our children in formal education earlier, keep them in school longer, and send a greater percentage of them on for so-called higher education than any other country. On the other hand, the teaching is so contentless that we seem to rely on the emergence of an innate goodness.

American education is strangely unproductive. It is not in backward, mountainous regions but in prosperous Virginia and Maryland that there was serious discussion in mid-1976 of introducing the "reform" of requiring ability to read for graduation from *high school*. Travelers in poverty-stricken India can observe little children, dressed in what is probably their sole garment, trudging down a dirt road, carrying their writing slates to a mud-walled communal school. Those children will learn to read and write in a complicated script having fifty letters and numerous variants for vowel sounds by the time they are nine or ten. American children, dressed in slovenly fashion in jean-type pants and flowered shirts, chosen from an ample selection, will be picked up by yellow school buses and transported to splendid, modern, air-conditioned, wall-to-wall carpeted buildings, where they will be occupied for twelve years and whence many of them will emerge unable to read a fairly simple language written in an alphabet of twenty-six letters.

Although education in America is showing signs of dramatic failure to do simple things that educators throughout history, and in much poorer settings, have succeeded in doing, such as teaching children to read and write, it has not lost its nerve, but is devoting itself to teaching something where it really has no mandate—values. Indeed, it is devoting itself not to reinforcing the traditional values of the home, as 19th-century education did, but to transforming them and replacing them. Sometimes the values public education seeks to impart are good, but the means are ineffectual or counter-productive: bussing for racial integration is a case in point. Frequently the values themselves are bad, although the means may be suitable for imposing them: much sex education offers a case in point.

The goal of promoting greater understanding and harmony between the races in the United States is certainly a desirable one. Unfortunately, because of the pragmatic bent of contemporary society, and the widespread refusal to look at traditional values and to consider their source, the means chosen to implement this goal are largely mechanical. In order to promote interracial harmony, our society would have to be explicit about the nature of man. Christianity and the Bible are explicit: Genesis tells us that God made man and woman—not any particular race—in his image (Genesis 1:27), and Paul told the proud Athenians, despite their disdain for other "barbarian" races, that God "hath made of one blood all nations of men" (Acts 17:26). The Bible would be a good source from which to substantiate the values of racial tolerance and mutual respect. But—unfortunately for its acceptability in our society—the Bible also promotes values that our society is unwilling to accept: respect for life, including the unborn, sexual self-restraint, marital fidelity.

As a matter of historical record, both white and black Americans overcame the tensions of the school integration and civil rights struggles and adapted best to racial equality in those parts of the country where the Bible and its authority were more widely accepted. But it has been extremely difficult for government to refer to moral values of Judeo-Christian origin to support its goals, for the new theory of government is that justice, rights, and moral principles are the endowment of government, not of God. In acrimonious Senate hearings on the human life issue in May, 1981, Senator Lowell Weicker (R., Conn.) repeatedly stated that Congress and the government have "nothing to do" with Judaeo-Christian values.

Because of its self-imposed isolation from the greatest source of moral values in our country, the Judeo-Christian biblical heritage, the government is in effect forced to pursue a moral goal—racial reconciliation—through an immoral, mechanical means—forced school bussing. The resort to mechanical means and physical force in an effort to secure racial harmony is so thoroughly entrenched in American government that in mid-1981, even after what might have been called an anti-bussing referendum in the 1980 presidential elections, at least one major metropolitan area, Chicago, is on the verge of dramatically expanded forced school bussing. The fact that such means have proved, time and time again, to be ineffectual if not actually counter-productive, seems to make little difference.

All this is clearly paradoxical. How is it possible that the world's wealthiest nation cannot teach reading and writing with consistent success in its schools? And how can it be that those same ineffective schools are supposed to be able to impart moral values by mechanical means, e.g., racial harmony by forced bussing?

This delusion is a consequence of our continuing national failure to define our values and to set our goals. In an earlier era, when most of the population was relatively wholeheartedly committed to one or another variety of the Judeo-Christian ethic and outlook, a reluctance to define values was not so serious. Even though they were not expressed in so many words, people were in such wide agreement about them that they prevailed without being expressed. Today we do not set clear, comprehensible goals because we no longer have an identifiable consensus on values.

Actually, as was indicated in the previous chapter, there really still is a considerable and vigorous American consensus on values, at least among a large and healthy part of the populace. But social developments have passed beyond the point where this value consensus can survive on its own, incognito as it were. From now on it must be increasingly identified, acknowledged, and expressed. Unfortunately, this is precisely what American society is unwilling to do.

Aristotle's Three Choices

Most teachers through the ages would fall into the third class mentioned by Aristotle: those who believe that goodness is taught. If we consider Aristotle's argument for a moment, we will immediately recognize that he presupposes that there is such a thing as goodness, virtue, and that it is *desirable*. He does not have to define it or justify seeking it. His question concerns where it originates and how it is to be imparted. The assumption that goodness is good would have been taken for granted during most of human history. There have been disputes as to how goodness is to be defined, where it comes from, and how it is to be imparted. But philosophers have generally taken for granted that "the good" is something that human beings need to, ought to, and will seek.

If asked to locate the philosophy of education in America within Aristotle's frame of reference, one would be hard put to give a precise answer. On the one hand, the tremendous emphasis on teaching and teaching methods certainly suggests a conviction that what is most valuable must be taught. On the other hand, the lack of emphasis on the *content* of teaching suggests that our American system is deeply influenced by the view that human beings are inherently good and need only be left to develop freely long enough for this goodness to come out. Of course any concept of the essential goodness of man runs counter to the fundamental Judeo-Christian conviction that man's nature has been damaged by the Fall. Christians and biblical Jews are characterized by long-range

74

optimism and short-range pessimism. They expect God's will to be fully worked out at the end of time. Prior to that, they count on a good deal of conflict, frustration, and trouble. They certainly do not think that anything as naive as simply providing a better environment will basically change people, since malice comes from within man, not from without (as Jesus said in Mark 7:21; cf. Jeremiah 17:9).

Probably the bussing situation in America is the clearest example of our nationwide failure to conceive and articulate values and means to attain them. Bussing is plausible only if one is persuaded first that the achievement of a measure of racial tolerance and compatibility is a value of a higher order, and second that bussing is a constructive means towards the achievement of that value. However, *if* one were so convinced of the supreme value of racial tolerance, it would seem that it ought to be taught in explicit statements, as well as sought by mechanical means such as bussing. This, however, is generally not done. Thus one has a paradoxical situation in which the architects of forced bussing live in regions that are isolated from bussing, or send their children to bus-proof private schools. Evidently they do not consider a multiracial experience such a high value that they seek it for themselves and their children.

The Machinery of Moralism

America as a country has the tradition of being highly moralistic, seeking to develop and impose moral values but unwilling to articulate them. Hence it resorts to mechanical means—in the clearest example, to bussing—to place people, namely children, in changed situations in which it is felt that moral values will spontaneously emerge.

Put this way, present-day public policy on bussing for school integration as a tool to racial harmony seems an absurdity. Indeed it is an absurdity. It reveals the typical American preoccupation with means rather than principles. But in this case, as in many others, the means are not merely not particularly helpful towards reaching the principles, but are actually incompatible with them or even counter-productive.

If morality is to be a goal of our public policy—which is not necessarily a bad idea—then it must be pursued, at least in large measure, by *moral* means, namely by persuasion, education, argument and good example. To think that we can achieve a moral goal by a mechanical means is an absurdity. It involves a less than rational, an unthinking commitment to this moral goal, for a rational, thinking commitment would naturally seek to *communicate* the goal in an expressed fashion and to propagate it by argument, education, and persuasion. (Perhaps it would not necessarily refrain from mechanical auxiliary methods such as transportation, i.e., bussing.) But if morality is to be a goal of public policy, then it must be expressed and acknowledged as such. However, few would dare to call integration a "moral" issue, because one of our official myths is that the law cannot deal with morality. Inasmuch as our society is determined to have integration, but cannot admit to being concerned about moral values, it must deny that integration is a moral issue and call it something else: a "civil rights" issue. But civil rights, on this view, is nothing but the expression of the will of the people, through the Constitution they have adopted. What happens, then, when the people oppose the "civil right" they are supposed to have enacted? It is enforced on them by bussing, or—in the extreme case—by tanks in the streets.

Among the many paradoxes of American politics today is the way in which *moral* considerations have been altogether ruled out as reasons for political action in certain issues, while in others a self-righteous moralism—never acknowledged as such—prevails. Thus, for example, foes of abortion are regularly charged with seeking to impose "a particular moral view" on society as a whole. This is supposed to be a sufficient reason to discredit the whole pro-life movement. The fact that millionfold abortion certainly must take place at *some* cost in human life, and thus might reasonably become the object of government regulation, is ignored. At the same time, many of the same people who vehemently oppose any attempt to regulate permissive abortion, which always takes human life, even in purely semantic terms, no matter how euphemistically it may be described, are equally zealous in their efforts to prohibit private ownership of firearms, which after all only take a rather small number of lives each year, compared with the total firearms ownership. (We can be sure that the mere expression "a rather small number of lives" will provoke a hostile reaction among gun control advocates, and to brand one who uses it, such as the present writer, as callous and heartless. But it *is* a rather small number of human lives, compared with (a) the total number of lives lost due to accidents and felonies involving the automobile, which no one is thinking of forbidding; (b) the total number of firearms owned without any cost to life; (c) the total number of human lives lost through late abortions in America, many of them not merely permitted but *paid for* by the government, at least until late 1980; (d) the much greater number of human lives, at least by biological and philosophical definition, lost through early abortions each—in excess of one million, according to recent and probably conservative estimates.)

The purpose of the preceding paragraph is neither to condemn abortion nor to oppose gun control, but rather to point to the fact that we do not achieve greater clarity in our political debates by decrying certain concerns as "moral" or "moralistic." We cannot avoid having "moral" concerns, whether they be to restrict abortion or the widespread possession of firearms. And a concern is not stamped as legitimate or illegitimate because it is moral any more than a man is identified as good or evil because he is "sincere."

No Concern for the Good?

The assumption that most if not all human beings will seek out and choose the good runs as a constant through human history. Poor education—in other words, a lack of knowledge about what is good—is seen as a principal reason for wrong conduct. Christians expect the natural man to "suppress the truth in unrighteousness" (Romans 1:18), and most philosophers understand how very hard it is to make knowledge of the good so overwhelmingly convincing that it will appear more attractive than what is bad. Nevertheless, the naïve assumption in most educational circles is that given the right knowledge, people will choose the good rather than the evil.

We have referred to the policy of bussing for racial integration. It may seem incongruous that so tangential and apparently secondary an issue could spark a major political battle. Actually, the disproportionate and unbalanced attention given to bussing perfectly reflects the confusion and loss of proportion that comes into human conduct when we feel morally obliged to fight for a certain good but are not allowed to think in moral terms nor to conceive of something as good because we now find it unsophisticated to think in terms of good and evil.

In May 1976, some rather embarrassing revelations were made concerning the private and public conduct of Congressman Wayne Hays of Ohio. When it was charged that he was supporting a mistress on the public payroll, hardly anyone characterized this conduct as *bad* in the moral (moralistic) sense. Most of the media were quick to state that Hays' personal moral behavior is his own business and that they were concerned only with a possible misuse of government funds. According to a contemporary *Washington Post* report, his Ohio constituents dismissed his liaison as a "peccadillo."[1] No one in public life would venture to say to

[1]*Washington Post*, May 31, 1976.

77

Hays what John the Baptist said to Herod, "It is not lawful for thee to have her" (Matthew 14:4), but only, "It is not lawful for thee to pay her from government funds."

What this incident symbolizes is a bit difficult to say. "Morality," the "good," is still important. That is why American opinion-makers see bussing as not merely desirable, but as something that must be enforced by law and promoted in all the important mass media. On the other hand, morals and the good are not to be defined in the received terms of our Judeo-Christian ethical heritage, which in the case at hand would condemn conduct such as Hays'. Or, if they are, then they are nobody's legitimate business but that of the one directly involved. But, if the good and morality are not defined by traditionally received moral values, what does define them?

One of the tremendous difficulties in selling the bussing decision lies, as we have seen, in the fact that it is essentially an attempt to impose morality. The imposition of certain moral standards by law is not necessarily a bad thing; in fact, all societies have to make some effort in this direction. Our prevailing public philosophy, heavily underscored by the leading opinion-making media, tells us that all such "moralizing attempts are wrong. But since it is still considered important to make *one* such attempt, namely to bus, we are forced to define what is essentially a moral quest as something else. Therefore bussing is promoted as required not by morality, but by the United States Constitution. Unfortunately, almost all Americans now understand that the Constituion no longer means anything *in itself*, but only what a majority of the members of the Supreme Court say that it means. Hence all realize that, in the case of the bussing decision they are being asked to bow not to the will of God, or even to natural law, or some other universally valid principle, but to the will of several men. In most of the hotly disputed bussing cases, they are being forced to bow to the will of a single judge.

Matters are made worse by the general recognition that bussing can by no reasonable stretch of the imagination be found in the Constitution; it must be read into it. But why read bussing into it, and not liberty of contract, as Archibald Cox asks in *The Role of the Supreme Court in American Government*? The real answer, of course is that the judges in question believe that they ought to find it there. But why *ought* they? Because something higher than the United States Constitution obliges them. One only has to be able to read to see what the Constitution *says*, but one must know something beyond the Constitution itself to know what it *ought to say*. The bussing tensions, like the Watergate scandal, reveal the continuing American concern about *moral* issues. But our sophisticated unwillingness to treat moral questions as such makes us disguise them as constitutional issues. This subterfuge then makes the attempt to enforce a moral concern appear as nothing more than the arbitrary oppression of the powerless by the powerful—which is just the way Judge Arthur Garrity's bussing decisions appear to the people of South Boston.

This is an extremely self-defeating process. One might properly describe it as slow moral and ethical suicide. *If* moral values are to be important to our society, then we must publicly discuss moral issues in moral terms. And since morality frankly does depend in great measure on our spiritual heritage and orientation, we are going to have to permit the introduction of spiritual and religious values into "public" debate. Otherwise we are put in the ridiculous situation of turning whole cities on their head to enforce a moral concern that is not part of the national consensus (or would not be recognized as such without considerable debate), is not required by any plausible reading of law, and does not appear to be very effectively attainable by the means we choose to attain it. We forfeit the chance of moral persuasion by not calling it morality, and hence appeal to force.

As we suggested earlier, one of the grave weaknesses of the capitalist West in its conflict with the Communist East is the diffidence of the West about stating the conflict in moral terms. One *might* make a case for bussing, but the only plausible case that can be made is a moral one. However, if moral concerns, by definition, are politically illegitimate in a "pluralistic" society, then we are forced, as we have said, to pretend that bussing is a "constitutional" concern. And this means that we must attribute a divine, quasi-religious significance to the Constitution, and see the majority justices as modern Moseses. This could be avoided if we would only take a simple, straightforward approach to our spiritual heritage. We need but acknowledge it to be what we all know it to be, basically biblical and Christian, Judeo-Christian if you prefer, and accept the fact that while it has been modified in various areas, it is the biblical heritage, not the Constitution, that is and remains the fundamental source of values.

8

The Government As Devil's Advocate

Just as Paul was about to speak, Gallio said to the Jews, "If you were making a complaint about some misdemeanor or serious crime, it would be reasonable for me to listen to you. But since it involves questions about words and names and your own law, settle the matter yourselves. I will not be a judge of such things." So he had them ejected from the court.

Acts 18:14 – 15
(New International Version)

There is an old Latin maxim, *de minimis non curat lex:* the law is not concerned with trifles. Turned around, it might say, "Whatever the law is not concerned with, is a trifle of no importance." Where the law claims to be unconcerned with morality, it is educating the public to believe that morality is of trifling importance. And this is the message that comes through in countless aspects of American public life. For example, morals are not important: money is. Thus the public outcry over Hays was not at the fact that he allegedly maintained a mistress, but that according to the charges this was done at government expense.

Instead of recovering and reinforcing the moral forces that still exist among the people, government in America, at its various levels, is doing a great deal to liquidate them. Of course, few legislators, administrators, and judges are conscious of doing this, or would admit to it. Few of those who become excessive drinkers are conscious of what they are doing, but their "innocence" does not prevent them from succumbing to alcoholism. Government has many ways to wear down and get rid of public value-structures, and the most significant tool for doing this is public education. Moral values have traditionally been taught primarily in the home and in church, but supported and reinforced by public education. When public schools were the affair of the community, locally staffed and controlled, nothing was more natural than that they should tend to uphold community standards. The progressive federalizing of education is now pushing such moral values and concerns more and more to the fringes of life. This process cannot go on indefinitely. When the old moral forces are sufficiently worn down, some new form of morality will have to be imposed to replace them, namely a "re-education." But for the present, we are in the period of wearing down. Three areas of present interest offer striking examples of this wearing down: (1) sex education in the public schools; (2) religious observances and Bible reading in the public schools; (3) public assistance to religiously oriented private schools.

Sex Education

The question of sex education in the public schools is a complex one. Its many implications have been discussed at length and heatedly. Alongside its commendable features, there is a certain quasi-religious enthusiasm about the sex education movement, as though in the millennia that mankind has existed on earth, people had somehow failed to get the word on sex. This particular "gospel," alone among religions, deserves government funding. Government must now step in to provide the missing information, and thus make real happiness and contentment possible for millions who missed it before. There is something very naïve—or perverse—about this, but for our purposes, we may ignore the controversy about the desirability of public-school sex education, and simply point to one inevitable consequence of introducing the theme of sexual behavior as a compulsory school subject without permitting it to be discussed in moral as well as physiological and psychological terms. We further downgrade traditional morality and create a hypocritical theory basing the good on the Constitution.

Beyond question, human sexuality and the issues relating to it have almost universally been considered a matter of morals and religion. With negligible exceptions, every organized human society regulates the expression of sexual desire, and does so for reasons that are considered moral or religious in nature. Most of the world has put a high premium on monogamous marriage and marital fidelity, with varying degrees of disapproval for extramarital and premarital relations as well as for homosexual behavior.

Throughout human history it has never been considered a matter of crucial importance to instruct people in sexual functions and technique, but it has universally been considered important to impress them with some rather definite moral principles regarding sexual behavior. These pricinciples have varied considerably depending on the culture, the age, and the general social situation, and some cultures and societies have exhibited standards differing widely from the general norm.

Even when societies have practiced a high degree of sexual freedom, it is common to see the best minds—philosophers, poets, and statesmen as well as religious leaders—calling for self-control and restraint in sexual conduct. Thus first-century Rome, although very liberal in its sexual practices (a few years ago, it would have been possible to say degenerate, but today we must content ourselves with calling them "liberal"), produced a number of intellectuals and leaders who called for a return to the older, stricter sexual standards of Rome's early days. Even people who took part in the general sexual looseness, such as the poet Martial, felt it to be wrong and expressed their disgust and dissatisfaction with the behavior they themselves were exemplifying. The modern West, including of course the United States, is remarkable less for the high degree of sexual license that is currently practiced, for Rome had it too, than for the fact that so few of our "best minds" find it objectionable or even questionable.

In any event, it is an indisputable fact that throughout most of human history, right up to the present, sexual behavior has been seen as a moral issue and society and the family have taken pains to instruct the young in what they considered a proper sexual morality. Indeed, it is surely correct to say that even today the vast majority of Americans still consider sexual behavior a moral issue. While there is a greater public tolerance of things that an earlier America generally branded as wrong, such as adultery, promiscuity, prostitution, and homosexuality, most Americans still believe today that all these things involve moral issues and that they have a responsibility to teach their children certain moral principles about them.

We have already noted that the greatest source of moral and ethical values by far in our society is the biblical tradition, or more specifically, Christianity. In contemporary sex education, a subject involving morals is taught in public school; at the same time, specifically Christian views on it are forbidden by law from being introduced. The net effect is to exclude not merely "religious" but all moral principles from the discussion. This is what many of the more moderate critics of public-school sex education fear. Certainly it is happening.

First, by bringing sex education into the public-school curriculum, the government has taken over an implicit responsibility for the transmission of moral values concerning sex that were otherwise transmitted by family and church, since such teaching in the past has always had a moral component — in fact, this was often the chief component. Now by systematically excluding all *religious* influences from public education, government in America has in effect de-moralized what traditionally has been one of the major areas of human moral concern through the ages. Whatever may be said of this policy, it should be evident that at the very least this is no contribution to the strengthening of moral forces in society at large. Moral principles are removed as a force that occupies the center of life. It is no accident that sex education of the type common in the United States and certain other Western countries, far from being duplicated in Communist nations, has no parallels there.*

In recent years, concern about the fact that public schools teach no values has led to a rash of interest in something called "values clarification," popularized by Harvard education professor Lawrence Kohlberg. Unfortunately, when Kohlberg's rather sophisticated analysis of values is applied in elementary and secondary schools, what it basically communicates is that values are important to have, but that what values one has is primarily a matter of individual preference and personal decision. In other words, values clarification, instead of reinforcing community values, promotes relativism, the idea that everyone should "do his own thing," or, in biblical language, whatever is "right in his own eyes" (Judges 21:25).

Sex education is naturally not the only field in which government attempts to teach in a value-free way have the effect of downgrading traditional moral values and, instead of "impregnating against rot," actively promote it. The fact that it is very difficult to teach sex education in

---

*In 1969 a tempest was provoked in Switzerland by the circulation of something called "The Schoolboy's Little Red Book" (*Das klein wrote Schülerbuch*), published in large quantities in German and French. The cantonal Department of Education in Bern made an attempt to suppress the book, printed by a left-wing publisher in Frankfurt, Germany, claiming that it would have a demoralizing effect on the young by its propaganda in favor of sexual license, abortion, and the like. Curiously, while the book was published in the West by Communist publishers, it could not be published or sold in a Communist-ruled state, where the official educational policy is nothing if not moralistic. (The morals taught differ at many points from those of Christianity, but Communist schools definitely teach a form of morality.)

isolation from religious values and still teach it in a way that does not adversely affect morality may not have been taken seriously enough by educators, most of whom would not consciously work to eliminate traditional Christian ethical values. On the other hand, the hope has been expressed by at least one prominent figure in psychology and education that compulsory government-sponsored sex education offers an ideal tool for getting rid of what he considers outmoded cultural values, not only in America, but indeed around the world.[1]

Abolition of Prayer and Bible-Reading in Public Schools

In 1961 and 1963, when it handed down the celebrated decisions banning prayer and reading of the Bible (as a form of religious exercise) in public schools, the Supreme Court was still the so-called Warren Court, famous for its judicial activism. Since then the makeup of the Court has changed markedly, with four of the current Justices, including the Chief Justice, Warren E. Burger, having been appointed by former President Nixon, and one since then by President Ford. Although the Burger Court is supposed to be considerably more conservative and to take more of a "strict constructionist" stand than the Warren Court, its May 19, 1975 decision on indirect state aid to religious schools indicated that it takes a very similar stand on First Amendment religious issues.

From the perspective of non-Christian religions, the widespread American practice of prayer and Bible reading in the public schools could appear undesirable, since in America as it is such observances were bound to have a vaguely Christian tone. On the other hand, many non-Christians felt that it is good to have at least some token acknowledgment of God in public schools if only to show that society takes divine worship seriously enough not to exclude it from schools, even though the form of the observance was not what they themselves would have chosen. From this viewpoint, to have the state acknowledge the importance of religion in the educational process is preferable to allowing it to ignore it.

Many Christians to whom their faith means more than a mere formality recognize that formal exercises such as an opening prayer or

[1]David R. Mace, United States representative at the World Health Organization, in his address "Sex and Culture" at the March 1972 Institute of American Sex Educators and Counselors in Washington, D.C.

morning Bible reading in the schools do no more for real Christianity than the formal pledging of allegiance to the flag every morning does to promote real patriotism. However, when there has been a long tradition of offering at least a token of recognition to God in the public education of children, the sudden official declaration that such recognition is "unconstitutional" seems to be saying that the Constitution is ungodly. Of course, the two Court decisions did not say that God is not worthy of recognition, but only that the state must not prescribe the form that this recognition is to take nor impose such a form in the course of an official state activity such as public education. Unfortunately, this theoretical distinction was certainly lost on most people. Those who hailed the decision called it a victory for "freedom of thought," which in the context meant a victory for secularism over religion. The general public, which disliked it, saw it as "putting God out of the schools." As the aftermath has shown, the general public was right.

This purging of the school system of vestigial religious ceremonies took place precisely at the time that educators were claiming the right to determine more and more aspects of a child's development (hence the slogan: "Give us the total child!"). Educators speak of "the child's total development—academic, athletic, and social." Of course such a list leaves out some important things. Besides "moral, spiritual," for example, one might wish to see "artistic" included. But whereas "artistic" or "musical" development could easily be added as an important part of the child's total development, "spiritual" would cause a "constitutional conflict." Naturally then, this does give the impression that, as far as the government is concerned, religion is of no importance to the development of children. The Court may well make a theoretical concession, as Associate Justice Tom C. Clark did in the majority opinion in *Schempp* v. *Abingdon Township*, and state that the proper place for religion is in the human heart, not in government schools, but this subtlety is lost on the public at large.

Of course, *if* the justices and others who favor the complete elimination of the recognition of God from the public activity gave him a conspicuous place in their personal lives, *then* the net impact of decisions such as *Schempp* and *Engel* v. *Vitale* could be quite different. By advocating the strict formal separation of church and state while showing on their own a personal commitment to faith and church life, they could have given the impression that both the church and the state are important, each in its own sphere. But simply to throw religious observance out, under the banner of separation of church and state, certainly suggests that religion is for the simple and backward, not for those who live in the great world of law, politics, and government—certainly not for Justices, endowed with the authority of secular Solomons. The personal motto of several Supreme Court Justices would appear to be that of the judge in the parable of Luke 18:2, "which feared not God, neither regarded man."

The Supreme Court as the Supreme Authority?

It is interesting that the Supreme Court, at one and the same time the nonelected branch of our government and the only one whose members enjoy life tenure, is to all appearances the least godly of the three branches. Virtually every president, and by far the majority of senators and congressmen, make some show of religious observance. While this gesture may be intended more for the voting public than for God, it is not without symbolic significance. The *Schempp* and *Engel* decisions do not by any means imply that the justices who voted with the majority against religious observances had no use for religion and no personal spiritual life. Nor can we assume that the dissenting minority was therefore composed of pious and godly individuals. Nevertheless, the decisions give the impression that the Supreme Court considers religion in general and Christianity in particular superfluous. (The practices the Court banned were in fact of Christian origin. This may be considered incidental, but that does not mean that it is without influence.)

The members of the United States Supreme Court, like popes and monarchs, are chosen for life. Their functions are invested with greater symbolic dignity. They are held in greater awe than either the president or members of Congress, who are elected and can of course be voted out of office. There is virtually no media criticism of individual justices, although the media are not notably reverent in their references to members of the other branches of the government. Decisions of the Court are eulogized as "the Law of the Land," a reverential expression seldom used of congressional enactments, for which it would be more appropriate. It is not *vox populi*—the voice of the people—but *vox curiae*, the voice of the Court, that is closest to *vox Dei* (the voice of God) in America. Therefore if the Supreme Court gives the impression that religion in general and Christianity in particular are the products of a wisdom inferior to its own, to be tolerated in America only where it is necessary to accommodate backward ("obscurantist"?) elements in the population, no amount of church attendance by presidents, senators, and congressmen can counteract the negative impression the Court makes.

Did the Old Observances Accomplish Anything?

The elimination of token religious observances from public schools may be thought to be of little direct significance. It would be hard to find an American in the country today who would claim to owe his religious convictions to public-school prayers and Bible reading. Throughout the country, the curriculum of the public schools — obviously much more important than formal opening exercise — was already completely secularized. But while we would not argue that the old observances did much real good, abolishing them did a great deal of harm, at least symbolically. And symbolism is important, even to modern man in the electronic age. For America to array herself symbolically against God cannot be good or what most Americans want.

There may be one positive feature of the Court-ordered abolition of the old practices. It has made it absolutely clear that public education is definitely set on a secularistic course, nor merely a religiously neutral one. This is certainly one of the fundamental reasons behind the growing interest across the country in parochial or other independent Christian schools.

The movement toward private schools in many communities where they had been virtually unknown is often characterized as an attempt to evade the consequences of an earlier Supreme Court decision, the 1954 school integration verdict. The desire to avoid accepting racial integration was certainly behind the establishment of many so-called Christian schools, particularly in the South. But the movement has gone on and expanded to areas where racial tensions are virtually nonexistent. The strength of the movement for independent Christian schools today derives directly from the desire of many parents to have an education for their children that will support rather than undermine the religious and moral values they hold.

While the older practices of perfunctory formal prayer and Bible reading may have done little positive good, they can hardly reasonably be called a serious affront to the minority of Americans who totally reject God. We have heard of very few children being withdrawn from public schools because prayers were occasionally said there. But millions have already been taken out and put into independent schools, precisely because prayers are now forbidden. It may be theoretically possible for the state and its functions, such as education, to be genuinely neutral toward religion, but it is no longer plausible to pretend that what our government calls "neutrality," the "separation of church and state," is really that.

While the hostility of American government, particularly of the Supreme Court, to any tokens of religious reverence in the schools has caused many parents to take their children out of the public system, the Court is also doing what it can to make the alternative systems as poor and as expensive as possible, and hence to force children back into the government system.

The 1975 School Aid Decision

On May 19, 1975 in a complex decision the Supreme Court prohibited several forms of indirect aid to nonpublic schools of a religious nature. The main opinion, written by Justice Potter Stewart, forbids states to aid church-related schools in many ways that might otherwise seem to be legitimate expressions of public concern for the general welfare. States are forbidden to supply publicly employed professional therapists and counselors to help parochial school pupils with learning problems or physical handicaps. The Court feared that pressure would be put on such persons to promote the religious doctrine that parochial schools espouse. Then, so the reasoning went, the state would have to try to make sure that the public servants did not succumb to such pressure, and thus would itself become too involved with religious education.[2]

Education has come a long way since the proverbial little red schoolhouse and the three Rs. Whether or not it has all been progress may be disputed, but there can be no doubt that schools now provide much more comprehensive education and many more services than in the past. Furthermore, these improvements and amplifications are extremely costly. It is not hard for a private school to duplicate or surpass the performance of government schools in teaching classical skills such as reading, writing, and arithmetic. It becomes much more difficult when it is a question of duplicating modern science laboratories, elaborate sports facilities, and the like. And of course the field of special and remedial education, especially where only a few students are involved, involves tremendous costs for a private school. Even Chief Justice Burger, who dissented from the majority in *Meek* at this point, found it hard to understand the reasonableness of denying state help in special and remedial education work to pupils in religious schools. The Court's argumentation seems rather contrived. However, whether it is sound or unsound, the decision has now become, as the reverential formula has it, "the Law of the Land."

[2]Meek v. *Pittenger,* 1975.

By driving vestiges of traditional religion out of the public schools, the Court ignored the complaints of those who claim that the schools now in effect teach another religion, contrary to Christianity or Judaism, that of secular humanism. The Supreme Court, together with lower courts, the old Department of Health, Education and Welfare, and other federal, state, and local agencies, has pushed large numbers of parents who take religious questions seriously into sending their children to private, religiously oriented schools. At the same time, by the constant expansion of public-school services, government is making it increasingly harder and more expensive for independent schools to compete. And where the people of a state or local community have desired, and the responsible authorities have agreed that it is proper for the state to provide certain services for pupils outside of the public system, the Supreme Court has now forbidden this.

What are the consequences? One is a tendency on the part of the hard-pressed independent schools to drop their religious ties and become completely secular, in order to receive the government assistance that seems to be becoming more and more necessary. Many denominational colleges have already become secular for this reason. A second is increasing pressure on parents to remove their children from religiously oriented schools and put them back into the government system. Both pressures involve government action against religion, whether acknowledged as such or not.

On the one hand, then, the government, or more particularly the Supreme Court and the lower courts, is making independent religious education increasingly expensive, and on the other it is requiring that public education be more and more militantly secular. What this amounts to is a government "front" against religion. Could such a policy be promoted by any elected officials? No. Could it pass a referendum in any state, or in the country as a whole? No. Is it in any plausible sense ordered by the Constitution or laws? No. Does it represent the will of the people? No. Why then do we have it? Because government by court, having turned away from the mainstream of our spiritual and ethical heritage in the Judeo-Christian tradition, is attempting to reconstitute moral principles by deriving them from, or rather reading them into, the federal Constitution.

All this is done, of course, in the name of neutrality and the separation of church and state. But what will the long-range social consequences be? Is it deliberate federal policy, after eliminating all vestiges of religious tradition from public education, to place so many burdens on private religious education that no one but the wealthy or those who are extremely deeply committed, to the point of making very substantial sacrifices, will be able to afford it? In the integration decision, *Brown* v. *Board of Education*, the Supreme Court looked beyond the formal equality supposedly provided by segregated educational systems ("separate but equal") to the social consequences of such separation, and based its decision on them. In its 1975 parochial school aid decision, *Meek* v. *Pittenger*, the Court ignored the social consequences of its decision and acted on the basis of a legalistic, we might almost say pharisaical, interpretation of the First Amendment. "Separate but equal" has now been recognized as a rationalization long used to deny blacks equality of access to educational benefits and thus keep them on the outside. How long will it take Americans to realize that "separation of church and state," at least in exaggerated form in which the Supreme Court has now cast it, is a device for relegating religion and those who take it seriously to the fringes of national life? When the powerful government declares "total separation," the result is not equality, but oppression.

"Goodness" by Grace of Government?

Traditionally American government has never established morality, in the sense of defining what is right and moral. It has taken what it found in the moral and spiritual heritage of the people and attempted, more or less vigorously, to reinforce it. It is a simple historical fact that most values in America, a nation of largely European ancestry and of British institutions, are biblical in origin. If we cut out or suppress the biblical sources of values, we are left with a vacuum. Some values will survive for a time, by force of habit, in individuals who have been cut off from their sources, but such values will not survive indefinitely.

The less a society possesses an effective, shared moral consensus, the more its government will be obliged to make use of compulsion and coercion. The use of tanks in Little Rock, Arkansas, to enforce school integration is a clear indication of the fact that no effective values consensus existed in Little Rock at that time. When the population does not accept a measure of social order on its own, because of values it voluntarily accepts, it is going to be put under coercion by its government. The only alternative is chaos. When values are strong and deeply rooted, a government needs to do little more than occasionally steer or give a slight shift in direction. But where values have decayed or been suppressed, the government must not only give the orders but must also supply the force to see to it that they are carried out.

Today, the attempts of our government to establish morality are really an attempt to redefine it. If we are in any doubt as to what is good, the government will tell us. Where a strong value-structure exists, a totalitarian system will attempt to break it down. Where there is no strong, shared value-structure—such as used to exist in the United States, but is vanishing—then there will be an increasing tendency to accept totalitarianism simply in order to have some accepted values.

In the United States, particularly since World War II, government at its various levels has been active in downgrading and pushing into the background traditional Christian values. In addition, these values are under attack by non-governmental forces, such as commercial interests. *Playboy* magazine and the vast commercial empire Hugh Hefner has created to develop and exploit hedonism has certainly done as much to debase sexual morality in America as the rather drab sex education programs of Planned Parenthood. Many of those engaged in undermining values are not fully aware of what they are doing; many, in fact, would be shocked to realize it. Some, of course, are doing it deliberately. The process is already fairly far along. When the old value-system is completely gone, what will replace it? Will the same government that has participated in its liquidation offer something to replace it?

Given our present governmental structure in America, the answer is clearly No. We cannot expect a complex, bourgeois governmental system based on the separation of powers and the balancing of conflicting interests to produce any kind of a comprehensive, reasonably self-consistent value system.

A government such as ours can function *within* such a value system; in fact, it cannot function without one. But it cannot *create* one, any more than the United Nations today can create a credible philosophy of world government. However, American society, like every other society, needs some kind of a generally accepted consensus on values to function, unless it opts instead for a very high degree of control and coercion. In other words, the present trend of government in America to participate in the active eradication of traditional Christian values, far from being something that will ultimately make government's task less complicated and hence easier, will instead make government as we still know it in America impossible. Government in America works as well as it still does—with a comparative minimum of compulsion—because a large measure of consensus on values still exists. But if the values are destroyed, the machinery of democratic government in America—a machinery that is adapted to balancing conflicting interests more or less fairly, but not to creating and maintaining spiritual and moral values—will not be able to replace them. When it becomes apparent that they are no longer present and functioning, it will have to substitute coercion—government force—for the motivation that used to be supplied by shared values.

For the moment, government in America is animated by a new spirit. It seems to be pulling back from fifty or sixty years of active wearing-down of shared values and traditional morality. But it is possible that this new spirit of restraint is largely the result of the charisma and tact of one man, President Reagan. Bureaucracy has its own momentum, and it is extremely difficult to stop it or to change its direction. If the trends that existed in full vigor until 1981 survive and recover their force, they will ultimately totally destroy the old American values consensus. Then, paradoxically, although those trends were fostered by "democratic" American government—in fact, more correctly, primarily by the unelected bureaucracy—they will ultimately make democratic government in the present sense impossible. There can be no representative, democratic government such as we have at present without a supporting structure of generally accepted morals and ethics. To participate in the ongoing destruction of what is left of the value system in America, or even to stand by as it is dismantled, supposedly for the sake of the Constitution, is to guarantee that within a measurable time, democratic government and the Constitution itself will become totally unworkable and irrelevant and will have to be abolished. Despite the fact that "traditional morality" and "Christian values" seem to many to be at odds with the newly-discovered constitutional principle of "pluralism," the fact remains that the United States Constitution can survive only among a people whose values permit it to survive, and that means only among a people who still share the same consensus of values that created it.

9

The Limits of Government

All dictators inflating bureaucracy do it with the cry: "Down with bureaucracy!"

Jacques Ellul
The Political Illusion

In the preceding chapter we examined one of the limits to the power of government, namely, the willing obedience that comes when a government has true moral authority. Government cannot avoid addressing itself to moral issues. If it decides to treat them not as moral issues, but as arbitrary administrative decisions or constitutional interpretations, it squanders its moral authority and will come up against a natural limit. It will be unable to lead the people and will be forced to rely on coercion. There is only so much that people are willing to accept and to do when they do not understand or accept the reason for doing it.*

Up to and through the Carter administration, the federal government was constantly launching itself against the natural limit of the people's failure to understand and reluctance to agree. Increasing frustration was expressed on the part of government officials—particularly judges—at

---

*The failure of the Volstead Act (Prohibition) offers an instructive example of the inability of a government such as ours to enforce measures with which the people by and large do not agree. If a Human Life (anti-abortion) Amendment should be adopted, it would be extremely difficult to enforce unless a very substantial number of people were persuaded that it is just and right. Of course, the Human Life Amendment is strongly rooted in both biblical and Hippocratic ethics, and hence is more likely to meet general approval, it properly understood, than Prohibition did.

the refusal of people in general to comply willingly with unpopular decisions, such as bussing. President Reagan has come into office with a reputation for being able to appeal to the people, at times over the head of the legislature. If he is able to persuade the American people of the wisdom and rightness of his policies, he will be able to accomplish tremendous things by leadership alone, and will not need to apply coercion. If he is forced to resort to a high degree of coercion, it will doom his programs and his vision, for the established agencies and mechanisms for coercion, i.e. the bureaucracy, are simply not capable of pushing the people hard enough to get them to cooperate and to work effectively at tasks they dislike.

In addition to the limit created by the unwillingness of people in general to follow policies when they have not been persuaded that they are necessary and desirable, there is a sort of natural limit in the nature of government itself, which we may refer to as the power and impotence of bureaucracy. A well-organized, highly motivated bureaucracy can achieve remarkable things, and therein lies the power of bureaucracy. By the remarkable things bureaucracy can achieve, it sometimes creates the illusion that it can achieve anything and everything, which is impossible, and by attempting more than is possible, dooms itself to frustration, failure, and contempt. Therein lies the impotence of bureaucracy—not that it can do nothing, for it can do much, but that it tends to try to do the impossible, i.e. to try to do everything, and thus fails so dismally that its genuine accomplishments are forgotten and ignored.

Bureaucracy is a remarkable instrument, a tool of great value. Yet it is held in contempt almost everywhere. Everyone is against bureaucracy, even bureaucrats. The word itself, derived from the Old French *burel*, a cloth used for covering a table, and the Greek *kratein*, rule, has a negative connotation: rule or administration by commission. In French, members of the bureaucracy are *fonctionnaires*, "functionaires." Bureaucracy is opposed on the one hand to anarchy—the situation in which there is no rule—and on the other to autocracy—"self-rule," i.e., the system in which all rule is centered in one person. It may be possible to have true "autocracy" on a very small scale—for example, at the breakfast table—but as soon as a social group becomes larger, some of the tasks of ruling have to be delegated. This is called management, or administration. A bureaucracy is opposed to a despotic system, in which the administrators have their power through their connections with the despot, and to a feudal one, in which the lower administrators hold it through their own hereditary right in that the administrative personnel are not favorites or vassals but professionals, chosen for their competence and ability, not for their ties to the ruler or family background.

In a modern state, a high degree of professional, specialized bureaucracy is absolutely necessary to achieve even a minimum of managerial efficiency. Although everyone accepts the inevitability of bureaucracy, just as that of taxation and of the police, it is if anything even less popular. As to the police, even in a police state prudence may generally keep one out of their way, and as to taxes, why, they are the fault of the bureaucracy—imposed to pay for its plans, and to pay the salaries of its *fonctionnaires*.

The Necessity of Bureaucracy

A state is powerless without bureaucracy. As Jacques Ellul continues his comment:

> All dictators inflating bureaucracy do it with the cry: "Down with bureaucracy!" This was one of Hitler's major lines, a subject of his most biting sarcasms against the bourgeois democracies. Then Stalin (at least ten times between 1947 and 1953), Khrushchev, and Nasser attacked bureaucracy, making it the scapegoat for all that was wrong. After them, as any good dictator must, Fidel Castro took up the same facile explanation in August, 1963: "The government's branches are full of people who do nothing . . . When these people find that their salary is secure, they no longer feel any urge to serve the public . . ."
>
> But all these leaders wisely returned to the road of bureaucratic organization because they had to. A state that wants to do everything and change everything, can do so only with the help of an enormous bureaucracy.[1]

But a modern state appears powerless to control or even regulate its bureaucracy. Can nothing, short of a total national catastrophe, stop the constant growth of administrative bureaucracy? Is there really a Parkinson's Law that requires bureaucracy to grow inevitably everywhere? We observe that in the United States, eight years of expansion and proliferation of federal agencies, services, operations and costs under the "liberal" administrations of Johnson and Kennedy have been followed by eight years of still greater expansion and proliferation under the "conservatives" Nixon and Ford. (The anti-Washington, anti-bureaucratic Jimmy Carter, as one of the

---

[1]Jacques Ellul, *The Political Illusion*, trans. Konrad Kellen (New York: Knopf, 1967), pp. 154–155.

first acts of his administration, increased the size of his own personal bureaucracy—the White House staff—and raised its salaries by up to 60 per cent. For the moment, President Reagan seems actually to have reduced the size of his bureaucracy. If this continues, it will be a real revolution against Parkinson's Law.)

The secret, of course, lies in Ellul's final sentence. *A state that wants to do everything and change everything can only do so with the help of an enormous bureaucracy.* The desire to cut waste, save money, increase efficiency simply cannot be reconciled with the aspiration to "do everything and change everything." But this is precisely what modern government claims to be able to do, and what the modern electorate, for the most part, demands of it. Of course everyone would *like* to have lower taxes, fewer forms to fill out, less bureaucratic interference in their personal and business affairs. But these things, which go along with bureaucracy—and indeed with organized government as such—are necessary means to try to accomplish the goal of "doing everything and changing everything." (We do not say, "means to accomplish the goal," for such a goal cannot be accomplished, only attempted. Whether we really have such a goal, or just pretend to have it to please the public, it makes a Parkinson-type bureaucracy inevitable.)

To say that one can expand a bureaucracy efficiently and economically is rather like saying that one can get drunk in moderation. It is of course theoretically possible to hold bureaucratic expansion and the scope of its activity within reasonable limits, just as it is possible to get only a bit drunk, and then stop. Unfortunately, however, there seems to be something intrinsically immoderate in bureaucracy, just as in intoxication, that makes "moderation" a very elusive goal indeed. The similarity is evident: both involve the quest for a goal—Utopia or euphoria—by means that appear to bring one closer to it, but in fact, once a certain point is reached, block the way. This leads to an intensification of the effort, an exaggeration of the means, but not to the desired result—only to disappointment and ultimately ·a hangover, administrative or alcoholic.

The Virtues of Bureaucracy

Bureaucracy is a necessary aspect of a government based on orderly procedures and law in a society possessing any degree of complexity. It is essentially a bourgeois or middle-class phenomenon. Bureaucracy is the middle class's method of structuring the responsibility for and the performance of government tasks. Duties and responsibility are assigned, in theory at least, on the basis of merit and performance, not birth or military prowess, as in the case of various types of monarchy, aristocracy, feudalism, etc. It depends in a large degree on the sense of integrity and responsibility of the bureaucrats; hence, bureaucracies in countries where the "Protestant ethic" or something similar has prevailed have frequently been *relatively* efficient and free from corruption. There seems to be some reason to suppose that Communist China, with its constant and repeated harping on moral principles as it sees them, may have achieved a considerable amount of integrity and efficiency within its vast bureaucracy. But bureaucracy by its very nature is bourgeois, hence antirevolutionary, no matter how much one may talk about revolution. (In another study, Ellul points out that this is one of the reasons why the bourgeoisie views an approaching revolution with less terror and apprehension than one would expect in the light of the revolutionaries' fury and fulmination at the middle class. The middle class instinctively realizes that no revolution can accomplish its goals of "doing everything and changing everything" without the service of a loyal, dedicated, selfless, disciplined, other-directed middle class.[2]

The fact that a measure of bureaucracy is an inevitable necessity, and the fact that only a class with middle-class characteristics can run a bureaucracy, indicate how difficult it is for a revolution to be truly revolutionary. But this is of scant comfort to those who are on the point of being smothered by bureaucratic proliferation.

A Matter of Appetite

According to a proverb engraved on the Busch-Reisinger Museum at Harvard University,

Es ist der Geist, der sich den Körper baut.

"It is the spirit that builds itself a body." The spirit of a nation does a great deal towards creating the political and administrative structure under which that nation lives — and towards determining whether that structure will be a support for a people's freedom and self-fulfillment or a straitjacket confining it narrowly into certain prescribed patterns. President Carter spoke of "a government as good as its people." If that is what he achieved, it is a sorry comment on the goodness of America's people. Actually, a government only just as good as the average of any

---

[2]Jacques Ellul, *Autopsie de la Révolution* (Paris: Calmann-Lévy, 1969).

people would be problematic enough, but recently we would have to say that American government does not even come up to the average standard of the American people where personal integreity, dedication, and willingness to serve are concerned. It is a sad finale to the political career of a distinguished former president, Gerald Ford, that he was unwilling to accept a call to a lesser post, that of vice-president, unless he was given guarantees of virtual co-presidential power. John F. Kennedy may have called on Americans to "Ask not, what your country can do for you," but that seems to be the password for many—not all—in high office.

The question is not merely a matter of knowing what is good. Virtually all of us, for example, know that it is good to be physically trim and bad to be overweight. But this knowledge does not necessarily determine how we will behave when we have an array of delicacies spread out in front of us on the table. How often the knowledgeable good intention of keeping one's weight down is overridden by the appetite for good food! Unless one is willing to give up the craving ambition to "eat everything and enjoy everything," there is no way to achieve the praiseworthy goal of avoiding excess fat. For government, the only way to cut waste is by first being willing to give up the ambition to "do everything and change everything."

Unfortunately, this is just what modern government cannot do. This is every bit as true of modern *democratic* government as of a dictatorship. Neither can government curb its appetite for expansion. A despotic or totalitarian government is psychologically unable to do it because the rulers, having virtually done away with the idea (or the mental reservation) that there is a sovereign God to whom they are ultimately responsible, automatically assume, no doubt unconsciously, that they should do God's job for him, and therefore that they can and ought to do everything. No task is too great for modern government.

What an autocratic government cannot do for psychological reasons, a democratic government dare not try for political reasons. Particularly since the plethora of Utopias that have been proffered to the American electroate for over forty years—New, Fair, Square Deals, New Frontier, Great Society, New American Revolution, and the like—the voters have been conditioned to expect from government the kind of fulfillment Christians used to expect only in heaven. Of course we Americans would not call our rulers omnipotent, and we would be quite alarmed if one of them claimed such power. In real life, we are constantly being disillusioned, not only by the disappointing accomplishments of those in power, but even more by what we constantly learn about their good will and ethical standards. Nevertheless, because we voters too have been conditioned for so long to think of no law in American above the Constitution, no authority in America above the President, no wisdom in America above the Supreme Court, even though we may know rationally that those institutions are flawed, fallible, and at times perhaps even malicious, because there is no one and nothing above them, we look to them for the attributes we ought to seek only in the Divinity.

How We Delude Ourselves

With the exception of a few still-enchanted liberals, virtually all Americans would passionately claim—like Hitler, Stalin, and Castro —to be opposed to bureaucracy, and especially to any further expansion of the Leviathan that already exists. We would all like to have lower taxes, fewer forms to fill out, less bureaucratic interference in our personal and business affairs. Of course, we know that we cannot dispense altogether with taxes, forms and administrative decision-making. These "bureaucratic" necessities are facts of life. If government is going to accomplish anything, it needs a measure of them.

The self-delusion is not in thinking that we oppose more bureaucracy and the higher taxes and greater government interference that inevitably accompany it. The delusion lies in our thinking that what we effectively communicate to our elected officials is anything other than the need for more of all these evils. Our legislators and administrators know what we think when we respond to polls. They know we think that further government expansion is bad. But they also know what we want, specifically that we have strong desires, so strong that we consider them necessities, and that what we thus "need" or desire can be given to us only by more bureaucracy. In other words, we are like the backsliding dieter at the banquet. Saying, and knowing, "I really shouldn't," he makes it clear by some very obvious actions—reaching for another helping—that he really will.

If the goal of government is to "do everything and to change everything," then a constantly expanding bureaucracy is inevitable. And "doing everything, changing everything" is what virtually all of us expect from our government. Even those of us who are most conservative, most committed to the free market, independent initiative, and self-reliance, to a great extent limit our pursuit of those goals to working for the election of a few people who will achieve them for us. In other words, even the conservatives frequently expect the government to "do everything and change everything," although they want it to do conservative things and change in a conservative direction.

Unless we control our appetites, we cannot control our government. We certainly cannot expect it to limit itself, because it senses our appetites far more strongly than it is persuaded by our claims that we are tired of bureaucracy, taxes, and government interference. If the ultimate goal of government is to "do everything and change everything," really an infinite challenge, then it will require an infinite effort—in fact, infinite taxes, infinite paperwork, and infinite interference: infinite in the sense that there will be no limit to them, no place at which people will say, "This is clearly all that we want or need," until the limits of exhaustion are reached. *Infinite goals mean infinite controls.* And infinite controls mean zero freedom.

This is a good reason to beware of all government policies, goals, and programs couched in open-ended and *positive* language, i.e., claiming to do or accomplish something that is not self-limiting. For example, in the matter of public schooling, a "negative" goal is to determine that the state shall not maintain separate schools for different races. This goal is limited and attainable. By contrast, it is a "positive" and almost unlimited goal to say that the state shall bring about even so apparently mechanical a thing as integration. If we view integration as simple mathematical mixing, it might look as though it could be achieved by mechanical means, such as pupil transfer and bussing. An ideal such as "integration," and even more, one such as "equality," commits the state to take upon itself an *infinite* challenge, i.e., one that has no natural limit or goal, no point at which one would claim success and relax. Such an infinite challenge will require infinite effort and sacrifice in the effort to meet it, effort and sacrifice without limit, with no point at which we can be satisfied with what we have already achieved and expended.

Of course it would be ridiculous to use the expression "infinite" taxation in the sense of mathematical infinity. If the government confiscated all the money and property in the country, that would be a limit—a rather final one, too, as production and work would immediately cease. But we can speak of "infinite" taxation, taxation without any *natural* limit, as a necessary consequence of "infinite" or unlimited goals and expectations.

For decades the greatest expenditures of the United States government were for national defense. Today, even though the defense budget is exceeded by that of Health and Human Services, it remains immense. Yet no one supposes that the size of the defense budget makes us *safe* in any absolute sense. If we wanted to do everything that we conceivably could to assure ourselves against foreign attack, there would be no limit to the weapons we could buy or to the money we could spend. Similarly, Health and Human Services can guarantee hospitals, but not health. The Department might conceivably guarantee the availability of a properly equipped hospital within a certain distance of every population center in America but it cannot of course guarantee that the taxpayers who make use of those hospitals will get well in them. It is one thing to say that the government may not *take* anyone's life without due process of law—a negative goal—as the Constitution states, or even that it may not take it at all, as opponents of capital punishment wish to establish. But if we were to say that the government must have the postive goal of preserving and protecting everyone's life, we would be setting an unlimited goal incapable of being fulfilled in this world, where there continues to be sickness, old age, accident, and crime. If the Supreme Court were to discover that everyone has a constitutional right to good health, for example, there would be no way to achieve it by human means—but a tremendous effort could be made in the process of trying. One unintended by-product of such sweeping goals is the temptation to eliminate those who fail to achieve them and thus spoil the average. The only realistic way to "guarantee" good health nationwide would be to eliminate those individuals who appear to be chronically or incurably sick or injured, just as generalized abortion "prevents" birth deformation. This is unfortunately not an altogether fanciful point. Observation: if health becomes something that the government must guarantee, ultimately we can expect to hear calls for government action to dispose of those who persistently fail to profit from the best treatment that can be given them.

The Power of Negative Thinking

The early amendments to the Constitution, especially the first ten, the so-called Bill of Rights, were limited in scope and essentially directed at restraining the government. They were thus *negative:* no censorship of the press, no establishment or persecution of any religion, no prohibition of the ownership of weapons. This was limited government. More recent amendments, instead of restraining government, were positive; they expanded its powers: the Volstead Act (Eighteenth Amendment) enabled government to enforce prohibition of the use or manufacture of beverage alcohol, and even more dramatically, the Sixteenth Amendment permitted the federal government to levy an income tax. (The Eighteenth

Amendment has been repealed, as not being enforceable; the Sixteenth is vigorously enforced, as not being repealable.)

Both of these amendments still fall in the area of limited goals, in that they premit or require the government to do *one* specific thing: beverage alcohol is a fairly well defined, easily identifiable substance, and so are taxes. If we were to suppose that an amendment were to require the government to guarantee good nutrition, to ensure that all citizens eat enough but only enough good, nourishing, non-habit-forming food, we would have the example of a "limitless" amendment. Because almost all money transactions mean "income" of some kind, the Sixteenth Amendment is closer to being "limitless" than most others. In addition, it is expansionistic, disregarding traditional concepts of national sovereignty, in that it reaches out beyond our own borders and taxes income earned outside the sovereignty of the United States. (To be fair, we must note that such taxation is in turn somewhat limited and moderated by agreements between the United States and several foreign nations, and frequently is less than their rates.) At the same time, as it has subsequently been worked out, our government assumes total jurisdiction over income earned by noncitizens within the United States, and sets up rather elaborate accounting, reporting, enforcement and collection systems to insure that income taxes are not evaded. We note that the USSR will not permit its citizens to emigrate without payment of large fees. The United States sets theoretically stringent requirements on aliens wishing to leave, although in general our authorities are fairly compassionate.

The Dangers of "Positive" Thinking: The Example of ERA

Despite certain tendencies towards greed, the tax appetite of the U.S. government is finite, and can be satisfied. Indeed, as we have said, although American taxes are much higher than ever before in history, they are still lower than those in many industrialized nations, who set out on the road of ultimate ambitions for government to do everything and change everything before we did. Currently there is a good deal of criticism of the Internal Revenue Service and its collection and enforcement practices. There are indeed abuses, and a number of practices that hardly seem to conform to the Constitution's promise of "due process." But two things should be noted: first, that the IRS in most cases only attempts to enforce the tax laws; it does not make them. Second, the tax laws are not written to correspond to some theoretical ideal of taxation, but are the direct result of the appetites of those who elect the legislators who adopt them.

More threatening than the present and possible abuses of limited power is the specter of limitless power, of asking the government to do something that is potentially impossible, or altogether limitless. The Twenty-seventh or Equal Rights Amendment currently in the ratification process is an example of a "positive" legislation with an open-ended and altogether unachievable goal. Hence it has great potential for launching us upon an ever-increasing, never-satisfied course of government regulation and control.

At first glance, the Equal Rights Amendment would seem to correspond to our criterion of limiting, or negative legislation. It denies the government power to make laws of a certain type, namely those that make distinctions between individuals on the basis of sex:

> SECTION 1. Equality of rights under the law shall not be denied or abridged by the United States or any state on account of sex.

It also empowers—we may read, requires—Congress to make laws to achieve that absence of denial or abridgment—we may read, to achieve equality:

> SECTION 2: The Congress shall have power to enforce this article by appropriate legislation.

One could understand the language of the Equal Rights Amendment and the intent behind it as the abolition of invidious legal distinctions based on sex. This is no doubt the goal of many of its supporters, and as such is a very commendable one. Its opponents have noted, however, that in fact it could and probably would be read as requiring the government to accomplish something that really does not lie within its power: the abolition of *all* distinctions based on sex. Since most, perhaps the majority, of such distinctions are based on tradition, culture, custom, and what we might call human nature, and some of them are clearly based on biological factors,[3] for government to attempt to remove them involves almost limitless positive intervention into human affairs, including but not limited to remaking the language which is the bearer of our culture.

---

[3] For a full discussion of the biological factor in sex roles, see Steven Goldberg, *The Inevitability of Patriarchy* (revised edition with appendices; New York: Morrow, 1974).

Mission Impossible?

The most serious flaws of the Equal Rights Amendment lie not so much in what it seeks to accomplish as in what it could be used to do. ERA advocates reject the warnings of a total overthrow of traditional patterns of the family, legalization of homosexual marriage, and the like, but it is hard to see what would prevent this, other than common sense. And common sense seems to have little part in our present court system. Above and beyond this, there is the universal quality of its promise to transform society in the area of relations between the sexes. This is something that it may prove difficult if not impossible for government to achieve under any circumstances. If people are led to expect that an amendment will do it, when the amendment fails to accomplish what has been promised for it, the result will certainly be a demand for more and more "affirmative action," in other words, for coercive measures to accomplish a rapid transformation of social reality. Of course, few of those in the Congress and the state legislatures who support the Equal Rights Amendment think that they are voting for extensive measures of coercion. In fact, many who vote for it would oppose any such coercive consequences. Unfortunately, once the provision is enacted, we will have to live with the consequences that may be derived from it, regardless of the expectations or reservations of those who participated in enacting it. The extension of time to ratify—but not to reconsider—the Equal Rights Amendment, voted by Congress in 1979 under considerable pressure from President Carter, certainly seems to violate the spirit of the amendment process, which is supposed to require a three-fourths majority of all the states, presumably at more or less the same time. It is a clear application of the principle, "The end justifies the means." As things now stand, however, enough Americans are coming to reject the end to leave ERA dead in the water and unlikely to be adopted in its present form.

In an important little book, *Science, Politics, and Gnosticism,* political philosopher Eric Voegelin likens the religio-philosophical movement that flourished in the pagan Roman Empire and rivaled Christianity for a time, Gnosticism, to many modern political movements, particularly Marxism.[4] Although Gnosticism was an esoteric religion and Marxism and most other political ideologies claim to be totally this-worldly and scientific, there is an important element of similarity: dissatisfaction with the world as it really exists. Dissatisfaction with the world is really a rejection of the

---

[4]Eric Voegelin, *Science, Politics, and Gnosticism,* trans. William J. Fitzpatrick (Chicago: Gateway Books [Henry Regnery], 1968).

wisdom of the Creator. Gnosticism taught that the maker of the world was not God, but a narrow-minded lesser power called the demiurge. The goal of Gnostic religion was to escape from this physical world and its demiurge to communion with the highest and most spiritual entity, God. Modern secularism, of course, does not believe in a half-divine demiurge, but like Gnosticism it repudiates the idea that the world as it presently exists is the product of a wise and good Creator. Secularism basically sees the world as the product of mindless, naturalistic evolution, and in the course of constantly changing for the better, through evolution. Hence neither the "order of nature" nor human tradition can be guides for present and future conduct; all is changing, and must change.

Voegelin sees this common rejection of Creation—he calls it a rejection of the order of Being—as a real hostility to what is, a rejection of the fact that there is an order to the universe, an order that we did not create or impose and that cannot readily be changed by us.

This rejection of the Creator goes farther than a mere unwillingness to obey the Ten Commandments and such other laws and principles as are thought too repressive. It involves a rejection of the fact that there are any laws at all, that there is any pattern to reality that we cannot alter or break at will. Much traditional religion and traditional human wisdom has been concerned with helping human beings to live harmoniously and happily in natural relationships—for example, those of parent and child, husband and wife, friend and friend, king and subject. Ancient Gnosticism and its modern parallels deny natural ties and make all obligations the consequence not of anything natural but simply of arbitrary government decree. St. Paul speaks of rendering "honor to whom honor is due" (Romans 13:7), and he has in mind the idea that a ruler, or at least his office, is *worthy* of honor. Modern government has very little sense of the *worth* that might merit honor, but only of the techniques for imposing compliance with its regulations.

If there really is a Creator, and if he has actually, really and truly made the world in one particular way and not in another—and this is the underlying conviction of all biblical thought, of Western civilization, and indeed of modern empirical science—then we cannot alter reality at will. We can only alter or suppress our perception of it.

The desire to have a different reality from that created by God manifests itself in contemporary culture in several ways, dramatically in the flight from reality through drugs. Resistance to the idea that there is a Creation order to which man ought by nature to conform is evident in the widespread abandonment of the idea that there is such a thing as a *crimen contra naturam*, a crime against nature. The practice of homosexuality used to be called unnatural vice (to distinguish it from natural vice). A child who turned against his parents, or a parent who destroyed his child, was called unnatural. Today it is considered, by the law at least, quite permissible for a mother to destroy her unborn child, and it is becoming possible for children to sue their own parents. In the former case the state intervenes to legitimize what human beings for generations have considered a dreadful act against the fruit of one's own body; in the latter, it rather logically declares the converse. Since the parents now seem to have the right to destroy their unborn offspring, the born offspring are no longer obliged to treat their own parents as having some special immunity. In both cases the State, a secondary human institution, breaks the bonds of the primary institution, the family, and does so not to protect a family member, but in effect to injure him. This is a paramount example of the way in which the modern state destroys all existing interpersonal ties and replaces them with bonds to itself alone.

The rejection of the concept that there is such a thing as an order of nature that ought to be kept and respected is frequently not seen as a direct attack on God, for modern man no longer links "Nature and Nature's God," as the Declaration of Independence did. During the eighteenth-century Enlightenment, when it ceased to be intellectually fashionable to speak of a personal Creator and a revealed Word from him, a sense of the Creation order and an attitude of respect for it were preserved, but it was called the order of Nature rather than of Creation. As time passed, it became less and less easy to defend the seemingly arbitrary relations in nature. They have to be accepted if they reflect the Will of an almighty Creator, but certainly they do not command the same reverent acceptance if they merely represent accidents of nature.

Since nature, as it is, is widely considered to be less than perfect, and since our ability to change it to our liking, despite all our scientific and technological progress, is still limited, there is a temptation to think that the problem is not with reality as it is, but with our perception of it. Christianity, like Judaism, is in large measure compatible with the received wisdom of mankind, and represented a clarification of it. Biblical religion does not tell us that nothing is as it seems to the natural human reason, but only that the natural human reason, although it is capable of accomplishing many worthwhile things, cannot attain the highest and most important goal unaided, namely the knowledge of God.

Reversals of Knowledge

There are two sides to a movement such as that represented by the Equal Rights Amendment. This duality illustrates the ambiguity that surrounds so much state and government activity in America today. It results from the fact that we are establishing programs without principles, so that the programs ultimately become their own principles. We create mechanisms without being altogether agreed on what those mechanisms are to accomplish. As a result, there is a very real danger that the mechanisms themselves will come to set the goal. This is the kind of thing that many people instinctively fear with a movement such as ERA. What it says it wants is reasonable enough, though that still might be open to debate. But the way in which it says it makes people fear that what is sought is really a total reversal, not of laws but of life, and naturally the majority of people are apprehensive, and many are altogether antagonistic, towards such a prospect.

Until the adoption of the Equal Rights Amendment, if it ultimately is adopted, the relation between the sexes and the roles attributed to each sex in the United States are determined as they have been in every other human society: by custom, tradition, religion, habit, and of course to a large extent, if we follow the view of Goldberg, by biological factors. Everyone has a general, not altogether uniform, understanding of that relation and those roles. But just as they are not spelled out in law codes or common law, nor in the Constitution, they are not explicitly worked out in detail in any generally accepted religious or philosophical system.

As long as these customary, traditional relations were not challenged, they could operate without being well defined. To a great extent they helped people to orient themselves in their world; to some extent, of course, they caused conflict, oppression, and unhappiness, as any set of rules will, good or bad, and as reality itself does. They were also flexible enough to allow considerable variation under them, and they were not incapable of evolution and change.

What the Equal Rights Amendment appears to threaten — or promise — to do is to install a well-articulated government dogma in the place of custom and tradition. If it promised merely to change certain specific things, there would probably be far less opposition to it than there has been. But it appears to threaten the fabric of human life, telling people that everything they have inherited from the past is wrong and must be radically changed, conformed to a newly discovered principle. This is tyranny — intellectual, legal, and physical.

Surely this is not in the minds of many articulate supporters of ERA. Equally surely, some such deep dissatisfaction with reality as it is *is* in the back of the minds of some of its advocates. It is this ambivalence about what sounds like a simple legal reform that makes it appear so threatening to many, so appealing to others, while the middle-of-the-road constitutionalists, who see it *only* as a technical legal issue, cannot understand why some people get into a panic over it and others reach a frenzy of quasi-religious enthusiasm.

What human beings have traditionally done or thought is not sacrosanct. Indeed, traditions in many areas are doubtless at variance with the facts; some have already been changed, and many still ought to be. But the fact that something has become a tradition indicates that people have learned how to live with it. People in general do not like their living patterns changed by government decree, and this is what many people fear with movements such as ERA. Perhaps everything that we think we know in a particular area *is* wrong and should be changed. But then it should be done first of all as an intellectual, educational matter and only subsequently, once its validity is ascertained, written into law.

Into the Abyss

One of the most baffling things about the enthusiastic support and almost universal official party endorsement that the ERA receives is that no one knows what it will do or where it will take us. Indeed, even its supporters are not at all united about what they expect or hope it to achieve. About one thing there can be no doubt, however. It gives the government—first of all the regulatory agencies, then Congress, and in the final analysis and perhaps most significantly, the federal courts—*carte blanche* to remake our social structure according to what they think ERA mandates. When we observe that father-son banquets were prohibited as "unconstitutional" under Title IX of the Secondary and Higher Education Act (a decree overturned by President Ford), we do not require a vivid imagination to conceive of what the agencies, and even more the courts, can and will do with the ERA. Since government's record in regulating less delicate matters, such as industrial and commercial relations, is not altogether brilliant, there is a reason to be apprehensive about what it will do to the traditional relation between the sexes.

It is not unreasonable to hesitate at the brink of the abyss, before plunging into a situation the real nature of which we can only suspect. When we note that ERA is the gateway to an adventure which—so far—even the most totalitarian of states have not ventured to pursue, there is real reason to ask ourselves whether it is sensible in a democratic society, or even feasible with democratic institutions as we know them. For a government to be able to "do everything and change everything," it is going to have to change itself, especially to the extent that its powers are, for the moment, constitutionally limited.

ERA and school bussing are different, yet related symbols for the transition from limited government to government that is totalitarian. Perhaps we should say ultratotalitarian, if such a super-superlative may be tolerated, because it goes beyond traditional totalitarianism in attempting to change fundamental realities, and people with them, without even naming the realities or informing the people clearly — something that more orthodox totalitarians did thoroughly through their propaganda machinery.

School bussing is the adoption of a mechanical means to regulate and change something that is very subtle and delicate: how members of various races perceive themselves and each other, and how they relate to one another. It says something about the state's view of human nature to presuppose that man's fundamental spiritual and emotional nature can be radically influenced by simple mechanical shifts in environmental factors. And it says something about the state's implicit claim to total dominion over its citizens, or rather subjects, that it takes for granted that it is entitled to change their basic self-image and interpersonal relations by crude manipulation without ever bringing it up to the level of discussion and dialogue either among the children or their parents. Thus the objection to school bussing in this context is not that it is ineffective, costs too much, is counterproductive, harms the children, or violates parental rights, though each of these objections may be argued. Our fundamental objection is that it is an attempt, largely unconscious but nevertheless serious, on the part of the state to redefine for people who they are and what their value is, without even giving them the courtesy of discussing it with them.

Bussing is a mandatory and a very mechanical means of trying to accomplish a moral goal. ERA seeks an ideal, a social and human transformation that would not be approved if clearly expressed, and that will require mandatory and indeed mechanical measures to implement. And both projects — if human nature really is anything like what human beings, through three millennia of civilization, have thought it to be — are either doomed to frustration and failure or will require the marshalling of hitherto undreamt-of measures of coercion, confirmity, and control.

Bussing and ERA, together with that other great attempted reversal of traditional values, abortion on demand, all have this in common: they are attempts to deal with a specific problem, but they are open-ended and potentially almost infinite in their implications. If the traditional American idea that government is "under God" and hence limited is to mean anything, we have to give serious thought to defining and enforcing those limits before plunging into the abyss of governmental efforts to transform the nature of reality. Government cannot make angelic beings of us, but in the effort to do so it can make slaves of us.

10

Government and God

On the appointed day Herod, wearing his royal robes, sat on his throne and delivered a public address to the people. They shouted, "This is the voice of a god, not of a man."

Acts 12:21–22
(New International Version)

Government, whether it sees itself as "under God" or not, cannot possibly "do everything and change everything," but it will attempt to do so unless it is rather forcefully limited. This means that if we in America really believe that government and the state are to be under God and therefore are not absolute, we must develop principles and procedures that will keeps them so. Otherwise their ambitions — or rather the ambitions we encourage them to have — will push them irresistibly towards absolutism and totalitarianism. In order to limit the ambition of government, we have to limit our own expectations, of which governmental ambition is but a reflection. Limiting our expectations means limiting our appetites, something neither our modern consumer society nor our ambitious politicians are eager to have us do. This means that our only hope to check the headlong rush of government into the abyss of unattainable goals and unbearable controls lies in our own willingness and determination to step off the conveyor belt, so to speak, to see where we are and where our movement is taking us. Only as Americans are willing to step out of the onrushing mob, to see where it is headed and when necessary to choose a different direction for themselves, will it be possible for us to challenge, and perhaps change, the direction that events seem to be taking. In order to do this, we must first pause to consider the nature of human civil government and its place—if it is to be where we say it ought to be, namely under God.

Key Passages Relating to Government

Historically there have been two basic attitudes on the part of Christians towards the state, or the civil government. We may call them obedience and rejection. They are opposed, but not totally so, for many times a Christian will be a paragon of obedience to the state—up to a point, after which he abruptly rejects its authority and may even rebel against it. There are two basic biblical texts that correspond to these views, both taken from the early days of the church's life, when the little Christian congregations found themselves facing on the one hand the glorious, worldwide Roman Empire, and on the other hand the impressive, self-confident religious establishment of Judaism.

Submission

According to Paul in Romans 13:1, "Everyone must submit himself to the governing authorities, for there is no authority except that which God has established. The authorities that exist have been established by God." This is the *locus classicus* for the idea that Christians should submit to the authority of the state. It is fairly sweeping—all the more so when we bear in mind that the state that Paul knew best was the Roman Empire, ruled at this time by Nero (A.D. 53–66). Nero, who came to the throne very young, at the age of eighteen, was viewed at first as a saviour, for it was known that he had had Rome's greatest philosopher, Seneca, as his tutor. But as everyone knows, Nero was led astray by his great power, and ultimately became one of the worst rulers Rome had, so that there was general rejoicing when he was finally driven from the throne and murdered. It is important to remember that Paul wrote Romans 13 when Nero was in power, not Augustus or the later philosopher-emperor Marcus Aurelius. If Paul could assert that *Nero's* authority came from God, one would think that he could say it of almost anyone.

At the same time, we must remember that every government is greater than its head, and almost every government, even autocratic and tyrannical ones, is staffed by administrators and officials who want to establish justice and to do as Paul says in Romans 13:3-4, i.e., to reward the good and punish evildoers. If one takes the punishment of generally recognized evil deeds, such as murder, assault, robbery and rape, as one aspect of justice, then one could correctly say that there are many dictatorial governments in the world today that go farther towards establishing that aspect of justice than the United States. The Roman government of Paul's day, despite its cruelties and excesses, did give the ancient world a measure of order, peace, and prosperity unknown before Rome and not achieved again until many centuries later.

Rejection

If Romans 13:1-7 provides the *locus classicus* to justify the Christian's submission to the state, the comments of Peter and John in Acts 4:19 provide the key theme for Christian resistance: "But Peter and John replied, 'Judge for yourselves whether it is right in God's sight to obey you rather than God.'" Clearly the apostles believed that they had the right, even the duty, to refuse to obey these human officials. Actually, interpretation of the text is complicated by the fact that the authority before whom the apostles had been brought, the Sanhedrin, had religious as well as civil power, and the reason for the apostles' summons was religious in nature: they had been preaching about Jesus. Thus it can be argued that Peter and John were not resisting a lawful civil authority but an illegitimate religious one. Essentially, however, it seems necessary to admit that the Sanhedrin, albeit in part a religious council, was also a civil body to which the apostles were refusing obedience. Their refusal to obey only came when the Sanhedrin attempted to forbid them to do something that God had expressly commanded them. And this is the place at which most Christian rejection of government occurs, when government attempts to prevent the preaching of the Gospel of Christ. But there is a small, yet impressive, group of Christians that rejects the civil state altogether, identifying it with the world from which Christians are to be separate. Such Christian rejection of the state is generally nonviolent: it involves rejection of the state's authority and withdrawal to an isolated or separated life much more often than any violent resistance to the power of the state.

The Legitimacy of Government

Government, biblically speaking, appears after the Fall of Man. In-

115

stitutions clearly established before the Fall—and hence not as the result of or penalty for sin—include marriage, the family, and work, both intellectual and physical, as something fundamentally right for man. The state or civil government—like crime—appears only the Fall. One may well speculate, with Robert Culver and others,[1] that some form of social organization would have been necessary even without the Fall, and this may well be true. Nevertheless, God did not expressly ordain civil government before the Fall, as he did ordain the family and the institution of work. We may infer from this that government is a secondary kind of human institution, and hence that it should not usurp the role or the powers of the family, a primary institution. Nevertheless, though secondary, government is a legitimate institution from the biblical perspective. Indeed, to quote St. Paul, "The powers that be are instituted to God." For "power" Paul uses the Greek word *exousia,* rendered into Latin *auctoritas,* authority, one of the most important terms used to describe the authority of the Senate, of the Emperor, and of Rome itself. As noted earlier, it signifies the ability to command respect and willing obedience, not the mere power to enforce them. The word *exousia* is also used of the authority given to Jesus (Matthew 28:18). There is no stronger clue to the legitimacy of government and its right to exercise power than these remarks of Paul in Romans 13.

Nevertheless, there is a tradition among Christains of denying legitimacy to the government. After all, as the Gospel narratives make plain, government at almost every level was involved in killing the Founder of Christianity: the temple police of the religious authorities arrested him; both religious and local political puppet officials heard the case; the imperial Roman government, which reserved to itself the right of capital punishment, appointed the procurator, Pontius Pilate. There was even "mass democracy" in the mob scenes in which Pilate wanted to release Jesus but was intimidated by the mob's shouting and the insinuations of the religious authorities. Nevertheless, depite the fact that Jesus was executed by the Roman authorities, the early Christians evinced little hostility to the Roman government until it began fairly severe religious persecution. Rising Christian antipathy to imperial Rome is reflected in the last book of the Bible, the Revelation of St. John, but it is couched in obscure, symbolic language. For most Christians, the government remained an authority deserving of respect. Several of the early Christain writers of the second century, the so-called apologists, addressed long essays to different emperors arguing, among other things, that Christians promoted the public welfare with their

---

[1]Robert D. Culver, *Toward a Biblical View of Civil Government* (Chicago: Moody, 1974).

prayers for the emperor. After the conversion of Constantine the Great (the date is uncertain; he was not formally baptized until near the end of his life in 339), the Christians entered into a long period of close cooperation with "Christian" rulers and governments. This so-called "Constantinian era" of Christendom, in which the government collaborated with one church or another, is supposed by some to have lasted right up to the present and to be only slowly coming to an end in our own day. As a result of this close liaison between church and government, dissident Christians found themselves at odds with the state, which sometimes persecuted them for the sake of religious unity within its boundaries. Dissidents of various sorts—orthodox Christians under Constantine's Arian son Constantius, Arians later under the orthodox, Donatists in North Africa and many others—endured varying amounts of government hostility without changing their fundamental conviction that government is God-ordained and deserves the loyalty of Christians. But some of the most persecuted groups, particularly certain branches of the Anabaptist movement of the sixteenth century, began to reject civil government altogether. Some looked on the state as a this-worldly institution with which true Christians should have nothing to do; others went so far as to condemn it as positively evil, "the woman drunk with the blood of saints."

However vivid their Christian imagery condemning the state, little groups of sectarian Christians had no real means to oppose it: During the Reformation period, as Europe was just emerging from the feudal system, some small groups of other-worldly Christians were able to organize separatist religious communities, some of them on a basis of religious communism. After the discovery of North America, a number of Anabaptist groups emigrated to the New World, where they found room and freedom to live their own kind of life with very little formal contact with the colonial and later the independent government. As government expanded the scope of its operations, both in the United States and elsewhere, it became less tolerant of those dissenting groups for their refusal to serve in the conscripted army, and sometimes even to pay taxes. The United States government has been relatively less severe on such mavericks than most other modern states have been.

The American Attitude

Traditionally representatives of the major Christian confessions in America have been consistently patriotic. The War of Independence was fought with considerable church backing, particularly from the Calvinists

(Presbyterians and Congregationalists), the largest American religious group at the time of the Revolution. As non-Calvinists—Roman Catholics and Lutherans—began to grow in numbers during the nineteenth century, they generally shared the unquestioning patriotism of the Calvinists. On the Union side, the War between the States was sparked by Unitarian Abolitionists, but largely fought by the orthodox Congregationalists and Presbyterians of New England and the Middle Atlantic seaboard, Irish Catholics, German Catholics and Lutherans.

During the two World Wars, there were some pacifist sentiments among Christians. William Jennings Bryan, devoutly religious, resigned his post as Wilson's Secretary of State because of his conviction that the president was not doing his best to preserve peace. But most religious leaders in America accepted the idea that the Allied cause was just, and supported America's combat role. In World War II there was some criticism of urban bombing from liberal Protestant leaders such as Harry Emerson Fosdick of New York's Riverside Church, but in general most Christians in America were so outraged by the enormity of the enemy's conduct that they overlooked Allied excesses, and even the mass murders perpetrated by the USSR. (As we now know, not a few liberal churchmen were sympathetic to Communism, and hence all the readier to overlook Russian excesses.) Roman Catholics, Jews, and the bulk of America's Protestants supported national policy through the Korean War, up until Vietnam, when the united front began to crack. Since the middle of the Vietnam War, there has been considerable retreat from the fundamental position of general church support for national policy. This began with the liberal Protestants and spread to both conservative Protestants and Roman Catholics. Among the conservative Protestants, those in the Reformed tradition, as well as the independent fundamentalists, generally continue to hold a high view of the state and to support it, but non-Reformed evangelicals are becoming more critical of it. In this there is a conscious tendency to recover the old separatist, antigovernment tradition of the Anabaptists. Clark H. Pinnock, of McMaster Divinity College, Hamilton, Ontario, is the foremost theological exponent of this Anabaptist mood; among spiritually active American political leaders, Senator Mark O. Hatfield (R.-Ore.) has shown some affinity for the separatistic, Anabaptist critique of the state.

Because the unified position is visibly crumbling, it is no longer possible to assume that Christians in America will automatically support "established government" in general or American government in particular. For this reason it is necessary for Christians concerned about society and the state to reexamine some of the most important aspects of the legitimacy of government under God.

Benefits and Punishments

As indicated above, Paul in his treatment of the lawfulness of government *assumes* that government will protect and reward the innocent and punish the guilty. This is a basic, essential function of government under God; without it a government cannot well claim legitimacy in God's sight. The establishment of justice is in theory a primary concern of government, but government in America is well on its way to standing the biblical requirement on its head, by protecting the guilty and punishing the innocent. For thousands of violent murders in America each year, only a tiny minority if any of the felons will be convicted and executed. But of the approximately 4.5 million human beings conceived in America each year, over one-third die before birth, killed by physicians at the request of the women who would otherwise have been their mothers. One and the same Supreme Court made it difficult if not impossible for society to take the life of a murderer, and difficult if not impossible for society to protect the life of a developing child, even if his only offense is being inconvenient. Faced with legal trends in America that seem to turn fundamental biblical values upside down, we must in all seriousness ask the question of whether the basic policies of our government may not shortly become so perverted that it will be impossible to continue to credit its authority as coming from God.

Punishment As an Element of Justice

The Bible plainly speaks of exacting punishment as one of the chief ways of establishing justice. Indeed, this corresponds to the ordinary wisdom of the man in the street. Asked what it means "to see justice done," most people will answer "to have the guilty punished." A major, even the primary, function of justice is seen as retribution, giving to each what he deserves. Walter Kaufmann, a trenchant philosopher and militant atheist, argues that the idea of justice is inseparable from punishment and ultimately from the religious view of a God who judges and punishes. Since the idea of God is unacceptable, Kaufmann would have us do away with the concept of justice itself, inasmuch as it depends on

God. He cogently argues against the idea of "distributive justice" as an alternative to the "retributive justice" that involves punishment. "Distributive justice," based on an equal sharing of goods, is a misnomer, for the idea of justice is inexorably bound up with punishment and with God. He favors such equal sharing, but says that we should not confuse matters by calling it justice.[2] While we do not agree with Kaufmann's atheism and his vision of autonomous man, we are grateful to him for his elucidation of the necessity of punishment to the establishment of justice, and for the ultimate dependence of justice on at least a minimum of faith in God.

The legitimacy of government under God then rests on a certain minimum of justice, and the goal of securing justice in turn on a certain minimum of shared religious conviction. Both these things the founders of independent America certainly had. But there is real question as to whether their successors in late twentieth-century America do have them. Speaking from the great heritage of Christian, biblical faith, we can affirm that civil government is necessary and even good, that it is ordained by God, and that we have a religious duty, as well as an enforceable legal obligation, to obey it. But government on its part must fulfil a certain role in order to be considered a legitimate government and to share in the favor of God.

It is evident that the role of the Christian under a government such as Paul describes is one of respect and obedience. But what is the situation when, as is surely the case in America, citizens not only have duties but rights and powers? At this point it becomes evident to us that the role of government under God involves an important role for the Christian citizens who make up the bulk of our nation's populace.

---

[2]Walter Kaufmann, *Without Guilt and Justice* (New York: Wyden, 1973), especially pp. 65–96.

11

Government and the Christian

The collapse of order brings good to no one.

Ernst Jünger
Auf den Marmorklippen

If we accept the fundamental principle that government is legitimate, ordained by God, and has a function assigned to it by God, it is evident that Christians are to have a positive attitude toward it. Precisely what form is this positive attitude to take? How is it to be expressed in terms of actual behavior? Paul makes it clear that the Christian is to obey the government, respect those in authority, and pay taxes (I Timothy 2:1–2), and Peter's teaching is very similar (I Peter 2:13–17). Is this all that can be said, "Do as you're told"? Indeed not. According to a famous line from the African Christian lawyer and theologian Tertullian, the Christian is to society as the soul is to the body: he is to have an *animating* effect, giving it the spirit by which it is to be governed (cf. Jesus' expression, "the salt of the earth," Matthew 5:13). Tertullian was writing in the primarily non-Christian society of the early third century, where very few Christians occupied influential positions. If he could speak of the Christians of that day as the "soul" of society, the body, what ought we be able to say about the impact of Christians on a society where they make up the majority?

The lines from Romans 13 quoted in the preceding chapter are frequently cited to support the idea that Christians should obey the governing authorities. This is a generally accepted view of Christians all over the world, both in democracies and in dictatorships. But mere obedience falls far short of qualifying Christians as the "soul" or the "salt." What more can be expected of them?

Obedience

First of all, it is necessary to stress that obedience to the lawfully constituted authorities is normative for the Christian. The Christian is to obey the law, show respect for the authorities, pay his taxes, and generally participate in the duties and responsibilities of a citizen. This obligation does not hold only in a society where the rulers too are Christians, or in one that Christians find congenial. For this reason Christians who take the biblical mandates seriously usually are exemplary citizens even in non-Christian societies. Despotic governments have generally found that they could rely on the mass of Christians to live quietly, do their work, and not be rebellious. As a result they have been fairly well tolerated in both right- and left-wing dictatorships, thus opening themselves to charges of compromise and collaboration. Although there may—and sometimes does—come a point where the Christian has to take a stand against his government, this point is not reached until serious efforts have been made to work out conflicts with the authorities.

A Bicentennial Declaration of Repentance?

Among the organizations celebrating the bicentennial of the American Revolution, churches and Christian groups of all kinds have been highly visible. Only eight years earlier, when the Vietnam War protest movement was at its peak, many of those same Christians denounced civil disobedience and other forms of resistance to government authority as illegitimate for Christians who are committed to obedience to the powers that be. Yet somehow they see no inconsistency between requiring support for the American government in 1966 and endorsing rebellion against in 1776. The usual arguments, that the colonies were fighting for freedom, that England was oppressive, and so on, really are not sufficient to outweigh the explicit New Testament passages calling for obedience to established authority. Christians who intend to take seriously what the Bible says about civil authority cannot help but feel a certain ambivalence about the celebrations of "revolution." Of course, once the

American revolution had succeeded, and the colonies had become a new nation, the loyalty of Christian citizens transferred to the new "powers," the states and the federal government. But the transition, from a biblical perspective, definitely is open to question. Perhaps it would not be amiss for American Christians in 1981 to set out a bicentennial "declaration of repentance." No earthly nation is without failings. The United States of America has a mixed record: our nation is less evil than the New Left portrays us, and less virtuous than it appears in many official histories. But even if the nation was born in what the British called "rebellion" and we call "Revolution," it is certainly a legitimate power on the earth today. Very few countries have as long an unbroken history of governmental continuity as we do; in the United Nations, we definitely belong to the older, supposedly counterrevolutionary group. Violent change of government was not unknown in Paul's day—both Nero and his predecessor the Emperor Claudius came to power in one coup, and each lost his life in another. Paul's command seems to be that the Christian must take government as he finds it, and is not at liberty to rebel against it, except—and then only on the strength of inferences—under very grave provocation.

The question of the degree and totality of the obedience a Christian citizen owes his government has been dealt with at length by many authors. Our general conviction is that while the required loyalty is great, it is not unlimited. The immediate cause for disobedience is that brought by the apostles Peter and John in Acts 4:19. When the governing authorities forbid the preaching of the Gospel, the Christian has no choice but to go on doing it. Indeed, it is probably at this point that most governmental conflict with Christians has occurred: at the point we might call evangelism or proselytization. It is rather less common that a government commands the Christian to do something that his conscience forbids. Christians in the administrative or military service of a non-Christian government are more likely to be faced with a conflict of conscience than the ordinary Christian citizen. Under Hitler, there were some Christians who felt that they had to refuse Hitler obedience, or even attempt to overthrow him, but they were few in number compared with those who obediently fulfilled their tasks right up to the end. In retrospect, we would say that many Christians in Germany carried the principle of submission to the powers that be to an altogether unwarranted extreme. (At the same time, it is noteworthy that many highly placed Germans held back from revolting against Hitler because they felt bound by their oath of loyalty to him; during the Watergate affair, there were several cases of American leaders breaking an oath under far less pressure.) In general, however, there is agreement that the Christian is to obey the constituted authorities of government, but must withhold obedience if they command him to do something that God's laws forbid.

Responsibility

The Christian in the United States is in a different position from the ordinary Christian in the Roman Empire, Nazi Germany, or the USSR. First of all, the United States has a representative form of government. This means that all citizens have a voice in determining the policies of that government, and therefore bear a responsibility for them. Second, in contrast to ancient Rome before Constantine, Nazi Germany, and the Soviet Union, the government is on record as being at least benevolently disposed towards the Christian view of life. Third—and this is most significant—the Christians constitute the great majority of American citizens. Well over three-quarters of all Americans are nominal Christians. The largest Christian confession, Roman Catholicism, alone commands the nominal adherence of one fourth of all Americans. Protestant .churches, many of which have different and more stringent rules for counting members, embrace at least one-third of the population. It is estimated that forty million Americans are evangelicals, thus making evangelical Christianity America's largest religious bloc.

Figures such as these show one thing clearly: if there is something wrong in America, Christians—nominal and convinced—must take responsibility for it. Our situation here is not like that of believers in the Soviet Union, who are expected to keep quiet on all political and government matters. In the United States *all* citizens are expected to play an active part in the process. If the largest group has nothing to say about the direction in which the country is moving, it is because of its own indifference and laziness. Except for those few Christians who hold that Christians should have nothing to do with government and hence cannot attempt to influence it, the rest—the great majority—have only themselves to blame if their government begins to undermine the institutions and values they cherish.

If the Christian communities in the United States are accountable, on the basis of what they do or leave undone, for the policies of the United States government, what measures and steps are in order for Christians to fulfill this civil as well as spiritual responsibility?

Witness

One of the clearest characterizations of the role assigned to Christians by their Lord is found in Acts 1:8, where Jesus tells them that they will be his *witnesses*. The Greek words for witness, *martur*, and testimony, *marturion*, originally meant nothing more than a reliable witness, reliable testimony, such as would normally be expected in a court. As a matter developed, however, when Christians gave their *marturion*, testimony, in court, many of them paid for it with their life—hence the change in the meaning of the word *marturion* from meaning testimony to what we understand by martyrdom. Witnessing seldom results in martyrdom in today's world, but the idea is always there in the background, that a forthright testimony might provoke opposition and lead to persecution. Important as this martyr-witness is, it is not the only type of Christian witness that may be required. There is another type.

Watchman Witness

This second type of witness is exemplified in the Old Testament, where prophets spoke to a people that were generally familiar with the laws of God and committed in a general way to obeying it. In Ezekiel 3:15–27, the prophet is addressed as a "watchman" to the house of Israel. He has this role because the Word of God has been entrusted to him. It involves warning his fellow citizens when they transgress against the laws of God. In the charge given him the prophet is told that if he fails to warn the transgressors, they will die in their sin, but he will bear the responsibility. This bearing witness to the law of God we may designate as watchman-witness to distinguish it from martyr-witness. The duty to be a martyr-witness to the Gospel is incumbent on all Christians, wherever and under whatever form of government they may live. The duty to be a watchman-witness is also incumbent on all those who have been entrusted with the Word of God, that is, upon all Christians, certainly when they are among people who claim to know something about the laws of God and to be interested in them.

The idea of the watchman-witness can take on fanciful, even ludicrous forms. Boston had its Watch and Ward Society, which numbered among its duties the task of protecting the citizenry from unsavory entertainment. Americans have come to ridicule the idea of having guardians in the field of entertainment, feeling that adults should be trusted to choose properly for themselves. But the idea of watch-and-ward lives on, although the name has been allowed to fall into oblivion. The whole consumer protection movement spearheaded by Ralph Nader is a form of watch-and-ward activity. What this suggests is not that Nader's monitoring is therefore harmful. On the contrary, it shows that even in our "progressive," "enlightened" late twentieth-century society, where people are supposed to have "come of age," according to the theological cliché, there is considerable demand for watch-and-ward activities to advise citizens when they are in danger of harming themselves. Because of the widespread fear of cancer, the mere suggestion that a certain product causes it may be enough to drive it from the market (as happened with cyclamates, the artificial sweeteners, but has not happened with cigarettes). There is a legitimate need for such watch-and-ward concern. But it can be carried out in two ways: one defines the principles that should be followed, and tells people what they stand to gain if they will live in accordance with them. The other places little if any confidence in the individual to make the right decision, and instead seeks to remove all the instruments and opportunities lending themselves to wrong decisions from his reach. Human beings need recognizable, valid principles on which to order their lives, not only as a practical matter but also for deep psychological or spiritual reasons. Such principles are not supplied by the government or bureaucracy, and they certainly are not supplied by consumer protection regulations. These principles, in the substance in which they gave backbone and character to Western civilization, are found in our biblical, Judeo-Christian spiritual heritage. Christians have custody of them and may not keep them as a mysterious secret lore for themselves alone, unless they are willing to deprive all their neighbors and society as a whole of the benefit of their knowledge.

Christians as Treasurers

Paul, speaking of the value of the Christian message and the relative insignificance of those entrusted with spreading it, wrote, "We have this treasure in earthen vessels" (II Corinthians 4:7). He was speaking specifically of the Gospel. The image evoked is that of the treasurer, or treasure-keeper, charged with keeping and preserving the treasure, and also with making it available for wise use. A treasurer or banker who accepted deposits only to make them disappear from circulation forever would be an embezzler or a thief. Christians are the people who, as a group,

126

are custodians of the fundamental values of our spiritual heritage. Malcolm Muggeridge refers to Jesus Christ as "the founder of our religion and our civilization." The combination is important. Christian faith cannot exist without Jesus Christ; this is a truism. But can Christian civilization exist without him? One may say, "We are not interested in Christian civilization, but only in civilization. Surely we do not need Jesus for that." The difficulty is that the only available civilization, as far as the United States at the moment is concerned, is Christian civilization. We are rather in the situation of theatre-goers attending a performance by La Scala. It is true that there are other forms of entertainment besides opera. But there is little use asking La Scala to change its program from Verdi to Shakespeare. The presuppositions simply aren't there. Of course, La Scala's singers might *learn* Shakespeare. But a considerable period of adjustment and adaptation would be involved, and a decent presentation of Shakespeare's Macbeth would be preceded by a good interval of hysterical noise and confusion. Cultures and civilizations can evolve and adapt, but what happens in Western Christendom when the Christian element is removed is not evolution; it is not even revolution. It is dissolution. One group of non-Christians in America, namely the Jews, is understandably sensitive and uneasy about proposals to make America "a Christian nation once more." It is impossible to deny that Christian-oriented governments of the past have discriminated against Jews, but it is worth noting that the two governments with the worst record of anti-Semitism to date first rejected Christianity as a standard before turning violently against Jews — Nazi Germany and Soviet Russia.

In America, Christians are custodians of the values of our civilization. If we exclude ourselves or allow ourselves to be excluded from participation in public policymaking whenever political and spiritual concerns overlap, then we are depriving our whole society of its richest source of ethical insight. In our civilization, the primary ethical contribution comes from Christianity and the biblical tradition. Secular humanism, rationalist and existentialist philosophy, and other sources are present as well, but their contribution is largely in the nature of a critique, criticism, or supplement. If the Christians, who have custody of the heritage, keep it under wraps and out of sight, then the debate on political and constitutional policies will be carried out largely in a vacuum. And this is precisely what is happening.

The wasteland of values that exists in America today exists very largely as a result of the abdication of Christians. Far from attempting to impose their values, Christians have been unwilling even to share them with others. While many of the more evangelical Christians take refuge in personal piety, others are influenced by a mistaken concept of separation. They feel that Christians should be "separate from the world" with the effect of depriving nominal Christians and non-Christians of all values drawn from the Christian heritage. Liberals, such as Arthur S. Flemming, chairman of the U.S. Civil Rights Commission and former president of the National Council of Churches, appear to be so dedicated to "pluralism" and the "separation of church and state" that instead of being advocates of the values they claim to hold, they actively work to exclude them from consideration when they are presented by others. Simply on the basis of an empirical comparison of value systems, Christian values are worthy of consideration in any objective choice among values to be applied in determining public policy. Naturally, non-Christians cannot be expected to be familiar with Christian values or to be particularly interested in advocating them. If the Christians will not advocate their own value system, they certainly cannot expect others to do it for them. Under such circumstances, the fact that Christians are so numerous in America has come to mean that it is all the harder for Christian values to get even the fair hearing that their objective merits would warrant. Instead of pushing them, Christians actively withhold them. The result, a combination of voluntary abdication of responsibility on the part of Christians and deliberate interference by some militant secularists, is what we may call the disfranchisement of Christians in America.

12

The Disfranchisement of the Christians

> But what authority can man's laws have, when a man may have the luck to evade them, again and again undiscovered in his guilt, sometimes to despise them, as he breaks them of choice or of necessity?
>
> Tertullian
> *Apology*

Where there is no self-control, external controls must be imposed. In ancient societies, there were no adequate means for surveillance, recording, and control of individuals' activities to make a high degree of authoritarian, external controls possible. Kings and other rulers might punish the infraction of their laws with the utmost severity, including death, torture, and vengeance against family members. But many crimes remained undetected, and the citizen who was determined to disobey them often found that he could despise them with impunity. Writing to the imperial Roman authorities at a time when the Empire's external power was threatened and its internal authority shaky, Tertullian appealed to them to recognize the social value of the Christian element in the Empire. Unlike those who obeyed human laws only out of fear of punishment, or who disregarded them when they thought detection unlikely, Christians obeyed human ordinances out of obedience to God.*

---

*In the New Testament and early church history as indicated in Chapter 11, Christians refused to obey the civil authorities only when they commanded something definitely forbidden, such as idol worship, or attempted to forbid something definitely commanded, such as preaching the Gospel.

Because ancient Roman society lacked the technical means for imposing extensive external controls on the citizens' behavior, its leaders were forced to appeal to the general population for voluntary cooperation in a wide range of concerns. In early republican Rome, the small and homogeneous population shared a common religion and values. As the Empire expanded to include the whole Mediterranean basin, and absorbed populations with the most widely differing religions and philosophies, several emperors made an attempt to require at least a formal acknowledgment of the imperial and Roman ideals from the entire population. Since these ideas were tied up with pagan worship, it was at this point that they ran into persistent opposition from the Christians. As Tertullian wrote early in the third century, "I will frankly call the emperor Lord, but only in the ordinary way, but only when force is not brought to bear on me to call him Lord in the sense of God."[1] After several bloody and prolonged attempts by Rome to coerce the Christians into acknowledging the divinity of the emperor and the absoluteness of the state, the first emperor was converted, Constantine. Accepting the argument put forward by Tertullian and other Christians, namely that Christians who refused to worship the emperor as divine would nevertheless be better citizens than pagans out of obedience to God, Constantine broke with the policy of persecution. The era that he thus inaugurated has been hailed by many as the beginning of a Christian civilization, and by others as the beginning of a sellout by the church to the state.

Whether or not Constantine's conversion and motivation were genuine, and whether or not the subsequent participation of spiritual leaders in political affairs was wise, it is a fact that for sixteen centuries since Constantine the influence of Christian teachings on obedience to lawful authority has been taken for granted as one of the foundations of social stability in the Christian West. Even in systems that have formally repudiated Christianity and attempt to suppress it, such as the Soviet Union and other nations of Eastern Europe, there is some recognition of the fact that committed Christians often contribute more, by their industry, responsibility, and obedience to law, than other segments of society.

In the United States, traditionally a more or less Christian society, there can be no doubt that most or all of the major Christian traditions have made an important and long-lasting contribution to the stability of the social order, to the observance of law, and to the moderation of social conflict. Even those minority Christians who regard war as forbidden to the Christian, pacifism as obligatory, and government as a world-

Tertullian, *Apology*, xxxiv:1.

ly activity in which true Christians should have no part, have made a recognized positive contribution to the welfare, productivity, and stability of society: noteworthy among them are the heirs of the Anabaptist tradition, including the Mennonites and Amish.

At the present time, several things are occurring in American society that, many say, mark the "end of the Constantinian era." Theologians who hold that the churches compromised their integrity by accepting the liaison with government begun by that emperor have rejoiced at the fact that the churches are now on their own, free of harmful reliance on the wealth and power of the world, as represented by the civil government.

There can be no doubt that the sixteen centuries of intimate church-state cooperation inaugurated by Constantine witnessed immense compromises of principle on the part of Christians. On the other hand, one certainly cannot deny the right of any human being to be genuinely converted and to turn to Christ. If such an individual happens to be emperor, it would be strange to expect his personal conversion to have no influence on his public policy. (In America, we often seem to expect that a political leader's personal faith should have no influence whatsoever on his conduct in office. What we now universally deplore as "Watergate morality" is in part a result of this tradition of moral and spiritual schizophrenia.)

The End of Church-State Cooperation?

Of course the policy of close association between church and state inagurated by Constantine involved many compromises and a considerable element of self-deception and hypocrisy, both on the part of churchmen who lent support to unjust activities of the state, and of political leaders who pretended to be motivated by religious or moral principles when actually acting out of personal or national self-interest. Nevertheless, there can be no doubt that the degree of moral training of the general population achieved by the churches, partial and inadequate though it has always been, has made a very positive contribution to social order and harmony through the ages, even, as already noted, in societies that have declared themselves to be anti-Christian.

As the "Constantinian era" supposedly draws to an end, its demise is being hailed and hastened both by secularists, who see it as emancipation from the hated tutelage of religious authority and principles, and by many Christians, who think that it gives them the opportunity to be honestly Christian without being compromised by support and benefits conferred by the state. However, a set of relations and attitudes that has developed over sixteen hundred years cannot be shucked off without some profound dislocations and upheaval. Before Americans, Christian and non-Christian alike, agree in principle to the complete severance of all affinities between the religious and the civil realms, between spiritual and political principles, it would be good to examine the consequences that the incipient divorce is already producing, and to ask ourselves what the long-range results are likely to be.

Undiscovered in Guilt

Whatever else is going on in American society, one of its most glaring features is the soaring crime rate. Rapidly rising crime statistics have occasioned a flurry of political rhetoric and a number of not particularly effective measures to reduce them. Unfortunately, after an apparent slowing of the rate of increase in the early seventies, the figures again show an immense increase, ranging between twenty and thirty percent, depending on the category of crime and the source doing the reporting. And a mid-1975 Gallup Poll indicates that actual figures are even higher than those published, as a substantial number of crimes is not even reported.[2] One household in four has suffered some form of crime during the past twelve months. While state and federal governments ponder various means of attempting to control crime, a substantial percentage of crimes goes unreported; a large percentage of those reported never leads to the apprehension of a suspect; and only a small number of suspects are convicted and serve a jail sentence, which—when and if it comes—generally begins so long after the offense that it loses most of its psychological impact, both on the criminal and on society at large. Apparently what Tertullian predicted to the Roman magistrates of his day is being demonstrated to the American magistrates of our own: man's laws can have no authority when a man may have the luck to evade them, again and again undiscovered in his guilt.

This marked increase in crime at all levels—not excluding, as we know, the highest echelons of government—happens (does it "just happen"?) to coincide with a systematic turning away from the principles of our Judeo-Christian spiritual heritage in law, the courts, the schools, and the media. Is there a direct connection? Ours is an age in which we are supposed to think highly only of those discoveries made in the last six

[2]*Washington Post,* July 29, 1975.

months. What a humiliation it would be to have to recognize again something that has been apparent for not merely hundreds but thousands of years, known not only to Tertullian and to the pagan politicians he addressed, but also to their predecessors since the beginnings of organized society: laws, even the best laws, accomplish little unless people are generally disposed to obey them. Government has certain resources to compel a willingness to obey, but when they must be broadened and extended to reach virtually a whole society, they are costly, burdensome, and incompatible with free institutions.

The astonishing frequency of serious crimes in the general population attests to a generalized disregard for the law, which is perceived as relatively impotent. Apparently this perception was shared by many of those entrusted with making or enforcing the laws, as evidenced by the high incidence of serious crimes at the highest level of government, both federal and state. The Abscam affair—so soon after Watergate—revealed beyond any doubt the ease with which people in high office can violate both general moral principles and direct public laws. The Watergate affair is remarkable in the annals of modern government in that the accused took no recourse to violence, even though what was at stake was control of the government of the world's richest nation. This itself is probably a testimony to the residual strength of American political ideals even among those who were in the process of undermining them. In the Watergate matter, the nation escaped without violence and civil conflict. But the fact that political leaders could resort to the measures they did shows the extent to which they too shared the contempt for the law of which Tertullian warned.

Admitting that some of the misdeeds cited in the Watergate matter may conceivably have been covered under the concept of *raison d'état* —particularly if one is willing to apply the flexible standards of situation ethics—it is still evident that many things were done by supposedly honorable men that are clearly contrary to both biblical and civil law and concerning the wrongness of which there could have been no reasonable doubt. Perjury, for example, was both advocated and committed by individuals of the highest rank, even by some in the Department of Justice. Perjury, of course, is clearly a transgression of one or two of the Ten Commandments ("Thou shalt not take the name of the Lord thy God in vain; Thou shalt not bear false witness against thy neighbor"). But in Watergate false swearing was so common that one may wonder whether having sworn testimony by accused persons served any purpose other than giving the government a new charge to bring against them, i.e., perjury. Even more remarkable than the readiness with which witnesses resorted to perjury was the fact that the news media were so little surprised by it. Perhaps this is the result of the fact that they too have come to rely on deception, and even on false swearing (as in the case of Representative Michael J. Harrington's violation of his oath not to disclose the contents of classified material as a condition for gaining access to it) to obtain the material they publish.

The question of perjury — false testimony under oath — reveals one of the breaking points of a system of government and justice based on the assumption of a general belief in and fear of God. The state's means of detecting and punishing perjury, short of the introduction of forcible interrogation using lie detectors, "truth serum," and other technical devices, are relatively slight. The value of requiring witnesses to swear to the truth of their testimony has clearly always lain in the expectation that the fear of God would compel them to speak the truth. As Tertullian says in the same context, speaking of the inadequacy of merely human laws to compel obedience: "We who are examined in the sight of God who sees all, we who foresee an eternal punishment from His hand, we well may be the only ones to attain innocence; since, at once from fullness of knowledge, from the difficulty of concealment, from the greatness of the penalty (not *long,* but eternal), we fear Him, whom he too must fear who judges us . . ."[3]

Against the background of these two facts of American life today — rising crime at every level of society on the one hand, and a general decline in the once general expectation of having to answer to God as well as to civil authorities for one's misdeeds — let us consider another prominent feature of our political and social development, one that is so pervasive that it is becoming part of our political and social climate rather than a disruption to be noticed. The general thesis of this book, already introduced in Chapter 2, is that the United States must recover a vision of justice and a sense of purpose, and that for many good and sufficient reasons this vision and sense should come not from an alien source but from the deep roots of our civilization and social life in our biblical, Judeo-Christian heritage. But instead of recovering that heritage, America is in the process of extirpating it. A major step in this direction is the silencing or disfranchisement of Christians in public life and affairs, a movement that is already well under way.

[3]Tertullian, *Apology,* xlv:7.

134

The Disfranchisement of Christians

There are several groups in America today, generally classified as minorities (although one group, women, is not a minority but the majority of the population), that are widely thought to have been deprived of a measure of their rights and dignity.* They are now in the process of recovering and reasserting them, sometimes as a result of special legislation, sometimes by direct action to earn respect and recognition. In order to obtain their rights, blacks have had to overcome the myth of white supremacy, a delusion once held by many whites and accepted even by numbers of blacks. Women, or at least a minority of them acting in the name of all, have found it necessary to struggle against what many now call "male chauvinism." These two struggles, although showing some similarities, reveal one marked difference. Blacks in general have always been aware of their oppressed lot. Women in America, by contrast, were for the most part not so deeply aware of being oppressed, or of the supposed severity of the oppression, and consequently one of the major tasks of the women's liberation movement has been what is referred to as "consciousness raising." The idea is to bring an awareness of the oppressed condition of women to their consciousness, and also to that of men, who as a class have always been attached to women and their interests by manifold bonds of sentiment, reason, and utility.

The problem with Christians in America is rather like that facing women a few years ago, at least in the eyes of various women's liberation movements: they are unaware of the extent of their own disfranchisement, and to the extent to which they are made to work in opposition to their own true interests. Unlike the blacks and the women, Christians in general have no powerful allies in the media; if they are to awaken to the reality of their own progressive exclusion from a share in American life, they will have to rouse themselves. In order to liberate themselves from the disfranchisement already under way, they must recognize and expose the anti-Christian mythology expressed, for example, in three currently accepted slogans: "freedom of choice," "pluralism," and "separation of church and state." Each of these concepts has a legitimate and valid use, but each is also capable of signal misuse, and today

*Whether women have historically been an "oppressed group," as everyone is now supposed to concede, remains an open question. It is interesting that Cicero said, before the birth of Christ, "We Romans rule the world, and our wives rule us." The evidence of history lends itself to various interpretations, as do conditions in American society today.

they are all being misused to force Christians—who after all constitute the largest element of American society—to withdraw to the sidelines and allow the society to be directed by those for whom Christianity and its principles are a source of amusement or contempt.

"Freedom of Choice"

Whenever the abortion-right to life issue is raised, most of those on the pro-abortion side deny that they favor abortion at all: no, what they advocate is merely "freedom of choice." One pro-abortion group has the slogan, "Choice is as American as apple pie." Similar language is used to argue for homosexuality: "freedom of sexual (or affectional) preference."

"Freedom of choice," because it is composed of two words with a high emotive value to Americans, "freedom" and "choice," will almost always have a positive effect when thrown into a discussion. Who could be opposed to freedom of choice in this great, democratic nation? Who indeed but petty tyrants, Puritans, authoritarians, and incipient fascists? Unfortunately, freedom of choice is an empty slogan. It can mean anything or nothing. Its emptiness would soon be exposed if it were also pressed into service to justify other things: "Do you believe in paying taxes?" "I believe in freedom of choice." "Do you believe in sending children to school?" "I believe in freedom of choice." A concept or principle that proves hollow when brought into play where second-order moral principles are concerned (the duty to pay taxes and to educate children) certainly should not be allowed to stand as though it were an argument or a proof in questions of a more fundamental nature.

Choosing between alternatives, in other words, decision-making, is the ethical *problem,* not the solution. Freedom to choose may imply one of two things: (a) the factual ability to choose between two or more alternatives, coupled with the duty to make a right choice. The physician, for example, has "freedom of choice" in deciding whether to treat a broken leg by splinting it or by prescribing aspirin. In this sense, freedom refers to factual potentiality or ability, and implies an accompanying responsibility. Freedom of choice can also mean (b) the moral freedom to choose between two or more equally acceptable alternatives: thus one may have freedom of choice in the matter of sending a child to a public or a private school. Although the doctor has the potential power to choose to treat a broken leg with aspirin, rather than setting it, no reasonable person would defend such an action on the grounds that it was merely a proper exercise of freedom of choice. A parent may object that while he has the right to send his child to a private school, its fees are too high. As a result, he has no real freedom in the matter. Most reasonable people will understand that what he lacks is not freedom but money — or the right priorities in the use of his money — which is not at all the same thing.

The introduction of the concept of freedom of choice as a principle into fundamental moral issues, particularly issues where our Judeo-Christian heritage characterizes one alternative as good and another as evil, not only confuses the issue but really constitutes a repudiation of the right of biblical or Judeo-Christian ethics to speak to the question. We do not speak of "freedom of choice" with respect to the options of murder or vengeance, even though the prohibition of both is found quite explicitly and forcefully in the Bible (although not only there). To make a principle of freedom of choice in such a matter is not to uphold the principle (unless by freedom we mean total license or chaos), but simply to remove the issue from the ethical and legal arena.

Since biblical ethics forbid the taking of innocent life,* an individual committed to biblical ethics can accept the practice of abortion only if it can be shown that the fetus or unborn child is in fact not innocent human life in the Bible's sense.** Much effort has been expended by pro-abortion forces to demonstrate this, most of it frustrated by the relative unanimity of medical and scientific evidence and opinion to the contrary. But where it has not been possible to convince Christians to withdraw their opposition to permissive abortion by showing that it is not killing — for it clearly is killing — large numbers of Christians have been reduced to silence by the slogan of freedom of choice. "You have no right to impose your morality, to violate my freedom of choice."

What this reveals is the fact that many American Christians, and indeed many Americans of all backgrounds, are unable to make simple logical distinctions and so fall readily into verbal traps created with catchy slogans. "Of course we are interested in the right to life," some

---

*Not, however, the taking of all life, as biblical regulations concerning capital punishment and the waging of war show.

**Historic Christian teaching has always made an exception for abortion in the rare cases where it is necessary to save the mother's life, when Tertullian, for example, refers to it as a "necessary cruelty." Cf. my essay, "What the Supreme Court Didn't Know: Ancient and Early Christian Views on Abortion," *Human Life Review*, I:2 (Spring 1975), pp. 15–18.

pro-abortionists will tell us, "but we are more interested in the quality of life." Life is an absolute, easy to recognize; "quality of life" is a subjective value, very hard to define precisely. When "quality of life" is allowed to supersede the right to life itself, reality has given place to rhetoric.

Slogans without a clearly understood, identifiable content are a menace to any discussion of fundamental principles in public policy. Slogans such as "freedom of choice," "imposition of morality," and "separation of church and state" have effectively muzzled many Christians in the right to life controversy, and caused them to acquiesce in a situation that they know is inhuman and odious to God, simply because they lack the logical tools and insights to disentangle themselves from the rhetorical coils of their opponents. What "freedom of choice" really means in the abortion issue is that no one is to be allowed to raise really basic and fundamental issues — such as those related to the beginning of human life and to its value.

A more recent tactic of the pro-abortionists, displayed in the U.S. Senate subcommittee hearings on the Human Life Bill in April and May of 1981, is to tell the legislators that "science has no criterion for determining what is human . . . it is a metaphysical question." If that testimony — made by a number of professionally eminent witnesses — were taken at face value, it would mean that science has no criterion by which we might judge the humanity of the witnesses, and hence that it would have no more objection to offer to killing them than, according to them, it does to killing developing fetuses. To the extent that America's Christians are browbeaten into silence by these and similar slogans, it will insure that Christians — who have contributed so much to the formation of the country and who still make up the majority of its citizens — will have nothing substantial to say about the formulation of national policies. If "humanness" is not a scientific but a metaphysical or religious question, as several pro-abortionists testified, then it is absolutely evident that the law will have to address "metaphysical" and "religious" issues, inasmuch as laws made by humans for the regulation of human society cannot do without a definition of what humanness is. Most of these slogans which we call formalistic or contentless¯either prove too much for the good of those who are using them (as in the case of denying the possibility of showing a witness himself to be human), or can be turned equally well to the other side. But this can happen only if Christians are willing to look squarely at them, see what they say and imply, and turn from a parroting of empty slogans back to a consideration of fundamental values, "the laws of Nature and of Nature's God."

"Pluralism"

The concept of "pluralism" may be considered another aspect of the freedom of choice fallacy. As we have already indicated, "pluralism" is a very flexible concept. Ostensibly it is intended to cover the diversity of present American society and to express a commitment that no single group shall impose its views on the others. Actually it is used to downgrade the deepest commitments of large numbers of Americans, sometimes even of a majority, to the level of mere opinions that have no right to be heard in the determination of public policy.

What the myth of pluralism, like that of freedom of choice, overlooks is that both our fundamental freedoms and the living together of varying religious and philosophical traditions in comparative harmony —which we now designate pluralism—could and did arise only in a society where there was mild diversity but considerable unity of opinion on basic values. The freedoms we now enjoy could never have been articulated and built into our governmental structure if there had not been a broad and deep consensus and self-discipline concerning the limits within which those freedoms should be expressed. That consensus was of course in the main a Christian one. While it did not suppress divergent views, it did not, at least not until the present century, accord divergent views the right to suppress it and to eradicate it from all expression in public law and life. Yet that is precisely what "pluralism," if the myth, without further definition, continues to enjoy its present status as a principle of American public policy, will do. In fact, pluralism would remain a livable concept even if it were taken to mean that while the theistic tradition of the majority would never be allowed to dominate public affairs, institutions, and expressions, it would never be excluded from them. But as things now stand, pluralism means that the majority tradition, which could contribute to the shaping of public policy with the least damage to the largest number of citizens, is precisely the one that must not be expressed.*

*An almost ludicrous—but significant—illustration occurred in Fairfax County, Virginia public schools at Christmas 1975. All references to "religion" were banned from the traditional pre-Christmas vacation observances. No Christmas decorations, such as manger scenes or stars, were permitted. The vacation was called the "End of the Year" vacation—a gloomier name, it seems, than that of the Communist substitute for Christmas, which is at least called "New Year." But curiously enough, certain Jewish symbols *were* used and Hanukah songs were sung and explained in at least one school (where the author's daughter attended), on the grounds that they were of "historic" significance. The implication, of course, is that the birth of Christ, according to which all our activities are dated, did not occur in history or has no historic significance. Similar situations prevail in many places across the nation.

As was recently brought to light in a series of articles in the *Washington Post* Walt Whitman High School in Bethesda, Maryland, perhaps the wealthiest public high school in the country, offers its teachers great freedom to instruct their classes as they see fit. One teacher makes use of this liberty to teach Marxism-Leninism. Every day his class performs Chinese-style exercises before a huge mural poster of Lenin and memorizes a slogan for the day from Mao's little red book.[4] This is considered acceptable, even commendable, under the rubric of pluralism and intellectual freedom. One can imagine the reaction that would take place if a teacher in the same school had his class kneel before a picture of Jesus and memorize a Bible verse every day — although one could argue, with equal plausibility, that such exercises would be quite helpful for an understanding of what Christians believe and think.

As things now stand, the concept of pluralism, supposedly evoked to prohibit the imposition of one set of values, actually functions to prevent their expression. Unless Christians rapidly awaken to the fact that what they consider a voluntary duty imposed by considerations of tolerance or modesty is rapidly turning into an obligatory silencing and disfranchisement, they will soon find themselves reduced to complete passivity in shaping the future of this complex nation of which they still constitute the largest part. In Portugal, we recently witnessed the sad spectacle of the attempted imposition, by military and police force, of the views of a small minority over the anguished but ineffectual protests of the majority. This attempt fortunately ended in failure in Portugal. In the United States, we appear to be witnessing the voluntary abdication of the Christian majority from areas of legitimate concern. One may say that Christians who will accept the slogan of pluralism as sufficient reason for lapsing into silence about their deepest convictions when they are discussed in the public arena deserve to be disfranchised. In any event, that is what is happening, and it is a trend certain not to be reversed unless those most directly affected by it recognize and resist it.

"Separation of Church and State"

As already suggested in Chapter 2, the concept of the separation of church and state — not found explicitly in the Constitution, but implied in

---

[4]*Washington Post,* June 8, 1975.

the establishment clause of the First Amendment—is legitimate and valid if it taken to mean that the two institutions are to be kept separate and not to interfere with one another structurally or organizationally. If, however, it is taken to mean that no principles, views, insights, or concepts of church, religious, or Christian origin are to be accepted or discussed in realms where the government is active, or on any square foot of government property, it is an obvious absurdity. Unfortunately, it is not an innocuous absurdity, since it can be used to drive biblical and Christian principles, many of them fundamental principles of our society and certainly the richest source of ethical and spiritual insight in our heritage, to the fringes of social life, to confine them within the walls of what Justice Tom C. Clark, in an expression intended to mollify Christian sentiment, called "the inviolable citadel of the human heart and mind."

The slogan, "separation of church and state," like "freedom of choice" and "pluralism," can mean everything or nothing. If taken to mean what the establishment clause of the First Amendment originally meant, that the federal government (and the states, by subsequent extension) may not establish a national or state church, it is legitimate and salutary. If taken to mean that there must be absolutely no overlapping of secular and religious interest, of state concerns with church concerns, then it becomes, in light of the ever-expanding nature of state concerns, a tool for the disfranchisement of Christians and their exclusion from full participation in national life.

The Sterilization of the Presidency

Perhaps the most striking demonstration of the disfranchisement of Christians in American political and social life is offered by what we may call the spiritual sterilization of the president. All of the presidents since Truman, who was rather diffident about his religious sentiments, have made a pretty strong display of their attachment to one branch or another of the Christian faith: John F. Kennedy, to Catholicism; Eisenhower, Johnson, Nixon, Ford, Carter, and Reagan to one or another branch of Protestantism. The late President Eisenhower, in fact, went so far as to be baptized while in office, rather like the first Christian emperor, Constantine. In a country in which, as of 1972, only about seven million out of a total population of over two hundred million formally designate themselves as non-Christians, it is not at all surprising that the chief executive would belong to a Christian church. What is rather surprising is that it should be taken for granted that, once occupying high public office, he should put aside his Christian convictions and attachments, and act no differently from a nonreligious humanitarian (a group, incidentally, that constitutes only a very small percentage of the American people).

When considering the religion of a prominent political leader, there is always a question as to whether his professed beliefs result more from genuine conviction or from expediency. This question is asked about Eisenhower as about Constantine, and will continue to be asked whenever a leader's professed spiritual allegiance coincides with that of a substantial number of voters. In this connection, it is particularly interesting to consider President Gerald R. Ford, who was catapulted into the nation's highest office by an extraordinary series of events without ever having been exposed to the glaring illumination of a national political campaign. Prior to becoming president, Mr. Ford was active in a local Episcopal church in Alexandria, Virginia and was well known to many members, including fellow vestrymen. There seems to be a consensus among those who know him that his Christian faith and conviction are genuine, not a posture he adopts for public relations purposes. Since becoming President, Mr. Ford continued his practice of regular Sunday worship, even under circumstances when attendance might have appeared to inconvenience him. But apart from his personal religious life, is there anything that distinguishes his conduct of the presidential office from what might be expected of an upright, nonreligious humanitarian? It is rather as though one were obliged, like the Protestant Henri de Navarre who had to accept Catholicism in order to become King of France (and made the famous statement, "Paris is worth a Mass"), to drop all practical demonstration of one's religious commitment and act simply as a good humanist in order to become President of the United States. President Ford has taken a number of stands as President that are altogether consistent with biblical Christian teaching, but he scrupulously avoids stating that he takes them for Christian reasons. Can one imagine President Ford commenting, for example, on capital punishment: "The Bible prescribes it for certain crimes; we may wish to refrain from it for various reasons, but we certainly cannot call what God commands 'cruel and unusual punishment'"? A Moslem could understand such a statement, and so could a religious Jew, but not, it seems, a Christian.

Jimmy Carter, the first president in memory to make a point of claiming to be born again, and one who continued to teach Sunday school while president, did little or nothing as president to demonstrate a strong concern for biblical values in public life. He "personally opposed" abortion but appointed pro-abortionists throughout Health and Human Services. Ronald Reagan, also a professing Christian, although less outspoken about it than Carter, does seem to be going about things differently.

It is a remarkable thing, when the at least second most powerful nation in the world, populated in its overwhelming majority by Christians and with an apparently genuinely committed Christian as chief of state, undertakes frequent efforts to protect members of one religious minority, the Jews, from oppression, for example in the Soviet Union, yet scrupulously refrains from mentioning the fate of Christians in that same land. There is a strong and active pro-Israel and pro-Jewish party in Congress, headed by Senator Henry M. Jackson, always ready to defend the state of Israel and to protest Russian mistreatment of Jews; there is no corresponding concern expressed — not even by outspoken Christians, such as Senators Hatfield and Thurmond and Congressman Quie — about continuing persecution of Christians around the world, and in countries with which we have extensive and intimate dealings. Why is it that Christians in America will protest the mistreatment of Jews in the Soviet Union, even to the point of seriously interfering with our current foreign policy of detente, while saying little or nothing about the more extensive Soviet repression of Christians? It is no doubt true that persecution of Jews is a more sensitive issue, particularly after the monstrous cruelties perpetrated by Hitler's Germany, and it may well be that Jews have greater access to media visibility. But this may explain the attention given to the plight of the Jews; it cannot be the explanation for the indifference and silence that greet the plight of Christians. Here it is certainly appropriate to address to highly placed Christians in American government Christ's rebuke to the Pharisees: "These ought ye to have done, and not to leave the other undone" (Matthew 23:23). By all means protest against the persecution of Jews in other countries. But by no means fail to protest against the persecution of Christians.

Is spiritual emasculation an unwritten condition for Christians seeking high public office, or for their conduct in office once they have won it? It would seem ridiculous to suppose that a small minority of committed non-Christians can effectively muzzle Christian leaders and reduce them to impotence and silence whenever it is a question of helping suffering Christian brothers and sisters or presenting the Christian point of view in political discussion. The blacks are a relatively small minority in America. No one would expect to make it a condition for electing a black to high public office that he agree to keep silent on all problems and concerns particularly affecting his fellow blacks. For example, former Senator Edward W. Brooke of Massachusetts was supposed, by constitutional theory, to represent the Commonwealth of Massachusetts,

143

but no one thought it strange when he made himself a spokesman for the interests of his fellow Negroes in the United States or even expressed the concerns of American blacks with respect to foreign policy in Africa and elsewhere. It would in fact be thought strange if he did not do so. Yet in the Senate and the House of Representatives — the latter body includes ordained clergymen of more than one denomination — Christians seem to have taken a voluntary vow of silence when it comes to speaking out on primarily Christian concerns. Even so humanitarian an issue as the persecution of minorities may be passed over in virtual silence, if the minority happens to be Christian.

If it is not a condition for holding national office that Christians keep their Christian ties and commitments out of sight, then let some of them begin to show as much interest in and loyalty towards their fellow-believers as members of other religions do for theirs. If there is an unwritten law, then let it be brought out into the open, recognized for what it is, and dealt with accordingly. The situation we now have amounts to a virtual spiritual emasculation of Christians in high office. As long as the general public, in its majority nominally Christian, is willing to tolerate such pusillanimous conduct on the part of its elected representatives, it means that Christians, as Christians, are accepting second-class status and are effectively disfranchised as American citizens.

The Reconstruction of the Republic

Since assuming office in January, 1981, Ronald Reagan has done all that he can to bring America's defenses back up to an acceptable level. This may secure the preservation of the republic. But mere adequate military forces cannot do anything to rebuild the nation spiritually. That can only be accomplished if there is a widespread recovery of America's spiritual vision, and specifically of the conviction that this is a nation under God, and that our laws should correspond to his Law.

We are not speaking of an establishment of Christianity as a national religion, nor indeed of any formal tie between religion and the state, but of an awakening of America's Christians to serious and mature participation in national life. Christians must recognize that when our leaders keep silent on issues of concern to Christians, they effectively disfranchise them. Christians should be no more tolerant of the commonly-accepted governmental and media pattern of keeping them "in their place" than blacks were towards white supremacy.

13

Responsibility or Control

A genius can do anything. A genius will shampoo a pig and curl and its bristles.

Walter Rauschenbusch
Christianizing the Social Order

Neither individual human beings nor any human institution can "do everything and change everything." Anyone who thinks otherwise is deceived, and anyone who attempts to do otherwise is doomed to frustration and failure. Unfortunately, the larger the scale of the attempt, the longer it may be drawn out before ultimate failure becomes evident, and the more frustrating that failure will be. Because American government is immense, it takes a long time to reach that point—as we did in the Vietnam War.

Not only is human power limited because we are finite beings, but human knowledge is also limited, and human wisdom to use that knowledge. There may be many things that, from the perspective of some ideal, we ought to do, but cannot. But there also are many things that we can do, but ought not to. The influence of technology tends to make us do all that is possible, regardless of whether it is beneficial.

Let us assume, for example, that our abundant society ought, as a matter of principle, to provide good medical care for all its citizens. Probably most of us will agree that the availability of such care is desirable, whether we hold that it should be provided privately, publicly, or by a combination of both means. But there is an immediate problem. Nobel Prize winner Dr. Jean Bernard of Paris has movingly pointed out in

Grandeur et tentations de la médicine ("The Grandeur and Temptations of Medicine")[1] that it is *physically and financially beyond the capacity* of a great industrial nation to provide for all its citizens all the medical services that our modern level of medical knowledge tells us will or possibly could be helpful to them. In past days, Bernard says, medicine was not very effective, but it was inexpensive. Today, in many cases it is amazingly effective — but it is also becoming prohibitively expensive. This is true in the United States, where a combination of government action and other developments have contributed to making medical costs rise far more rapidly than other costs. It is also true in Europe, although there health care costs have not risen as drastically as in America. What we "should" provide, we cannot. And unfortunately it is impossible to predict that we ever will be able to do so at any time in the future. Just as in the past, when the rich could pay for specialists the poor could not afford, there will simply never be enough of certain kinds of specialized medical services for everyone. Many will continue to receive care that they do not need or that does them no good, and others will continue to lack care that might help or cure them. We *can* improve our performance. We can make progress in the direction of trying to meet more people's needs, of trying to insure that no critically ill patient is denied hospital care, of trying to provide preventive medicine on a large scale. But there are simply limits to our resources, time, and energy. We inevitably reach those limits before we have made an end of human suffering. Medical care provides only one graphic example of many needs that no modern society, capitalist, communist, or anything in between, can fully meet.

One rather macabre development in health care is the recurring tendency, in the abortion discussion, to bring up cost-reduction that this procedure achieves by reducing welfare and other costs. The implications of this line of thought are evident. In view of the policies already in effect requiring the government to provide public assistance to the old and infirm, it is probably only a matter of time until the various proposals for the legalization of euthanasia start to be promoted on the grounds that they will save society money. Of course they will. People are expensive.[2]

---

[1] Paris: Buchet-Castel, 1973.

[2] The legal, medical, philosophical and psychological connections between abortion and euthanasia are brought out by Helmut Ehrhardt, M.D., Ph.D., in "Abortion and Euthanasia," *Human Life Review,* I:3, Summer 1975.

The Limited Larder

The list of things that society simply cannot do, even though they might be desirable, is virtually inexhaustible. It is not financially possible, for example, to provide "free urban public transportation." It would be possible to establish a limited, tax-supported public transportation system in large cities, but it is becoming increasingly evident that any good system will run up immense costs. If it is no good, no one will use it, and costs will quickly outstrip the system's usefulness.

The limits we encounter through lack of resources or energy are an obstacle that no government, democratic or dictatorial, can brush aside. There is another kind of obstacle to the omnipotence of government. Since it is an obstacle we create, we can do something to remove it, but since it is rooted in human nature, this removal is hard. The effort it requires is too much for the possible good we may accomplish.

A Human Obstacle—Stubbornness

We all acknowledge that human beings cannot do everything. America could put one man on the moon, or a dozen, or perhaps even a thousand, but cannot move its whole population there. There simply are certain limits that we cannot bypass. Over and above strict physical and economic limitations that are impossible to overcome, human nature itself seems to create limits that cannot be passed, at least not in the context of freedom.

Although Americans as a group show little interest in learning a second or third language, evidence from around the world shows us that almost everyone who can learn one language can learn another. In Europe it is not uncommon even for uneducated people to speak two or more languages. In India, where there is no common national language, tens of millions of people speak not two but three or four or even more. Affluence and leisure to study are not a requirement for being bilingual or multilingual. What seems to impede bilingualism is human stubbornness. In Canada, bilingualism is official government policy; educational standards are high, and the populace is well-educated and affluent. Yet millions of Québecois seem to find English an insoluble mystery, and countless Anglo-Canadians appear to be baffled by French. Of course a government can compel an unwilling people to learn another language, just as the old Imperial Russian government compelled its minorities to learn Russian. But where the people are unwilling, for whatever reason, the resort to compulsion will be difficult and will spell the end of much civil liberty. Canada's turmoil over bilingualism—paralleled in Belgium—shows that a democratic government that is unwilling to use brute force on its subjects may by stymied in some of its praiseworthy goals by simple human stubbornness.

There are two possible solutions to human stubbornness as an obstacle to government plans—one is compulsion, the other is persuasion. One might naturally assume that persuasion rather than compulsion would be the natural method in a democratic society. Yet paradoxically, in the United States, confronted with public resistance to a serious government concern—racial integration—the government has more readily resorted to coercion than to persuasion. In order to persuade, one must appeal to shared values and commitments, and this is precisely what the new slogan of pluralism has rendered unthinkable. So compulsion remains the only alternative.

Up to the present, it has proved impossible to achieve true racial integration in the United States. We have achieved an end to most formal segregation, but even if we take integration to mean nothing deeper or more profound than a relatively uniform mechanical mixing according to prescribed quotas, we do not have it—primarily because it is not widely desired. It has been possible to abolish arbitrary *barriers* to racial integration, but it is quite a different matter when it comes to effective promotion of integration. Public policy in the United States appears to presuppose the basic agreement of the public. But if the public fails to demonstrate the "good will" government gave it credit for, officials resort almost immediately to measures of force. One of the curious features of American governmental policy is the government's willingness to coerce with overwhelming force. President Eisenhower immediately resorted to overwhelming force, including tanks, against an unruly Little Rock population. Such measures frankly amaze European democrats. According to Kenneth Macksey in his history of armoured warfare, "Civil policing at its most sophisticated is the effective application of minimum force."[3] In the United States, we have maximum force against relatively innocuous citizens. The federal government almost immediately resorted to massive armed intervention, including tanks, at the first substantial evidence of public hostility to public school integration. Macksey comments: "Tanks represent the pinnacle of aggression and are anomalous to crowd control—their use by the British against Egyptians, by the Russians against East Berliners, Hungarians, and Czechs, and by the Americans against their own countrymen, may have restored a veneer of order, but no more; the appearance of tanks in the streets as counter to revolution or insurrection is

[3]Kenneth Macksey, *Tank Warfare: A History of Tanks in Battle* (New York: Stein and Day, 1972), p.251.

148

but a sign of transient dictatorship on the march."[4] We are a "free society," but with surprising evidence of the iron fist beneath the velvet glove.

Nevertheless neither maximum force, i.e., tanks in the streets, nor the more moderate application of police power, as in Boston, has succeeded in bringing about the desired mixing of the races in American schools. Americans are still relatively free in some respects and still have the options of private schools or of moving. Large numbers of them choose such alternatives instead of accepting government policies to which they object. The use of minimum force can be very effective in keeping order when most people *favor* what the government is trying to do. The use of maximum force is really a tacit confession that the government is acting tyrannically. The resort to overwhelming force against the citizens makes it much harder to persuade them that they should willingly accept government policies. By using massive force to impose "constitutional principles," the government is indicating that not only does the Constitution at those points conflict with the will of the people, but the people are not amenable to reason but must be coerced.

Unfortunately, the degree of coercion which would be necessary to accomplish the desired result would be politically suicidal in America. Thus at the moment the worst solution is what we have: a questionable policy, which would be good only if it worked, i.e., were effectively implemented, is ineffectively imposed by tyrannical coercive measures. We lose freedom but do not gain integration. As a result, relations between the races as well as trust in and sympathy for the government among large elements of the population are effectively undermined.

If there were such a thing as a government psychologist (by which is meant not a psychologist on government pay, of which there are many, but someone examining the psyche of government, trying to get at the hidden motives behind its mysterious actions), he might well discern in the whole school integration-bussing tangle a subconscious desire on the part of American government to punish itself—at least vicariously, by punishing the general public—for its guilt feelings on the racial issue.

Bussing Again

When the United States Supreme Court decreed, by a unanimous vote, in *Brown* v. *Board of Education* (1954) that the legal separation of the races in public school education violated the constitutional provision

[4]*Ibid.*

of equal protection of the laws under the Fourteenth Amendment, it certainly was engaging in a rather imaginative interpretation of the amendment. It may be good ethics, but it is bad logic, history, and law. Nevertheless most Americans, including a substantial percentage of those in the states then practicing segregation, now feel that the decision was morally right. The judges were making good the legislators' failure to act. Since neither the individual states nor the United States Congress seemed likely to do anything constructive, the Supreme Court took it upon itself to remove what was generally considered to be an unacceptable evil. Judicial legislation followed legislative indolence.

Although there was much dismay in legal and other circles at the sweeping nature of the *Brown* ruling — recently criticized again by Harvard law professor and former Watergate Special Prosecutor Archibald Cox[5] — it *was* enforced, even with the use of tanks. One of the reasons why such a ruling could be enforced, despite all the misgivings about its technical, constitutional legitimacy and its social implications, was the obvious and general agreement that school segregation, as practiced in the South and Border States, was wrong. And a second reason lay in the fact that the rigorous enforcement was, at least in 1954 and the following decade, limited to the South. The agreement that forcible integration measures were right and desirable began to crack as integration measures were introduced in other states as well, where a considerable amount of racial separation ("de facto segregation") did and does exist. How can public resentment fail to mount as it becomes generally known that almost none of those public servants — judges, senators, congressmen — who have been imposing integration, including forced bussing, send their own children to such schools? This resentment has reached a climax thanks to bussing, with the Boston situation being the most acute, as discussed earlier. It should be obvious even to a casual observer that what is going on is the exacerbation of the tensions between the races, not a constructive contribution to racial harmony. What will be gained by it? No immediate practical value is apparent. Some people, parents and children, have been forced to make a rather costly sacrifice in the name of an ideal, racial justice. But it is not an effective sacrifice, for while it costs much, it produced little. And it is also true that the individuals and the groups who determined that the sacrifice must be made are not the same as those who pay the price. And what is saddest in the whole situation is that no one in government addresses himself to the main problem, namely changing the heart. The emphasis is on changing the

[5]A major theme of Archibald Cox, *The Role of the Supreme Court in American Government* (New York: Oxford, 1976).

location. People are treated like laboratory animals, as though their attitudes blindly followed their environment. There is also the apparent assumption that black children must have white companions to learn. Since this assumption is clearly racist, it is not stated expressly, although it does come out in a round-about way.

Powerful and Impotent

The school bussing situation is but one example pointing to the power and the impotence of the complex federal constitutional system in this country. Europeans from countries where direct democracy via popular referendum is practiced, or where the government can be thrown out in mid-term if really serious public objections to its policies develop, are astonished at the fact that our American government can impose such peculiar measures on a generally hostile public and get away with it. Of course most decisions are made by federal judges, who are appointed, not elected, and really answer to no one.

Probably a majority of Americans would have accepted the idea behind the Supreme Court's verdict on public school segregation in 1954. Without question, a substantial majority in America today *opposes* the currently popular method of applying that decision, namely compulsory bussing to achieve "racial balance" in public schools.

Indira Gandhi has recently given the world several interesting illustrations of the power and weakness of supposedly democratic rulers. Threatened by investigations into some of her electioneering practices, Mrs. Gandhi declared a "state of emergency" and pretty well assumed dictatorial powers for herself. The middle classes in India had the intelligence and the democratic commitment to resist her, but instead for the most part dropped their voices and grew strangely silent as she began to call into play some of the bureaucratic resources of a modern government. But when she attempted to promote sterilization, sometimes apparently by force, as a means of dealing with India's population problem, there was widespread popular revulsion and she was driven from office. The next government proved inept, and Mrs. Gandhi is prime minister once again, although apparently somewhat moderated in her attitudes. It is important to note that when her government fell, Mrs. Gandhi could have kept herself in power by force — she had the wherewithal to do so. But she was sufficiently committed to the principles of democracy to be unwilling to maintain herself by force when she saw that her leadership had clearly been rejected. Force is always an alternative to persuasion,

151

but it destroys freedom. It is perplexing that in democratic America the government at least occasionally resorts to rather drastic measures of force instead of making a serious attempt at persuasion.

Mrs. Gandhi, although she made herself a virtual dictator and was effectively ruling by decree, still considered herself sufficiently responsible to the will of the people to surrender her power when they clearly signaled their rejection. In the United States, even presidents have to do this: Johnson stepped down from the 1968 presidential campaign when he felt that his leadership was repudiated, and Nixon resigned the presidency itself in 1974. But in the United States there is an institution that is potentially more powerful than the Indian Prime Minister or the President, and one that is far less subject to recall than prime ministers and presidents. We are speaking, of course, of the judiciary in America, and most particularly of the United States Supreme Court, which sits at the top of the pyramid — not infallible, but capable of being overruled only by the cumbersome expedient of a constitutional amendment. Thus one of the major branches of government is no longer merely independent: it is virtually irresponsible. It need not give an accounting of its stewardship to any man, and tenure is limited only by the eventual approach of death.

Yet this very arbitrary power of the judges, illustrated by their ability to impose many hateful, costly, and self-defeating regulations on large numbers of unwilling citizens without having to answer to anyone for it, is final evidence of government's impotence.

The irresponsible access to power — i.e., having power for which you must answer to no one — makes possible a degree of control over people that is incompatible with the idea of representative government. In a republic, the people agree to obey their rulers on the principle that the rulers are ultimately answerable to the people for their stewardship of the power entrusted to them. But when much or even most of the effective power to control and compel people is no longer in the hands of responsible public officials (responsible in the sense that they must answer to the public for their stewarship), but in the hands of appointed judges and administrators — as is certainly the case in modern America- — then this principle has been violated. Irresponsible authorities mean increasingly authoritarian control.

Paradoxically, the very power that judges and federal and state officials have (particularly the functionaries in the Internal Revenue Service and the Department of Health and Human Services, makes their true impotence all the more evident. For it is abundantly evident that the bussing for racial balance decisions made by federal judges in Charlotte, Detroit (since overturned on appeal), and Boston are not, in fact, achieving their goals but are actually producing a worse situation than the one they were supposedly intended to correct. Nor have antidiscrimination verdicts fundamentally changed our social situation.

The government's inability to achieve its goals stems in large measure from the fact that it attempts to achieve a *moral* result by a *mechanical* means. It deals with man's environment but neglects his heart, mind, and spirit. In one respect, the bussing issue is a fortunate example, for in it the case is clear: the means is mechanical conveyance. There are many situations in which government is likewise attempting, in effect, to transform people's minds and hearts by putting them, as it were, where they have no choice but to respond as government wishes, but nowhere is the incompatibility of the means chosen with the end desire more obvious.

14

Ethics: Means and Ends

We have found that moral excellence or virtue has to do with feelings and actions. These may be voluntary or involuntary. It is only to the former that we assign praise or blame.

Aristotle
Ethics

An entire government, or individual branches and agencies, that is not held accountable for its conduct of affairs is by definition *irresponsible* and free to exercise as much control and coercion of the people it rules as it desires. It is self-evident that the larger the government agency, the more centralized its operations, the greater the difficulty that will be encountered by an individual citizen in calling it to accountability. One of the largest and most powerful of all the branches of the American government in fact, the one on which all the rest depend for their very existence — is the Internal Revenue Service of the Treasury Department. The IRS is generally thought to be run in a conscientious way. The occasional abuses of its collecting and investigating power that are reported are few in number by comparison with the magnitude of its task. And Americans who have run into the more prying, officious, and hostile type of IRS officers will find that most of their stories can be matched ten or a hundred-fold by the experience of people in other major industrialized nations with their respective fisc.

Despite its many good qualities, at least by comparison with revenue officers in many other countries, the United States Internal Revenue Service offers a typical example of a largely *irresponsible* agency. First of all, because it is an immense agency, centrally organized, and operat- ing not on a local basis but from several regional headquarters scattered about the country, it is difficult for an individual taxpayer to make con- tact directly with the agency to resolve a problem that *he* has. However, it is very easy for the agency to send its agents to make contact with the taxpayer with whom *it* has a controversy. The "normal" collection proce- dures of the IRS in connection with what it considers unpaid taxes quickly run to confiscation, garnishment, tax liens, and forced sale of property. An individual has very little recourse other than to pay the taxes — or submit to the various enforcement procedures and subsequently seek re- lief through the courts. Our system of justice is good enough for him to have a good chance of ultimately getting fair treatment. However, if it should turn out that he has been incorrectly, or even negligently, as- sessed, garnished, locked out of his property, or whatever it may be, the agents and officials who might be thought responsible are in fact not held responsible. He will get his money back, and the government is re- quired by law to pay interest. But except in the case of flagrant miscon- duct by officials amounting to malicious abuse of the taxpayer and his rights, the IRS personnel may withdraw into the anonymity of their great organization without suffering any equivalent penalty or inconvenience to compare to that through which they have put the taxpayer.

Here then, we have control without responsibility. The fact that the control is no more onerous than it is, and generally as decently handled as it is, is evidence of the self-restraint of the taxing authorities, not of the taxpayers' power to bring them to account by any feasible procedure.

For the most part, it is self-restraint on the part of the rulers of a "democracy," not commitment to democracy on the part of the people, that prevents abuses of power.[1] The fact that France today is a free, open society with functioning democratic institutions and liberties is due less to the determination of the French people to preserve freedom than to an unwillingness of General de Gaulle to destroy it. During the several crises through which he guided the Republic, de Gaulle had many op- portunities to assume absolute, dictatorial power. But despite his author- itarian bent, he never did so. Former President Nixon resisted being forced from power over Watergate for over a year, but he never made any attempt to keep his power by assuming the role of a dictator. How quickly democratic institutions and freedoms can wilt in the face of a naked use of police and military power has been demonstrated by Indira

---

[1] Helge Pross points this out clearly in her book, "Capitalism and Democracy": *Kapi- talismus und Demokratie: Studien über westdeutsche Sozialstrukturen* (Frankfurt am Main: Athenäum Fischer, 1972).

Gandhi in India. Admittedly, democracy was younger in India and the politically conscious, educated, active middle class is far smaller there, in proportion to the total population, than in the United States. But we should not deceive ourselves into thinking that such authoritarian measures could not be duplicated in America.

The Vulnerability of the Bourgeoisie

In imposing arbitrary and dictatorial measures throughout India, Madame Gandhi found her task facilitated because the group that was most likely to understand her measures and see the threat they pose was also the group that was most vulnerable to her measures of control and coercion, namely the Indian middle class. Because India's situation is an extreme one and her problems so immense, the relevance of the Indian example to American circumstances may not appear evident. Nevertheless, precisely because India's situation is extreme, we can observe in stark outline certain factors that are also present, although less strikingly obvious, in the United States.

India's population exceeds six hundred million, of which perhaps ten percent — sixty million — belong to the middle class and to the tiny upper class. What we have to observe about the middle class applies with even greater force to the upper class, which is even more readily identifiable and even more vulnerable than the middle class. Hence we do not need to consider it separately, at least not for India (in the United States there may be better reasons for considering the upper class of wealth and power to occupy a different situation from that of the American middle class). These ten percent are relatively well educated, and enjoy a modest standard of living and comfort — very modest indeed, by comparison with the industrialized West, but splendid by comparison with the lot of five hundred and fifty million Indians living in poverty. A member of the Indian middle class is confronted on every side with examples of the misery into which he could be plunged if he lost those privileges of rank and property that distinquish him from the rest. When Mrs. Gandhi's first government was toppled, it was not the educated middle class but the uneducated masses that brought it down.

In any highly organized, centrally governed modern state, there are tremendous facilities available for those who would like to impose an authoritarian regime. Of course, there is a level of popular resistance above which it is extremely difficult for a government to impose its will. But the awakening and mobilizing of such resistance depends on various structures which are in themselves rather frail and easily subject to destruction. In the United States, the major communications media are virtually essential for the mobilization of popular sentiment on any issue. A kind of communications "underground" does exist, but the so-called "underground press" that came into existence during the Vietnam era is in fact not underground at all, just somewhat different, and could be repressed almost as easily as the more conventional media if the government desired.

Government Self-Restraint

The rhetoric of freedom, revolution, and violence may be exciting but experience in scores of "revolutionary" societies has shown that free democratic institutions seldom emerge from revolutionary upheaval. The American Revolution was not really a revolution in the sociological sense; it is more correct to call it the War of Independence. The French Revolution was more revolutionary. Free and democratic institutions came out of it only after a reign of terror, dictatorship, the establishment of Napoleon's empire, a virtual world war lasting twenty years, restoration of the monarchy, several coups, plebiscites, and a lost war. Democracy emerged in Germany following World War I but it was unstable, led to Hitler's dictatorship, and was finally reestablished, in the western half of the country only, by the influence of the occupying foreign powers. The democratic institutions that Britain and France thought to perpetuate in their former colonies have not long survived the end of colonialism.

Members of the middle class are readily identifiable. They pay taxes, own bank accounts, have permanent addresses — may even own real estate — have positions, own a certain amount of good clothing and household furnishings. They may own books, subscribe to magazines, belong to clubs and societies, and generally show considerable interest in obtaining a good education for their children.

Because of all these things, members of the middle class are also especially vulnerable to government control. The government may have a member of the poverty-stricken class beaten for taking part in a demonstration, but it cannot fine him or confiscate his property, for he has little or none. He does not write books or articles that could be censored; he is probably not trying to send his son or daughter to a university. There are very few mild but effective measures that the Indian government can take to control its lower classes: if they became seriously disaffected, it would have to resort to brutality and violence to repress them. An unemployed untouchable,* for example, is not likely to feel seriously threatened by a citation to appear before a magistrate. If he is not punished on the spot, it will hardly be worth the government's time and expense to attempt to locate him and bring him to trial. On the other hand, a middle-class citizen can easily be identified, and nothing is easier than to discipline him. If he is a civil servant, he can be transfered, demoted, or fired. A businessman or self-employed professional can have his tax returns examined, his license revoked, the admission of his children to university-level education brought into question. Additional taxes can be assessed, with the threat of financial ruin, either through the assessment itself or through the costly and time-consuming attempt to fight it in the courts.

It is remarkable that India, which for all its faults had a lively tradition of freedom of speech, opinion, and debate, should have been so quickly subdued into a docile silence under Madame Gandhi's dictatorial measures. We see the reason when we recognize that those who have the background, the education, and the civic spirit to reject her usurpations are also terribly susceptible to coercion, confiscation, and blacklisting, without the necessity to resort to imprisonment—a recourse which, nevertheless, India's ruler did not appear to shun. Since her return to power, she seems to have grown more cautious.

The American Middle Class

The middle class in the United States is vastly larger than in any other major country. If we think of middle-class status in terms of income, educational and other opportunities, and a measure of vested interest in the preservation of society and the status quo, then a substantial majority of Americans are middle class. (If we wish to define the concept of middle class in America as the French, for example, do their *bourgeoisie*, in terms of other-directedness, deferment of present pleasures for future goals, self-discipline, a systematic and calculating approach to the challenges and opportunities of life, then the number of Americans who are genuinely *bourgeois* is of course smaller, but it is still very large by comparison with the relative size of the bourgeoisie

---

*The status of "untouchability" has been legally abolished in India, but the concept remains.

almost anywhere else, except of course Switzerland.) Unfortunately, America's middle class is afflicted by many of the same frailties that beset India. The student protester can make his oppositon to government policy felt, but runs some slight risk of academic discipline by contrast with a nonstudent dropout. The situation of the middle-class homeowner, businessman, professional, bureaucrat, or educator is quite different. If he is cited for even a minor violation, there is no need to arrest him: the government automatically holds his home, his possessions, his bank account, his livelihood as surety against his fulfillment of the obligation it wishes to lay upon him.

The North American economy is so productive that it was possible for a substantial number of draft evaders, resisters, and military deserters to drop out of sight during the Vietnam era and nevertheless maintain themselves, sometimes including a family, with some semblance of comfort. Such a course of action was far more difficult for those who had already established themselves as part of the middle class — military officers, professional men, academicians, businessmen. During the Vietnam protests, the representatives of the middle and upper middle class who joined the protest usually did so only verbally. If the United States government had dealt with those expressing their discontent verbally as dictators routinely do, then we can well imagine that the level of even verbal protest among the bourgeoisie would have dropped rather quickly here as well.

Power, Responsibility, and Vulnerability

The implications of all this are evident. Even though the middle class in the United States is large, self-confident, well-established, and thinks of itself as committed to freedom, it could still prove tremendously weak and diffident in the face of any determined effort by the government to silence it. People with much to lose are generally quite vulnerable to control. Although a very substantial number of U.S. physicians hold abortion to be killing, only a small number actively protest abortion policies, because a doctor who challenges the system runs some danger of being rejected by it and becoming an outcast.

In order for a democracy to function, it must possess a large number of citizens with what we have called middle-class or bourgeois virtues — wealth, education, training, willingness to work hard, discipline, the ability to build for the future and to wait for rewards rather than demanding instant gratification. A strong, self-reliant middle class is a necessity for a highly-organized, free economy. Unfortunately, the strong, self-reliant middle class often turns out to be quite vulnerable to government pressures. Herein lies the paradox: it is only those who possess one or more of the characteristics of the bourgeoisie who have the ability to influence government and its institutions, but it is precisely the same bourgeois citizens who are readily subject to pressure, coercion, and control by the government, without any need for the government to resort to drastic police measures.

At the present time, the middle class in America is virtually entirely intact. But it no longer is the strong bastion of freedom and of moral values that it might be. The American middle class is no longer on the upswing, economically, educationally, culturally, or spiritually. It feels its very existence threatened, not by any revolutionary upheaval, but by mounting pressure of petty obligations and details in every area of life. Although an independent-spirited middle class may have caused revolutionary upheaval in England, France, and the North American colonies, today the middle class is being largely deprived of its potential for spiritual leadership because it is being put under such tremendous pressure, particularly in the economic arena.

Responsibility or Control?

In a previous chapter, we considered the tension between the responsibility or answerability of government and its agencies and the degree of control it exercises over the lives of those it rules. Now we shall examine a different relationship between responsibility and control, this time on the level of those subject to rule. We may say quite simply, the greater the individual responsibility shown, the less the need for government controls. Where responsibility fades into nothingness, controls become absolute. To the extent that citizens assume responsibility in society, the government can leave them free from elaborate controls. It will not need constantly to check up on what they are doing, and it will not have to coerce them to fulfill their obligations. To the extent that citizens fail to conduct themselves as though they were aware of their personal stake in the maintenance of society and its institutions, they will increasingly be placed under more and more stringent controls. Even when a relatively large percentage of the populace does act responsibly, the irresponsibility of a small number can lead to the imposition of generalized controls. Only a very small percentage of handgun owners use them for acts of violence, but the irresponsibility of the few may well lead to rigorous controls for the many. Only a tiny percentage of airline passengers ever seek to hijack an airliner, but the small minority of those who do has brought about the imposition of controls on everyone who flies.

In the United States, the federal income tax is based largely on the principle of self-reporting and self-assessment. But in recent years a variety of factors — increasing tax burdens, increasing complexity of tax laws, and a decreasing sense of personal morality and social responsibility on the part of many ordinary citizens — has begun to produce a situation in which the government is exercising tighter surveillance and increasing control over individuals' income and expenditures. People have discovered and are making use of a wide range of subterfuges to avoid or evade taxes. The government has reacted by the imposition of increasingly explicit and elaborate requirements for reporting not merely salaries and wages, but payments of all kinds, and has required banks and other financial institutions to collaborate in furnishing complete and detailed information on their clients' transactions. The next step in this developing control would be to require *all* institutions making payments to individuals to deduct a certain amount as income tax and forward it directly to the government, an obligation attaching only to employers at present. When control is "perfect," no one is personally responsible — just properly programmed.

Ideally, greater responsibility on the part of individual citizens and taxpayers would alleviate the increasing burdens on government and business alike caused by extremely detailed reporting, withholding, and the associated functions. There was once a point at which the level of individual responsibility and integrity was sufficiently high that it seemed neither necessary nor financially efficient for the government to engage in extensive measures of income surveillance, investigation, and control. As more and more people, including millions with no experience in or tradition of accounting and fiscal responsibility, were obliged to pay increasingly higher income taxes, the point was reached where the government could no longer content itself with spot checks but felt the necessity of routinely investigating an ever-larger number of taxpayers. The growth of mechanical and electronic methods of reporting and analysis, of course, has made this possible on a vastly enlarged scale. We can assume that the cost of collection of taxes, involving as it does ever-increasing expenses for both employers and other payers, taxpayers, and the government, is gradually becoming large enough to in turn require an increase in the tax rates to compensate for it.

Authority vs. Power

Responsibility or control, means vs. ends, automatic collection rather than willing payment: all these are aspects of the conflict in government between *authority* and *power*.

Authority, properly understood, is necessary in a free society. It is not necessary in a slave society, where power alone is enough to guarantee that the will of the masters will be fulfilled. But such is the modification of words and the emotional response we have to them that most Americans react negatively to the very idea of authority, never realizing that it is a necessary foundation of the freedom they cherish.

The word *authority* is derived from the Latin *auctoritas*, and is distinguished from *power* (Latin *potestas*). It is the ability, the right, to command voluntary agreement and obedience. There are two aspects to authority: the character of the one having authority, and the character of those responding to it. In the Roman Republic, the Senate was supposed, in theory at least, to have authority by virtue of its dignity or moral worth that commanded the respect of the rest of society. When the Republic became a principate, headed by a single ruler (*princeps*, Caesar, or Augustus), his rule was initially thought of as leadership. Being *first* in the commonwealth, the prince led; the people, attracted by his moral stature, willingly followed. In this his authority consisted. Authority, as opposed to power, is essentially a personal quality. An evil man may obtain and wield power, but he cannot possess authority. In this sense, former President Nixon's frequently voiced concern for "the authority of the presidency" was altogether wrongheaded. In the first place, the "presidency" cannot have *authority*, but only *power*. Power goes with the man's office, authority with his character. Of course there is a tendency for us to treat those with power as though they also merited authority. Thus it happens that whoever occupies the presidency is frequently asserted by public opinion polls to be the nation's most admired man. As far as the true authority of a president is concerned, Nixon did more to destroy it than almost anyone else could have done. Needless to say, his own merited loss of authority was increased by the unremitting glare of publicity focused on him by hostile mass media. Other presidents may also have demonstrated a lack of the moral worth, *dignitas*, that creates authority, but as their deeds, motives and thinking were less publicized, they continued to enjoy an authority that they did not really deserve.

To true authority there is a *response*. This is the responsibility, or better, responsiveness, of the governed, contrasting with the responsibility of the ruler mentioned in the preceding chapters. Where the ruler has the appropriate character to inspire willing compliance with his instructions, the governed must also have the appropriate character to respond. An irresponsible citizenry will make it impossible for a ruler to govern by virtue of his authority, and will force him to resort to the use of power, to coerce obedience. Thus authority also calls for a particular character in the governed, in the citizenry.

Among the many ideas of ancient statecraft and civilization that were taken for granted was the idea that the people would respect virtue. While many ancient rulers fell far below the level of personal worth that would have won them general authority, education in antiquity held before those in high places the ideals of nobility, courage, generosity, justice, and mercy. All this was far from perfect, as indeed nothing is perfect in a world of fallen human beings. But it was a strikingly different orientation from that characterizing contemporary Western and particularly American society. From a ruler we expect conformity to the standards of the mass; we may expect style, and respect someone who seems to have more of it than others, such as the late President Kennedy. But we really do not look for true nobility of spirit in a leader, nor would we be likely to recognize it where it exists. The media make a business of exposing the feet of clay of those in high office, and in one way they do well to do so. No one should be allowed to think of himself as more than human, or—like the later Herod in the Bible—to be flattered as speaking with "the voice of a god, and not of a man" (Acts 12:22). There is another side to the matter, however. All of us have weaknesses and faults of character mixed with strengths and virtues. It is certainly possible to dwell on the faults of a virtuous man so as to conceal his good qualities and, which is perhaps even worse, to dishearten him and discourage him from exercising them.

The long series of scandals that has marked recent American political history offers no startling surprises by comparison with the past, unless it be that they are becoming more frequent, more severe, and affect more people. What is perhaps new about them is that they pass with scant public condemnation: there is much excitement, but little genuine indignation, and what there is is largely reserved for those offenders who also happen to be one's political opponents. Highly placed political leaders have maintained mistresses since time immemorial, and many of them have found ways to divert public funds to their private amusements. Several things stand out in the Hays-Ray affair, or rather in the public and media response to it. First, while Hays was disgraced, Miss Ray became an instant celebrity, her fame earned by her share in pursuits

—and her skillful publicizing of them—that, by common standards, ranged from the immoral to the possibly illegal. Second, although to all appearances evidently involved in conduct that is, to say the least, hardly honorable, Congressman Hays claimed he did not feel that the loss of honor in any sense disqualified him from continuance in office. Nor did a majority of the voters of his party, who nominated him for another term before he decided to pull out of the race. Indicted Congressmen have frequently been returned to office while awaiting trial.

Such a figure may wield considerable power, but he has no *authority* in the traditional sense. If he is an isolated figure among over half a thousand legislators in Congress, if he does not have countless mirror images in the bureaucracy and in the several states, then the disgrace of a man like Hays will not destroy the authority of government. But if the immediately preceding president, Nixon, had thoroughly discredited his own claim to authority, and if Hays is considered, judging from the popular response, to be a somewhat extreme but not particularly unusual example of high-level governmental conduct, then we are dealing in the United States with a situation in which the authority of those "in authority" has reached the vanishing point.

A consequence of the loss of authority is the increasing resort to raw power. We have already referred to the immediate resort to overwhelming force by President Eisenhower in Little Rock. Eisenhower was not a philosophically inclined man, and may not have understood the implications of his action. But what he was saying by his actions was that he had no confidence that the people of Little Rock, or of America in general, could be persuaded to follow the laws, or the Supreme Court's interpretation of them, on their merits. They had to be forced.

Needless to say, no society composed of human beings can run on authority alone. There will always have to be some application of force. But it is evident that if force has to be used to compel compliance with what ought to be some of the recognized basic assumptions of a democratic society, such as the equality of all in the eyes of the law, or the citizen's responsibility to pay taxes, then force will have to be used for everything. Where power alone prevails, we can no longer speak of freedom.

There can be no democracy, no freedom, where there is not a measure of authority. We need not speak of "respect for authority" as though it were something that could be coerced by the police, as ancient Asian potentates forced their subjects to touch their forehead to the ground at the potentate's passage. We speak of respect for authority that is deserving of respect. This means the education, cultivation, and development

165

of leaders who can lead because they have the qualities, or rather virtues, that men admire. And it also means that the general population must once again find it natural to admire virtue, rather than labeling it silly.

This means a restructuring of our outlook to include room for values worthy of admiration — and to cultivate in ordinary citizens what used to come naturally, in a ruder and healthier age: ungrudging respect for true worth.

15

Self-Restraint

Conversely we may see thousands who are cowardly, intemperate, foolish, unjust, and irreligious at heart, but unable to display the ugliness of each vice, because of the inconvenience of their opportunities for sin.

Philo of Alexandria
On Sobriety

A certain level of conformity and predictability in the behavior of its citizens is a necessity for the existence of a civilized society. Such conformity and predictability may be obtained in a variety of ways: by regimentation, which is at its maximum in a military unit; by unquestioning adherence to tradition, which has prevailed in certain isolated societies, but which is hardly a possibility in today's world; by a strong sense of personal values on the part of a majority of the citizens, resulting in their voluntary adherence to productive and socially harmonious patterns of living.

Traditionally, most societies have used a mixture of the three factors: some regimentation, particularly for the unrulier members, reaching its extreme in prison or corrective labor camp; some tradition, followed by people more or less voluntarily, but without much reflection; finally, a measure of deliberate personal decisionmaking, based on personally held values. The second factor, tradition, is the one that is least serviceable in the modern world. We might well wish for a situation in which people would have a deeper sense of the value of the "old ways" and be readier to follow some of the customs, manners, and habits that used to make interpersonal contacts smoother and less problematic. But adherence to tradition depends on a variety of things that hardly exist in the modern world, and certainly not in highly mobile, media-dominated modern American society. Tradition is an effective force only in small, self-conscious communities with a strong sense of identity, such as Orthodox Jews or Amish. Traditions cannot be created and imposed or standardized for people who have no organic relation to them. This is one of the problems with the honor codes at the service academies, West Point, Annapolis, and the Air Force Academy. Earlier, these honor codes were only a highly developed, rather extreme formulation of the idea of honor that prevailed, or at least was traditional, in society as a whole. But now that American society has virtually abandoned the concept of personal honor and integrity, it is increasingly difficult, and increasingly meaningless, to try to impose it on young men and women drawn from the general pool of society's youth.

The service academies, rather like certain spiritual and religious communities, are intended to train a kind of an elite for hard service. Hence they feel justified in calling on their trainees for a level of personal commitment and a standard of behavior superior to that found in society as a whole. This would not be a difficult point to make. The problem comes when the standard that is called for seems to be entirely different from what prevails in society as a whole, even at the highest levels of those who are commanding the commanders of the academies and directing the rest of government. The Wilbur Mills-Fanne Foxe affair seemed rather an isolated incident when it first happened in 1974. But when the Hays-Ray uproar began in 1976, it was immediately followed by a number of other sex-related exposés of misconduct in high places, more recently by the Abscam affair. It really has begun to seem as though restrained, sexually continent behavior would be hard to find among the powerful on Capitol Hill and elsewhere in government. And the problems did not merely involve sexual immorality, but apparent intimidation of employees to secure sexual favors, as well as misuse of government funds to provide highly paid official positions for those supplying the favors.

"Representative" Representatives?

In the midst of the uproar, the insinuations, charges, denials and countercharges, the Washington press corps and the media generally found it more difficult to muster the same kind of indignation for the sexual and financial misdoings of prominent congressmen that it had earlier found for abuses of power under then President Nixon. The usual reason given for the contrast between the hot pursuit of Nixon and the rather mild treatment of Mills, Hays, and others is that one involved political, the other personal, morality. This may not be a valid distinction. Noted Roman Catholic lay theologian Michael Novak voiced the opinion early in 1976 that an individual's moral character is not divisible into compartments, and that turning a blind eye to the violation of traditional standards of public morality facilitates the violation of accepted standards of public morality. Needless to say, he was roundly criticized by others in the media, who want sexual conduct that Novak considers immoral designated only as an acceptable "lifestyle." The point Novak was making—but which is now generally rejected—is that the same moral sense and the same ethical teaching that tell us that bribery is wrong tell us that adultery and homosexual behavior are wrong. If we want to accept the latter as perfectly tolerable "alternative lifestyles," we find it hard to think of plausible reasons for condemning bribery. After all, bribery too can be a way of life, or life-style, as it certainly is and has been in many societies and sometimes seems to be in our own.

Writing in the *Washington Post*, noted political analyst David Broder brought up the interesting argument that since society as a whole contains many people who have problems with alcohol, behave irresponsibly, engage in sexual immorality and otherwise fall short of traditional standards of behavior, one should expect a similar proportion of our Representatives to display similar behavior patterns, and really ought to find nothing objectionable about it.[1] Of course to carry this argument to its logical conclusion would produce an absurdity. A certain percentage of society's members are mentally ill, and some are criminals. Other members—quite a large number—have violent prejudices and antipathies of a racial and religious nature, not to mention a host of other personality factors that do not necessarily seem suitable for high government officials. Would one argue that the House of Representatives should contain "representatives" of all those tendencies and behavior patterns? Surely not.

But what Broder is really implying is rather important: moral excellency, goodness—what an earlier generation called virtue without being embarrassed—are not particularly desirable qualities in our leaders. But what he, with so many of the other liberal writers who really do favor free institutions, fails to see is that without moral worth, goodness, and virtue, political leaders can have no authority in the sense discussed. And where

[1]*Washington Post*, June 19, 1976.

there is no authority, there will necessarily be more and more of the control that most liberals sincerely think they detest.

One of our major problems in attempting to define the kind of person who will be able to exercise authority, as opposed to power, by winning our respect, is that we are no longer clear about what constitutes goodness, about what we should admire. This is certainly true of society as a whole, and often is true of individuals as well.

In the passage cited at the chapter's beginning, Philo of Alexandria, a Jewish contemporary of St. Paul and of the pagan philosopher Seneca, like them one of the most learned men of the ancient world, illustrates this point. Philo took it for granted, without feeling any need to explain or defend his views, that certain things—cowardice, intemperance, folly, injustice, impiety—are ugly vices and that all persons endowed with common sense will recognize them as such, even those who fall into them. The Christian Paul and the pagan Seneca would have agreed with him. In fact, Philo's expression "the ugliness of each vice," is both typical and very significant. He took it for granted that beauty is an attribute readily recognizable by ordinary people, and that virtue will be found beautiful, even by those who lack it, while vice will be found ugly, even by those who engage in it.

In modern America, by contrast, we admire many of the things that Philo abhorred. Cowardice so called is not generally considered a virtue even today, it is true, but "being afraid" is widely accepted as an excuse for almost any misdeed. The opposite of temperance is extravagant self-indulgence, particularly in food, drink, and sexuality, and such self-indulgence is widely admired as an achievement. Much modern entertainment —much even of what is accepted as serious art—consists in playing the fool, or in treating one's audience as fools. Justice, always considered among the highest virtues in antiquity, is less admired today than the ability to get away with one's crimes. Being irreligious is considered a sign of intellectual maturity. Finally, we are not even agreed on what is beautiful, nor in aversion to ugliness. Many in our society positively seek out ugliness in everything from fashions to "art."

In other words, there is a general ethical and aesthetic confusion in our society. Hence it is no longer possible to rely in general understanding, common sense, and tradition to give people a certain set of values and to get them to practice them. The failure of traditional ways of seeing and of evaluating things is far more significant than the loss of traditional niceties of behavior, for it is the loss of the foundation upon which the behavior was built.

The direct result of this confusion is the ethical and moral anarchy out of which so many of the abuses in our society arise—from Watergate to bussing-related mob violence, from sexual immoralities and misuse of entrusted funds to cheating on taxes and exams and falsification of records and claims, all the way to violent crimes against the defenseless and weak. We still recognize most of these manifestations as evil, but as a society we find it very hard to identify what precisely is wrong about them. Although Nixon is no doubt correctly regarded as having "broken faith" with those who elected him—to borrow Theodore H. White's striking language—he might never have fallen from power had the government's lawyers not taken advantage of breaches of faith and even perjury by those who had once aided him. As the Hays-Ray affair has shown, one can commit some rather reprehensible acts with impunity if one is prompt enough to offer to give state's evidence in exchange for promises of immunity from prosecution. One of the ironies of Watergate is that although the general excuse given by the subordinates for their misdoings was loyalty to then President Nixon, the one who stayed longest in jail is the only one who was consistently loyal enough not to turn state's evidence, G. Gordon Liddy.

Although the 1976 presidential campaign was marked by a great concern for ethics, morality, and even spiritual values, and its outcome was in no small measure influenced by this concern, it is noteworthy that for most of those involved, those terms were merely slogans without any identifiable, definite content. Even if one elects—as we hope that we have done—national leaders with high moral and spiritual values, if these values are not expressed in some kind of a coherent framework, they will neither be very significant in government policymaking nor influential in helping mould the character of the citizenry as a whole.

Contemporary American society is losing, if it has not totally lost, its sense of appreciation for what used to be called virtue. Unfortunately, one of the main virtues—trustworthiness or fidelity—that is now considered outmoded is a necessity for the exercise of freedom in responsibility and freedom from surveillance and coercion. The terms "fidelity" and "faithfulness" are considered so out-of-date in one area, that of sexual conduct, that they have become almost ridiculous and are virtually unusable in other areas where they are no less needed, those of business and public life. Virtue cannot easily be recovered by a crash program to increase it, but it does arise and grow where people have the appropriate spiritual values. Hence we may say that spiritual renewal, far from increasing government control in our society, can increase individual responsibility and reduce control.

Government Coercion or Persuasion

As Ernst Jünger wrote, the destruction of order brings good to no one. And no society, democratic, oligarchical, or tyrannical, can survive without a large measure of order. How will American society in the 1980s go about establishing and maintaining order? Tradition is gone. The only remaining choices are coercion or persuasion. Coercion is readily possible for a modern government with all the techniques of surveillance, record-keeping and enforcement available to it. But if our American government goes much farther down the road of control—even if it is very mild-mannered and not at all brutal—there will soon be little left that we can recognize as personal freedom. On the other hand, persuading people to do voluntarily what government in the extreme case may have to force them to do against their will presupposes a receptivity on the part of the public to moral appeals. Apparently our government does not assume any such responsiveness on the public's part, as its prompt resort to force rather than long-term moral suasion in racial conflicts indicates. Perhaps its unreflecting assessment of the situation is correct. Perhaps the American people, despite its Puritan heritage and its strong preoccupation with morality, really is indifferent to moral arguments and can only be moved by force. However, if that is really the way it stands with us as a people, then we might as well abandon all pretense to have and keep a democratic society and republican institutions. In such a situation, it can only be a pretense, and a costly and useless one at that. Unless the population can respond to a moral appeal, it will be brought to heel by force. Morality does not hamper freedom; it makes it possible.

Control and Self-Control

There are two meanings to the verb control, still preserved in the use of the French *controller:* one is to observe, to keep track of; the other to direct, to regulate. The first meaning has been more or less lost in modern English usage. By control we really mean rule, regulate, dominate. There must be a measure of such control in all societies. The only real question is where it will come from: who will be the controller? Here there are two alternatives: external control and self-control. External control we might divide up into enforceable government control and traditional or habitual control through voluntary associations, such as churches or cultural groups. But insofar as membership in all such groups—except society as a whole—is largely voluntary, being controlled to any great extent by such a group is really a form of self-control, since it is voluntarily assumed. It requires a certain understanding of oneself, one's place in the scheme of things, of values and of the meaning of life. All this it has in common with self-control. Control by government requires little or nothing on the individual's part; on the government's, only sufficient power.

Self-control only exists when individuals know, either consciously or implicitly, who and what they are and what their life means. This government cannot tell them. Indeed, if government begins to tell them, then it will become hard to distinguish the "voluntary" self-control resulting from government indoctrination from outright government control. This then brings us to one of the fundamental questions of philosophy and religion: what is man?

The Question of Human Nature

One of the reasons for the continuing failure of idealistic Communism lies in its misunderstanding of the nature of man. Not having an understanding of man in his relation to his Creator, not believing in sin and the Fall, Communism assures the goodness and perfectibility of man (aided by government). But government is a human institution, and hence also afflicted by sin and the Fall. Imperfect institutions cannot produce perfection, but they can make a tremendous effort in that direction, institute mammoth controls and repressive measures, and generally wear everyone out trying.

Is man his own god? Are we autonomous, a law unto ourselves, in Muggeridge's words, "our own gods in our own universe"?[2] The vast majority of Americans do not believe that we are. We think of ourselves as creatures, in the real sense of the word: beings made by a Creator, not the accidental products of matter, time and change. Most Americans are theists of some kind: they believe that there is a God, and that we owe our existence to him and are in some sense responsible to him. However, only a minority think the matter through and express these views in a coherent way. Many of the rest are content to let matters rest in a kind of nebulous area of personal faith. We never articulate the doctrine of Creation, the idea that there is a God who made the world, that it did not make itself and is not eternal. Hence we do not recognize that such a presupposition is crucial for the way we approach the rest of life.

[2]Malcolm Muggeridge, "What the Abortion Argument is About," *Human Life Review,* I:3 (Summer 1975), p. 6.

The government, on the other hand, although it no longer speaks of the Creator, or Nature's God, as it did in the Declaration of Independence, so far has not expressed any official State Doctrine denying the reality of God, or claiming the world to be autonomous, self-created, independent of him. If the government as a whole or its various agencies were to set up any such doctrine of secularism as stated policy, it would be immediately rejected by the majority of America's people. Unfortunately, what it does not do in so many words, it can do equally effectively over a long period of time by degrees. Since World War II, and noticeably in the last ten years, the whole of our education system, from the lowest grades to the university level, has been more and more strongly proclaiming the idea that man is fully and satisfactorily explained as one animal among many: not a creature with a Creator, but simply a lump of matter on its own in an impersonal universe. The widely used and much disputed educational program funded by the Department of Health, Education, and Welfare, *Man: A Course of Study,* is inspired in part by the ideas of noted secularist psychologist and philosopher B. F. Skinner. Skinner, in his programmatic essay *Beyond Freedom and Dignity,* defined freedom and dignity as illusions, and harmful ones at that. They are illusions which prevent man from properly taking charge of his own affairs.

Is it not paradoxical that a democratic society based on the principle of responsible exercise of freedom and the equal worth (dignity, from Latin *dignitas*) of all human beings, should instruct its children in a philosophy that holds that both freedom and dignity are dangerous illusions?

The only alternative to more and more state control is a higher and growing degree of self-control. But self-control depends on understanding ourselves as responsible individuals—responsible in the sense that we must answer to an authority, or better, to the Authority, God, and also in the sense that we ourselves have derived authority if we attain a certain level of excellence of character. We have passed the stage when we could absorb such an understanding from tradition. Now it is challenged. It is in an area of conflict. Now it is no longer a question of tradition and culture, but of challenge and decision.

A restored republic can come only from restored self-consciousness on the part of enough citizens to make generalized state control, instead of more and more necessary, less and less so. This self-consciousness will come only when we have a clear understanding of the nature of virtues and of the ugliness of vices. Or, to put it another way, in more philosophical terms, of the nature, destiny, and dignity of man. But these are not merely "philosophical" questions. They are fundamentally religious ones.

Unless the republic is restored, it will inevitably turn into a technocratic tyranny more extensive than any the past has known. But it cannot be restored by technology or tradition. The only answer to the problems of the republic remains fundamentally a religious answer. Unless people have spiritual roots, they require social and governmental controls to keep them in line.

A Religious Answer in a Free Society?

Is it possible for society to find answers that are valid for enough people to give that society stability and character without having to enforce them as official "state church" doctrine? The answer is amazingly simple. Of course it is, for America was an example of such a society, at least for the first hundred and fifty or sixty years of its existence. We had no "establishment of religion." We had the constitutional principle of separation, institutional separation, between church and state. No one was coerced or penalized by government for his religious beliefs or lack of them. Religion, and religions, flourished in America. The United States are known as the home of a bewildering variety of cults and sects, many of them originating here, many imported from abroad. But alongside this proliferation, orthodox, traditional religion has prospered. The two great branches of Western Christendom, Catholic and Protestant, have expanded and flourished side by side, and coexisted reasonably harmoniously with the numerically smaller Eastern Orthodox churches as well as with the heirs of an earlier biblical tradition, the Jews.

A religious answer clearly *was* possible in a free society. There was a religious consensus through most of our national history. It was not without inconsistencies. It was not universally understood or expressed. In fact, in many cases, it was rather below the level of consciousness. But it existed. Today it has been challenged, partly by default. As society has become more and more disoriented, the failure of Christians to express and articulate their position has seemed to many an admission that they have no position. At the same time, official government "neutrality" on religion has been transmuted into official government hostility to religion. Of course, the United States government is not hostile to religious *institutions* — far from it. There are countless favors and benefits enjoyed by churches and religious institutions in American society today. But it *is* hostile to articulated religious *faith*. And the media are almost as hostile as government. It will matter little for government to go on tolerating religious institutions for a few decades longer, if it succeeds in driving from the consciousness of everyone educated in government

175

schools or dealing with government agencies the awareness of religious faith as a reasonable and defensible approach to the question of man, his meaning, and his destiny.

There is no answer to the restitution of the republic other than a religious answer. There is a religious answer that would be bearable, although not necessarily altogether appreciated, by those in our society who do not accept it. And those who are unwilling, for reasons that we must honor, to agree to an articulated religious answer, must face with all seriousness the question whether the society that we are building without religion, "beyond freedom and dignity," is one that they can endure.

The frantic attack on the Moral Majority, spearheaded by the ACLU, reveals a dangerous misreading of the political and spiritual climate in America. By opposing "morality" in the name of "freedom," the ACLU and similarly-motivated groups are doing their bit to help make the American people so immoral that they will be ungovernable except by extensive controls and coercion—controls and coercion that will spell the end of the ACLU and of all civil liberties.

16

Men, Deeds, and Ideas

My father made your yoke heavy, and I will add to your yoke: my father also chastised you with whips, but I will chastise you with scorpions.
> Rehoboam, Solomon's son, to the people
> of Israel after his father's funeral.
> *I Kings 12:14*

By July 4, 1976 the presidential primary campaign had settled down to three candidates—two Republicans, one Democrat. Each of them was a man of fairly well-known conservative Christian convictions, i.e., an evangelical Protestant. It was Southern Baptist Jimmy Carter who made much of his personal faith, and spoke openly of being "born again" and of his "personal relationship with Jesus Christ." But, although it was less publicized, Gerald Ford, an Episcopalian, also has had an evangelical "conversion experience," and has been active in small-group prayer and Bible study. Even less publicized, but no less genuine, was the Christian commitment of Ronald Reagan, a Presbyterian.

Thus, even prior to the actual nominating conventions, it was evident that the candidates of both major parties would be evangelical Christians who take their faith a good deal more seriously than most of their predecessors and their colleagues elsewhere in public life. The cumbersome presidential electoral process had finally done its work, and we then knew which man's faith would be subjected to the strains and temptations of one of the most exalted and powerful offices in the history of the world. Would he continue, as Gerald Ford did, to set a high standard of personal conduct, contrasting favorably with the ambition, pride, and sometimes even venality of earlier presidents? Would he in any sense fulfil what surely was the hope of those who elected him, that in choosing an identifiably Christian and religious man, American government, not merely America's ruler, would be brought closer to biblical principles? Much lay in his power. Not everything, it is true. For the American government, by a wise foresight of the founders, is a complex mechanism, and just as an evil president is hindered in the exercise of evil designs, the best of leaders will encounter obstacles in carrying out good ones. But perhaps more than anyone else the president—especially in an age of mass media and instant communication—is capable of being a leader for the national spirit. There is no doubt that Ford did much to heal the wounds our nation's spirit suffered. His successor had the opportunity to build. Would he do so?

The Carter administration now belongs to the past, although its history has yet to be written. But it seems to have passed, rather sad to say, almost as a dream in the night. Despite President Carter's evident personal qualities, like others before him, he relied on controls rather than on cultivating a renewed sense of responsibility. His administration seems to have involved four wasted years. Can President Reagan succeed where Carter drifted? America's future depends on it; there are only a few years of grace left.

By Their Fruits

A clearly stated biblical principle, reiterated by Jesus in the Sermon on the Mount, is that a man's deeds will reflect his character: "By their fruits ye shall know them" (Matthew 7:20). During the 1960 presidential campaign, when Richard Nixon faced John Kennedy, Kennedy was subjected to criticism because of his Roman Catholic faith and the fear that he might prove unduly complaisant towards the wishes of the Catholic power structure. At the same time Nixon, of Quaker background, was queried whether the pacifistic bent of his religious heritage might not disqualify him as commander in chief responsible for national defense. Both candidates replied, in effect, that if elected, they would not be influenced by their religion. At the time, more than one observer remarked that he would have been much happier to hear them promise that they *would* be influenced by it. With hindsight, we can see that it would have been much better had they been, for each had a chance at the presidency, and each was removed from it—one by an assassin's bullet, the other in the familiar crisis known as the Watergate affair.

178

Sixteen years later, in the bicentennial year of American independence, the most outspokenly religious of the candidates found words to declare that he too would not be affected by his religion if elected—although undoubtedly he owed his success to the votes of those who did not believe his words and expected him to go on being influenced, in line with Jesus' words in Matthew 7:20. Now that the election is history, the president had an opportunity, for a brief time at least, to make it clear that there *is* a correspondence between the character of the man and the nature of his deeds. If this is done, it will be an important step in the turning of America from a secular state in rebellion against God to a nation that knows itself to be under him. If it is not done, it will be a tremendous disillusionment to that great and growing body of Americans who are serious about their Christian commitment, who make genuine if inconsistent and often unsuccessful efforts to match their deeds to their profession of faith, and who can expect no less from another Christian elected to the nation's highest office. Carter did not—perhaps could not—do it. Will his successor be able?

Integrity

Before he decided to step out of the 1968 race for the Democratic presidential nomination, Lyndon Johnson had come to be regarded as someone who could not be trusted. Having opposed Barry Goldwater in 1964 as the candidate of peace, he had embroiled us in a losing war about which he seemed incapable of telling the truth. By the time he was forced out of the presidency in mid-1974, Nixon had won an even more dubious reputation. In retrospect, it seems that the judgment of the day may have been too hard on both Mr. Johnson and Mr. Nixon, but it cannot be doubted that by the time each left office, he had forfeited the respect that confers what we mean by authority. Gerald Ford, in his two-and-one-half years' presidency, did much to restore a measure of dignity to the office. But—perhaps because Ford had been chosen by Nixon and subsequently gave him a presidential pardon for everything connected with the Watergate affair—there was still considerable dissatisfaction expressed about his personal trustworthiness. Certainly one of the reasons for Ford's slim loss to Jimmy Carter in 1976 was the fact that the untested Carter seemed less tainted by politics and its corruption than anyone else.

Prior to the 1976 campaign, no politician had worn his religion on his sleeve. As a candidate, Carter frankly described himself as "born again," and won the approval of millions of conservative Christians both for his faith and for his frankness in confessing it. Large numbers of Protestants and Catholics voted for him in 1976 in the expectation that he would "bring God back into government." Yet as things developed, Carter made a point of keeping his personal faith out of his public life. Like others before him, he kept assuring the electorate, explicitly as well as implicitly, that his faith would not affect his politics. For many who voted for Carter in 1976 in the expectation that his faith would influence his public conduct, this was a disillusionment, and in his 1980 campaign the support of evangelicals was far less in evidence.

Even though Carter was by far the most outspokenly religious of the major candidates of 1976, both Ford and Reagan were also known to be Protestants in the evangelical tradition and regular churchgoers. When Carter faced Reagan in 1980, however much they differed on political and economic matters, both adhered to essentially the same religious position. It is beginning to look as though some kind of an evangelical commitment is a requirement for the presidential nomination of a major party. Even independent candidate John B. Anderson is a well-known evangelical churchman. Is this simply a coincidence? Or can it be that the voters in both 1976 and 1980 were looking for more than political and administrative qualities, namely for spiritual convictions and commitment, and the candidates' evangelical affiliations gave voters confidence that they possess them?

Whatever the strongly evangelical coloration of the presidential slates in both 1976 and 1980 may mean, it seems fair to say that voters were beginning to look for certain personal qualities in their major candidates, qualities that seemed to be promised by a commitment to evangelical Christianity.

This does not mean, of course, that many Americans—if any at all—wanted or expected a candidate to abolish the First Amendment, institute a state church, and turn the country into a theocracy. But they definitely did want more concern for biblical and Christian values in high office—and, for the time being at least, it appears that they got it. Carter, after being inaugurated in 1977, made a point of telling the people that he would not be influenced by his religious affiliation, and in the long run discovered that this disconcerted more supporters than it reassured. Reagan was less outspoken about his religion than Carter, but he has been considerably less inhibited than Carter in making appointments and decisions that reflect a Christian orientation and concern.

Does this violate the establishment clause of the First Amendment, "Congress shall make no law respecting an establishment of religion"?

Certainly not. The Amendment was intended to prevent the State from dictating to the conscience of Americans in telling them how to worship. It certainly was not intended to suggest to them that they ought not to worship. Nor was it intended to tell American Christians that their conscience might not speak to the State. Unfortunately, the First Amendment has gone far towards accomplishing these two things it was never intended to do.

The First Amendment and the Conscience of Americans

It would have been inconceivable for eighteenth-century Americans to think that the voice of their conscience—which in the case of the majority was a Christian conscience—would not be allowed to speak to the civil government. Had the First Amendment been presented as meaning such a thing, it would never have been accepted. Nor could it have been voted in any state legislature or in any popular referendum at any time since 1787. Unfortunately, that is the way it has turned out, increasingly so as we near the end of the twentieth century and set out, somewhat apprehensively, on the third century of American liberty. From a purely numerical standpoint, the conscience of most Americans is in some sense Christian. If the Christian conscience may not speak to the nation as a whole, then the voice of conscience is reduced to a whisper. The consequence, as we have already said, is the effective disfranchisement of the majority of Americans. If their spiritual heritage is important to them —and surely those Americans whose spiritual heritage does mean much to them are precisely the ones most concerned about questions of conscience—American citizens may not address their representatives. To listen to them would be to breach the "wall of separation" between church and state.

The direct consequence of this is that the state and society are thereby deprived of every insight that has spiritual roots. In a country grounded in Christian civilization, which America is and which cannot be changed by legislation forbidding us to acknowledge the fact, the simple truth is that much of the most valuable insight concerning the meaning and purpose of human life comes from spiritual sources. Under the presently prevailing rules—rules that were never adopted by any democratic process and that would not win a majority vote today—we cut ourselves off from our spiritual roots. The result is that in the clash of world empires, we confront a strong, vigorous, full-bodied foe with

an emaciated shadow, a bloodless wraith. In such a conflict, the outcome
is a foregone conclusion.

Representatives or Reflectors?

The classical, Burkean idea of an elected representative proposed
the election of a man in whom the voters have confidence. He was then
expected to act on the basis of his convictions and his best judgment in
representing them and their interests. If they had occasion to be dissatis-
fied, they could subsequently vote him out of office. This Burkean idea
is reminiscent of the Roman concept of authority, in which an individual
had authority because his character was such as to inspire voluntary obedience. This is, we might add, somewhat the approach used by Carter in
the 1976 campaign, for he clearly sought to sell himself as a man of
character and integrity, a man who could be trusted, without telling the
people in detail what to expect from his administration.

But Burke lived before the age of telecommunications, rapid means
of transport, and the public opinion poll. Even in Britain, it took some
time for news of the actions of a member of Parliament to trickle back to
his constituency, and longer still for him to become aware of popular
reaction to them. But today, especially in the case of a controversial decision, news of a politician's stand can quickly be telecast back to his
constituents, even if they are across a continent or an ocean. He can be
among them in a few hours to "test the water." Even more significant is
the continual taking (and reporting with considerable fanfare) of public
opinion polls. Pollsters have determined that a "scientific sample" of the
population—perhaps 1500 in number, sometimes more—can be trusted
to give responses that will reflect what the population as a whole would
answer if asked. These poll results are then widely publicized, with the
result that before a representative can make up his mind on the merits of
an issue, he already knows what his constituents want, or at least what a
more or less scientific opinion survey says that they want. It is taken for
granted that a politician, once he knows what "his people" want, can be
expected to vote that way himself.

There are several disadvantages to such government by poll. First of
all, it completely negates any superior attitude the elected official himself might have for making the right decisions. He may be of mature
judgment and have greater experience than his constituents, and he certainly ought to have access to better information than most of them do.
If his major function is not to decide, but simply to reflect the prefer-

ences of his constituents, then there is no need to seek out a superior individual, morally, mentally, or otherwise, to represent us in government. He needs only to be able to read a poll and act accordingly. Indeed, with modern means of communication, it is not really necessary to have a Congress at all. Polls could regularly be taken in each district, and votes cast by a single teller, or even by a computer, according to the outcome. Such a suggestion clearly makes a mockery of our political process. Yet it is only the logical outcome of our increasing preoccupation with public opinion surveys as a substitute for rational and responsible decisionmaking.

A second danger of government by poll is that it places tremendous power in the hands of the pollsters. The outcome of a poll may be managed, at least to a considerable extent, by a skillful wording of the questions. One example will illustrate:

POLL "A"
Question: Do you think that an abortion decision should be a matter for a woman and her doctor? ____ Yes ____ No ____ Undecided

POLL "B"
Question: Do you approve of the Supreme Court ruling that permits infants to be destroyed by abortion shortly before birth? ____ Yes ____ No ____ Undecided

It can be predicted with confidence that POLL "A" would produce a majority of "yes" replies, or close to it, almost anywhere in America, and that POLL "B", put independently to the same kind of people, would produce a majority of "no" answers. It takes a certain amount of skill to understand what a poll means, and even with care, one cannot always be sure that the question means the same thing to the interpreter that it did to the respondent. Recently a poll was circulated to a group of surgeons. As their answers were tabulated, it began to appear that the majority endorsed and even practiced infanticide. The questions were rather complicated and hypothetical, and the final opinion of those who commissioned it was that it did not mean what it appeared to say. It was thrown out and another attempt will be made. Unfortunately, many polls that are probably no more reliable than this are published and become the basis for political decisionmaking. And of course polls influence those polled, in that persons holding to a particular idea may be encouraged or discouraged from holding it as they get the impression that it is popular or a lost cause.

The result of all this is to reduce political leaders to mere reflectors of public opinion. To hold office under such circumstances, only minimum qualifications would be necessary. All that we would need is to find "representatives" in David Broder's sense, as described in the preceding chapter—persons who reflect their constituents, both their virtues and their faults. If really dependable reflectors could be found, it would make the public opinion poll superfluous: instead of a sample of 1500 consulted by Gallup, we would need only the five hundred and thirty-five Senators and Representatives chosen to "reflect" the population as a whole.

Despite what certain people may say to explain the fact that our elected officials sometimes exhibit vices that we would shun rather than virtues for us to imitate, in reality very few of us would want our representatives to be nothing more than reflectors. We instinctively feel that the leadership of our society should be drawn from the best we have, not be the perfection of mediocrity.

An answer, then, to the problem of integrity in public office would be a conscious decision to understand and vote for the "whole man." If we were voting for a person to whom religious commitment is important, we would expect that commitment to be reflected in the way he conducts himself in office. We would not elect a strong Christian and then tell him that we would expect, after his election, not to be able to distinguish him from an indifferent Christian, a pious or a nonpracticing Jew, an atheist or a person indifferent to spiritual questions. If we genuinely believe that a person in public office should in no way be influenced by religious convictions, then we should be honest enought to elect someone who shows no signs of such influence before his election. It is a form of democratic thought-control to elect someone to public office and then treat him as though he must change his convictions in order to be so colorless that he will annoy no one. Furthermore, since spiritual and ethical convictions are hard to separate, we should beware of persuading a candidate to renounce part of what he supposedly believes for the benefit of getting elected. He may later turn out to be willing to renounce other things, things that we thought he would keep, such as telling the truth and shunning bribes. Military chaplains, who of necessity serve units where many or most of the personnel may not share the chaplain's faith, are not advised to reduce their faith to a lowest common denominator. On the contrary, the Roman Catholic chaplain is told that the best way he can serve the Protestant and the Jew in his unit is to be a good Catholic chaplain. And something similar may be said to those we elect to public office: do not try to reduce your spiritual convictions and ethical ideas until they are representative of the lowest common denominator of all those who voted, or could have voted. Keep them clear and identifiable, so that when we vote we will know what as well as whom we are electing, and after your election, continue to adhere to them. If the people do not like it, they will find a way to tell you, and you will not have bartered away your personal spiritual integrity for the pottage of political popularity.

An individual's deeds should reflect his ideals and ideas, and these in turn should be consistent with his total personality. A political figure must necessarily have a private life. Indeed, we would do well to guarantee our political leaders more privacy in their personal lives, keeping them free from the prying of the media. At the same time, their character should be such that we can expect their private and public life to exhibit the same ideals.

Certainly one of the reasons that a politician likes to show something of his home and family life is to demonstrate—or at least give the impression—that he has a good home life and practices the traditional virtues in that area of life. And undoubtedly one of the reasons why the great media organs make so much of the disruption of a politician's home life or of moral deviations on his part is the awareness that this will almost inevitably hurt him politically. But when it comes to the repeated, almost tedious revelations of sexual immorality on the part of once-admired public figures, even those of the recent and more distant past, it sometimes seems as though the media were unconsciously trying to tell us that our leaders, far from exhibiting virtues that make them stand out among us, only use their power as convenient occasions to engage in common vices. This apparent attack on virtue as something practiced by almost no one is of course also an attack on authority; if we are once persuaded that there are no and never have been political leaders worthy of respect, and hence having a natural authority, the result will be a further decline in that fast-disappearing commodity. Unfortunately, the unrecognized after effect of the discrediting of authority is that society will have to replace it with force and coercion, since no society can exist without a measure of obedience on the citizens' part. Where there is true authority, much obedience will be voluntary and willing. Where there is no authority, much obedience will be obligatory and coerced.

There are people of integrity who have no professed religious commitment. However, because the greatest and most persistent teachers of the moral virtues are in fact the religions, it is logical enough to expect that a large percentage of those who make an effort to exhibit a life of integrity do it for religious reasons. If we desire, as part of the recovery of values necessary for a revitalized republic, to elect officials who have personal integrity, it is very relevant to ask them what they believe, and to try to discern the extent to which they live out their beliefs in daily life. It is not unreasonable to ask a candidate what he *knows*, as that will be an indication of what he is *able* to do in office. It is no less unreasonable to ask him what he *believes*, as that should certainly furnish a clue as to what he will be *willing* to do in office. Blacks in America do not limit their support to other blacks, but it would be hard to get them to support a black who had evidently sold out to an antiblack way of thinking. Christians in America should by no means exclusively support other Christians, but it is certainly reasonable for them to inquire, when confronted with a Christian candidate, about the way his practice corresponds to his posture.

We cannot exclude all knowledge of a candidate's religion from our political decisionmaking. Even if we were willing to remain ignorant of it, the media would tell us what it is — as has been the case with Jimmy Carter. This forces us to take a position on it. Hence it becomes relevant to know whether the position is genuine or a pose, and, if genuine, whether the influence that it exerts on the candidate's life is one that we would like to see represented in government. There should be no "religious test" for public office, but there can well be an *integrity* test, and one major aspect of a person's integrity lies in the way his religious profession corresponds to his performance. The media have thrust the religious question upon us. The way to deal with it is not to throw it back again with embarrassment, but rather to pursue it a bit. Find out more than the label. Find out how seriously the candidate takes it, whether it influences his daily life, and if so in what direction. As James wrote, "You have faith enough to believe that there is one God. Excellent! The devils have faith like that" (James 2:19). In the preceding verse, he had challenged, "Prove to me that this faith you speak of is real." We cannot rid ourselves of the "religious issue" in politics. The media would not allow it even if we wished to do so. Since it has been thrust upon us, we can use it as an indicator of a candidate's character and integrity. The conscience of Americans does have a right to speak to the state, and those of us who only elect officials and do not occupy offices have the right, indeed the duty, to know that we have at least some officials whose consciences are sensitive to the same influences that mould our own.

17

Communities

A house divided against itself cannot stand.

Matthew 12:25

According to the perceptive analysis of Hannah Arendt, one of the major steps on the road to totalitarianism is the reduction of society to what she calls an "atomistic mass." Existing loyalties to smaller groups and communities, to family, church, ethnic group, social circle, and the like are broken down. The individual is left with meaningful ties to the state alone. And because no individual on his own can debate the state, nothing remains to such an isolated, atomistic individual but to take the state's orders. This is the beginning of totalitarianism.

An antidote to the spread of totalitarianism, then, is the maintenance and strengthening of smaller communities within the state. But all modern states, and the United States among them, are engaged in weakening and destroying their smaller, natural, and voluntary communities. (A natural community is one to which one belongs naturally, as one's family or ethnic group, and sometimes one's religion; a voluntary association is one one chooses, such as a profession, a club, and more often than not in religiously free America, one's church or religion.) These intermediate communities are being broken down by social, economic, and cultural factors over which the state may have little control, or only indirect influence. The state is not alone at fault. The rapid mobility of Americans is not something that the government planned; this mobility itself, quite apart from other factors, has a very destructive effect on family and community ties. In addition to things that are happening in our society over which government has little control, government is also intervening directly to cut down the remaining natural ties. This intervention may not be consciously planned, but that is of secondary importance. It is real, and it is having its effect. The only way to counteract it is by reinforcing existing communities, and where there is a genuine place for them, helping new ones to form.

The earliest and most pervasive human community is the family. Most societies of the past and many of the present are characterized by what is called the extended family, including grandparents as well as parents and children, and collateral relatives—uncles, aunts, cousins, and more distant kin. American society, like that of modern Europe, is typified by what is called the nuclear family, or the family of procreation—parents and young children. The reasons for our transition from a society with extended family structures to one with primarily nuclear structures are many. Chief among them are industrialization, high mobility, and the reduction of family size. Children are no longer an economic asset in most families, but a very substantial financial burden. The older generation, once it is no longer productive, is often cared for by the state and is not considered primarily the direct responsibility of its adult children. When children go far away from home to school, to military service, or to work it is natural for them to marry partners from distant places. Frequent changes of residence destroy the cohesiveness of the extended family, and build tensions within the nuclear family. Indeed, as is well known, the nuclear form has not stood the strain of modern living well. The number of marriages that last "till death us do part" is dwindling, and according to some sociologists, a minority of American children today will be raised by the same parental couple that brought them into the world.

Religious Communities

The greatest voluntary association in America is the church. According to the classic definition of the great sociologist of religion, Ernst Troeltch (1865–1923), a "church" differs from a "sect" in that one belongs to a church by reason of one's background or nationality, while one joins a "sect," usually by a dramatic break with the "church." In his terminology, the church is hardly a voluntary association at all. This definition really does not fit the American situation, where despite high church attendance there is no established church. No one is forced to remain in the church into which he was born, baptized as a baby, or dedicated. Every church in America has large numbers of dropouts, and most also have a substantial number of converts. For this reason, it is correct to call the churches of America voluntary communities, unlike one's family or ethnic group. Quite apart from the soundness of their doctrines and beliefs and the praiseworthiness of their members' lives, we may make the sociological observation that the strength and vitality of the churches in America is a kind of barometer of the strength of the principle of voluntary association and hence of civic freedom. Where the churches and other voluntary associations flourish, one may assume that citizens are exercising a measure of freedom and responsibility to shape their own lives; where they are in decline or are suppressed, one may say that the citizens have either lost interest in freedom or have been deprived of it.

Small groups and communities, natural and voluntary associations, give individuals three very important things: identity, values, and a sense of security. The more stable a society is, the greater and more lasting is the influence of such communities. The greater the mobility of a society, the more individuals lose the sense of identity with small, knowable groups and the more dependent they become on the state—which is not a community, but an atomistic mass. Needless to say, we do not wish to restrict the mobility of individuals—neither physical mobility, i.e. their ability to move from place to place, nor social mobility, their ability to rise from one social or occupational class to another. But it is very important to recognize that as mobility is emphasized, true community ties are broken and the atomistic mass emerges. The end product of the atomistic mass is a society that organizes everyone and controls everything, in other words, totalitarianism. It is important to recognize that the march to totalitarianism cannot be blocked simply by "voting for freedom." No matter how one votes, no matter who wins the elections, no candidate can preserve freedom for a people where individuals have lost their sense of personal identity and worth and have become part of an atomistic mass. It is important—and we should be the last to deny it—to elect candidates who really do prize individual dignity and freedom. In this respect, the 1980 election of Ronald Reagan to the presidency can certainly be seen as a major step towards the preservation of true freedom in America. Nevertheless, no president, not even the most passionate lover of freedom, can keep a people free when the people itself has lost the strength to live in freedom.

189

Numbers and Names

European governments, and more recently, North American governments as well, give individuals an "identity" in the form of a passport that enables them to be recognized and respected among people with whom they have no natural ties. At home there should be no need of such a document. But modern governments are finding it expedient to give people such "identities" even at home: the *pièce d'identité*, *Ausweis*, or identification card has become universal in the non-English-speaking democracies. It is a token of residual freedom in the United States that there is as yet no national identification card, for despite the usefulness such a card could well have, it would also be symbolic of the individual's growing isolation from his fellow-citizens and his increasing dependence on the central government, even for his personal identity. In the United States, the Social Security number is becoming more important than an individual's name as a means of identifying him; by a macabre twist, the same type of number in Canada is called one's SIN (Social Insurance Number). It certainly is not a sin to have a Social Security number, but if one reaches the point of trusting in government rather than God as the source of all good, including one's personal identity, that certainly comes close to the basic sin of idolatry. Without becoming obsessed with the meaning of such symbolism, we should note that names reflect one's family, one's heritage, one's parents and their tastes, and perhaps even one's own character, in the case of nicknames —numbers reflect nothing but one's accidental location in the vast machinery of the state.

National Identity

Since World War II, but particularly during and since the Vietnam War, Americans in large numbers have become ashamed of their national identity. There was a time when it would have been better if Americans had been less boastful and more aware of their national failings. But today the reverse is true. One can frequently see an American hitch-hiking in Europe not with the American flag on his pack, but with that of his real or adopted ethnic origin, or even that of a country with with which he has no real connection. Identity has become a problem on a nationwide scale. It is not our purpose here to suggest the intensification of feelings of national identification *as Americans*, at least not without a simultaneous strengthening of local and voluntary community ties.

For pure identification with the nation leads to totalitarianism. American-made totalitarianism would not necessarily be greatly preferable to one imported from abroad.

Instead of seeking to reinforce national identity, which all dictatorships take as a high-priority project, Americans concerned with the survival of freedom must seek a *recovery of local community identity*. A network of family, local, and voluntary community ties enable an individual to know who he is and where he belongs. An individual with secure roots in his family, ethnic group, local community and religious fellowship can be a loyal and effective citizen of a great modern state, but he will not easily become the victim of a descent into totalitarianism, because he will not be an "atom."

A vital community spirit is largely a result of a community's vitality. The national government cannot create or share what it does not itself possess. National spirit can be fostered by indoctrination and propaganda, and it may be stimulated (or destroyed) by a national peril, such as war. But fundamentally the *esprit* of a nation must begin with local community *esprit*. Although government cannot create true community and the spirit that results from it, it can do much to foster it where it exists—and even more to frustrate and destroy it. Because individual, local and group identities in America are constantly being weakened by the process known in German as *Vermassung* (turning individuals into an amorphous mass), it is crucial for government to recognize this and to do what it can to reverse the trend.

Familiar Ties

Traditional social structures, even in independent America, depended to a great extent on naturally existing relations. The family unit was responsible for the care not only of its minor children, but also of its elderly and the handicapped members. In a family unit, persons whose age or infirmity might make them appear useless to industrial society can often make a very valuable contribution. Mentally handicapped people, for example, may be willing and able to assume the care of a chronically sick old person and thereby find a rewarding task where others would sense only a burden.

The family was traditionally responsible for providing education for its children. Of course this leads to great disparity in educational opportunity, as parents vary widely both in their ability to pay for education and in the value they place on it. On the other hand, this arrangement created a continuing relationship of mutual dependence: the parents had an ongoing responsibility to their maturing children, while the chldren could not but recognize the continuing concern of their parents. The family was to a great extent responsible for the conduct of its members. Parents may still be forced to pay for damages caused by their minor children, but with the lowering of the age of majority and the adoption by many localities of what is called self-emancipation (the principle that a child can become "emancipated," i.e., mature, simply by repudiating parental authority), parental responsibility has been diminished.

The state in many cases intervenes between parent and child. Sometimes, as in the case of a serious parental irresponsibility or incompetence, this is for the protection of the child. Sometimes, however, it is simply the expression of a social theory that holds, in effect, that the child is an "asset of the state" and to be protected from unwelcome parental influence. The very term *emancipation,* borrowed from the legal language related to slavery, implies that a child's submission to his parents is a form of bondage or servitude. It would be wrong to read too much into the use of such terminology; nevertheless, the choice of words does seem to correspond to an identifiable attitude on the part of many lawmakers and administrators, who feel that the state's interest in the child comes before any interest or rights the parents may have.

In a less mobile society, children naturally develop close neighborhood ties with people they know all their lives. Friendships and even long-standing rivalries give a sense of identification and community. The greatest force in rupturing such ties is the voluntary mobility of the American population. If we recognize that the promotion of such bonds is of great social value, we will deem it in our best interest to structure government in such a way that instead of furthering such rupture, it fosters and helps to maintain natural ties. Such restructuring of government will involve both attitudes and policies.

Citizen of Virginia (or Maine, or . . .)

The Fourteenth Amendment provides that "all persons born or naturalized in the United States . . . are citizens of the United States and of the State wherein they reside." The purpose of this amendment was to ensure the full citizenship, national and state, of freed slaves. It was intended to prevent individual states from setting different standards of citizenship from those of the national government in an effort to deny citizenship rights to former slaves. At the time of its adoption, in the aftermath of the Civil War, the population was relatively stable, at least by today's standards. People did move from east to west, but having arrived at their destination, they tended to stay there. As a result, the ordinary individual might not necessarily remain in one state during his entire life, but he would probably not be a citizen of more than two or three states in a lifetime. Today, however, it is not unusual for a child to be born in one state, attend elementary and secondary school in two or three different ones, college in still a different state, and during his adult life work in several more, never returning to live in one where he had lived already, and finally to retire to still another.

Such mobility makes state citizenship relatively meaningless. It does much to impair the continuity and vitality of state institutions. They simply lose track of their people. We are familiar in recent times with the way in which individuals who have made a name for themselves nationally can move into a state where they have no real ties in order to run for an office such as that of senator, even though constitutionally, it is precisely the Senate that is supposed to be the assembly of the states, and the senators who are charged with representing the interests of "their" states.

Amending the United States Constitution is an extremely difficult process and often consumes an inordinate amount of time — except when the amendment has broad nationwide support and the endorsement of the major opinion-makers. Thus the eighteen-year-old vote was adopted comparatively rapidly, but even ERA, the Equal Rights Amendment, is making but slow progress through the state legislatures despite the almost universal endorsement of major political leaders and the media. Because the amendment process is so difficult, and particularly because the Fourteenth Amendment enjoys almost sacral status in contemporary American political mythology, it would be rather enterprising to propose revising it. Yet it is precisely at the point of making state citizenship meaningful that this amendment has become pernicious in its effect on the country as a whole. An individual can move to Vermont from Tennessee, for example, and "instantly" he is as much of a citizen of Vermont as someone who was born there. To become a citizen of the country, however, one must go through a five-year process or meet other detailed conditions.

Evidently, then, citizenship in a state is regarded, in the light of the Fourteenth Amendment, as a mere convention. The amendment could be revised to make an individual a citizen of the state in which he is born or takes out his United States citizenship. Persons moving out of state would have the option of retaining their ties with their native state, and participating in its government by absentee ballot, or of transferring their state citizenship papers to their new state of residence. This transfer could be made simple and straightforward, in order not to add a great bureaucratic burden to moving. But if it were necessary to ask for a formal transfer, it would clearly create the attitude that state citizenship implies more than mere physical presence in a particular state, and this would be a very good concept to have. Certain countries, such as Switzerland, for example, go so far as to have *communal* citizenship, with an individual remaining a citizen of the town or commune of his ancestry unless he goes through the formal process of transferring his citizenship to a new residence. Such a constitutional change would do something to anchor individuals to their place of origin and would provide a source of continuity. The formality would be enough to symbolize the importance to a stable society of a tie otherwise easily lost.

As things currently stand, most American communities derive the major part of their revenue from property taxes. Those owning no property therefore contribute much less to the support of community services than property-owners. (Renters, however, do contribute through the property taxes their landlords pay, which come out of their rents.) At one time, many communities required property ownership to vote in local elections. Today this has vanished. This situation could become awkward, for example, in a college town, where students living in tax-exempt school-owned housing may make up a majority of the voting population. They would evidently be in a position to vote in extravagant community services for which they themselves would be required to pay nothing. A slogan of Independence was "No taxation without representation!" There is also something to be said for no representation without taxation, at least when the alternative is for people to have a determining voice in decisionmaking without being responsible for the decisions they make. This is the case when expenditures are voted by people who do not contribute to paying for them and laws are passed by those who need not keep them. This particular situation has not reached the point where it could reasonably be described as a major abuse, but the possibility illustrates the merits of binding a person, by one tie or another, to a particular community where he feels and exercises a certain responsibility. According to this proposed revision of the Fourteenth Amendment, a student in a college town could choose to have his citizenship transferred there, or he could elect to continue to vote in his home state by absentee ballot. Either way, he would be declaring a certain commitment to a specific community.

Welfare Migrants

Beginning during the 1940s, a new reason for migration began to appear. Instead of fleeing persecution or seeking new opportunities, some people began to move where they knew that they could find better welfare benefits. Such a motivation is not necessarily unworthy. To the extent that a community believes it should provide benefits, it is proper to make them available to residents on the basis of need, not necessarily on length of residency. Yet we can well understand that if a community resolved, for example, to pay all residents unemployment benefits to the level of their last regular income, it could speedily be bankrupted by the influx of a large number of unemployed who had not made previous contributions to that community's public wealth. If benefits are to be made available to all those who happen to be physically present in a particular community or region, and if there is a great deal of moving about in search of benefits, the only long-range solution will be the complete nationalization of welfare funds, a development towards which we have already taken major steps. But what such a development means is that the individual loses his ties to his community of origin, his claim on the support and encouragement of his friends and neighbors, and is related only to the state. There are many things to be said in favor of a totally nationalized welfare system. Among the objections, one is very significant: it moves society in the direction of Hannah Arendt's atomistic mass, where everyone relies not on natural bonds but only on the state for security.

We have noted many ways in which modern America resembles ancient Rome — a multiracial melting pot of ethnically and culturally diverse peoples. Rome, unlike modern America, had no highly developed welfare system. The famous "bread and circuses" were limited to the capital. As a result, many people organized voluntarily into benevolent societies where the members were pledged to sustain one another and share the losses in times of need, rather along the principle of a modern cooperative. All these voluntary societies were surpassed by the early Christian church, however. Its members' care and provision for one another were exemplary. Later, as more and more people were converted and finally the state itself adopted Christianity as the official religion, such mutual assistance became institutionalized and also declined in effectiveness. But even today there are religious and other communities where members can be counted on to take care of one another. Even the federal government recognizes the exemplary mutual support of members of certain religious denominations by allowing them exemption from Social Security taxes. Inasmuch as they have shown that their promise to take care of their own is good, the government refrains from taxing them to provide them with a service they are actually providing for themselves.

If smaller, voluntary communities are to be significant, they must have more than merely social and ceremonial functions. They have to be more than mere clubs. One of the chief values of a community is its support, practical and moral, of its members. To the extent that many or most of the citizens of a society belong to one or more such sustaining communities, the extent to which the mechanism of the state will have to assume responsibility for their security and welfare is reduced. In any society there will be some loners who do not fit into any well-defined small community. As a result, no matter how strongly small communities may develop, we can expect the national government always to retain some residual welfare responsibilities. Indeed, for the foreseeable future it is probably realistic to expect the role of state and national government in welfare to continue to increase. But we may at least limit that increase. If local and voluntary community ties can be strengthened to the point where such communities begin to assume some of the task of caring for some or many of those in difficulty, then it will eventually be reasonable to expect the government to reduce its outlay accordingly.

The Role of Christian Churches

So far in this chapter we have spoken in general terms of different kinds of intermediate and voluntary communities. And we can say with confidence that a free society can remain free and strong only when it consists of a large number of mutually interacting, independently healthy and vigorous smaller communities. While not overlooking the fact that some communities—such as street gangs or criminal bands—are destructive in their impact on society, we must maintain the assertion that the state cannot be healthy and free unless it provides a wholesome environment in which smaller communities can flourish. From this perspective, Christian churches are only specific examples of a general case. Their continuing vitality is useful to a healthy and free social order in the same way as is the vitality of ethnic groups, unions, social service organizations, and other independent associations.

Nevertheless, it is important to direct our attention specifically to Christian churches, for two reasons: first, the present work is addressed

196

primarily to Christian readers, who will naturally be concerned about the contribution they can make as Christians and church members to social and political reconstruction in our "pluralistic" society. Second, while we admit that the church resembles other voluntary associations *sociologically*, as Christians we contend that it has a resource that other associations lack, namely the promise and power of Christ, "the gates of hell shall not prevail against it" (Matthew 16:18). What this means, quite simply, is that while secular power can crush most voluntary associations —just as some universities have crushed Greek-letter fraternities—in the last analysis the world cannot destroy the church, for it is God's building, not man's. Christians as individuals and the churches as voluntary associations do have a hidden power to resist the mandatory conformity that the state seeks to impose. Even a ruthless state with unchecked internal police powers, such as the Soviet Union, has been forced to live with this reality. But—since the state officially looks on the church as just another voluntary association with no specific, God-given privileges —when the state finds that it must grant a measure of toleration to the church, it often also grants similar toleration to other voluntary groups. Hence in fighting for their own freedoms, Christians are also in effect fighting for freedom and openness in society.

This sometimes appears paradoxical, even self-contradictory. Can the power and influence of the church actually be a force for freedom? The growing influence of conservative Christian groups in American life —of which the Moral Majority is a paramount example—has been viewed with alarm by various professional advocates of "freedom," from Harriet Pilpel of the American Civil Liberties Union to Hugh Hefner of *Playboy* magazine. Full-page advertisements have been purchased in major newspapers, such as the *New York Times,* depicting a fat fundamentalist preacher holding a cross and riding piggy-back on a dejected Uncle Sam. Former Senator George S. McGovern, attributing his defeat in the 1980 elections to the forces of the "religious right," has launched a militantly secularistic counter-group with the rather unpromising name, People for the American Way. Such people obviously look on any increase in political influence on the part of religious groups as a threat to their freedom. And in some respects they have a point—at least to the extent that they wish to pervert freedom into social and sexual license, into abortion and pornography. But if we understand by freedom those things the Founding Fathers held dear—freedom of speech and thought, freedom of worship, freedom of association, the right to plan and work for one's own future—then neither the Moral Majority nor any other Christian-oriented group represents a threat to their freedom. In fact, we

197

can assert that to the extent that Christians do the job that Christ has assigned them, the power of the state will remain somewhat restricted, and the freedom of all citizens—non-Christians, even militant secularists, will remain stronger for it. In Soviet Russia there is no Russian Civil Liberties Union, no *Soviet Playboy,* and defeated office-holders do not found organizations called People for the Russian Way. Politically active Christians may be a nuisance; they may even interfere with some profitable commercial activities, such as pornography, but basically their strength enhances true civil liberty in a society by the simple expedient of keeping the state under some restraint and making the development of its police powers seem less necessary.

To the extent that political and social liberals, and especially moral and sexual libertines, feel threatened by the conservative, "reactionary" tendencies of Christian political activists, they will not be readily placated and won over by comments such as those in the preceding paragraphs. Nevertheless it is important for Christians to know, and confidently to assert, that their presence in society, like the presence of salt in food, does have a preservative effect on fundamental freedoms. In a chaotic society, freedom becomes impossible. The atomistic mass is the forerunner of chaos, and hence of totalitarianism and the extinction of freedom. To the extent that Christians keep society from deteriorating into an atomistic mass, they enhance freedom for all of society's members, not for themselves alone. It is important for us to see this fact clearly and to state it with confidence. If we do, there will be many libertarians who will ultimately come to recognize its validity, even though they may not like Christianity any better for it.

A vital element in the reconstruction of the Republic will be the *recovery of the church.* Specifically, the church—or rather the churches, denominations, and particularly individual congregations—must recover a sense of themselves *as a community.* From an historical perspective, it is only the churches in America that presently constitute a community broad enough and strong enough to give a large number of Americans that sense of identity, security, and values that individuals must recover if the Republic is to survive in freedom.

We have already mentioned the loss of pride in being an American. This does not affect the whole population, but it often does affect the young, idealistic, and sensitive members of it. This lack of pride, which sometimes amounts to a positive sense of shame, may be unwarranted, but it is real. Many people are ashamed to be identified as Americans. Such national celebrations as the Bicentennial have their uses and their joys, but this type of self-celebration can hardly be expected to restore

198

lagging national self-respect, any more than attendance at a spectacular Easter service can be depended on to revive fading religious faith. A presupposition of the hope that a reconstruction of this republic is possible on a nontotalitarian basis is the recovery and restoration of the vitality of many of its constituent parts — and not merely of its political subdivisions, such as states, cities, and counties, but of its intermediate communities, and foremost among them, of its churches.

Much has been said about the need for individual, personal religious awakening on a large scale for the restoration of vitality to America. In theological circles, there is an ongoing discussion between "personal salvation" and "social action." Proponents of personal salvation are supposed to want to change society only indirectly, by first changing millions of individual lives, while the social-action group is supposed to be interested only in changing structures without considering individual lives. Actually, most Christians would seek ultimately to do both, but certainly among conservative and Bible-centered Christians the emphasis has been on first changing individuals, who then will ultimately change society.

In this debate, what has been overlooked is the middle. What lies between the transformed individuals and the massive, centralized state? The answer, in a free society, consists of all the intermediate structures and communities of which we have been speaking. It is impossible for the individual to confront the state alone, except as a martyr. He needs the support of intermediate structures. There must be interplay, development, reinforcement and mutual correction between the individual and such intermediate community institutions. Then these institutions and communities can interact with one another, and finally with the great state and the nationwide society that surrounds them.

If we were simply to say, "Changing the church is the way to transform society," it might sound hopelessly idealistic. But if we first make it plain that the church represents a very important intermediate structure, and that what it alone does also affects other voluntary communities, it may seem more plausible to say that the transformation of society at large, is but a major step towards achieving it.

Identity, Security, Values

If Christian churches — and, *mutatis mutandis*, other communities with similar sociological features — were to recover the sense of community that they are supposed to have, they would begin to supply three things that the isolated individual greatly needs, and that the state should not give him. From this association he would receive his identity and sense of worth (or *dignity,* to use the Latin homonym). He should learn to wear this identifying label *Christian* as an honor, just as Americans used to boast of their American citizenship. From this identity he should also receive a large measure of his emotional and some of his material security. If the congregation is truly a community, a genuinely sharing fellowship, it will voluntarily assume a large measure of the responsibility for helping its members in sickness, adversity, and old age. The knowledge that one is part of a sustaining community will give individuals a greater sense of security than the mere confidence that there is a government agency to supply support checks. This is not to say that the sustaining voluntary community can or should eliminate all need for government-funded support, but merely that where such a vital community exists, an individual can feel far more truly secure and established then when he can rely only on the largesse of a giant, impersonal government bureaucracy.

Finally, the community should help an individual identify and maintain the *values* by which he will conduct his life. The Christian community tells its members that they are creatures of God, made in his image, called to be his children, with privilege, responsibility, and an assured inheritance in heaven. From this perspective it gives them a value system consistent with that self-understanding. American government, with no declared philosophical foundation, can give its citizens nothing better than statistics as the basis of a value system. The prophetic word, "Thus saith the Lord," typifies the biblical world and life view, and gives substance to the biblical value system. The statistically-based warning, "The surgeon general has determined that cigarette smoking is dangerous . . ." typifies the only type of ethics that a secular state can propagate: not ethics but statistics.

To the extent that they debate one another and force each other to justify and defend their respective value systems, a plurality of self-respecting communities living side by side in a free republic is a desirable thing. Only if they begin to quarrel so vigorously that they wind up by discrediting and disillusioning each other does pluralism become destructive. However, if we recognize that there is a solid, vital and living Christian basis to our society, despite the overlay of many variant and secularistic traditions, we will recognize that if pluralism really means free discussion and dialogue, some kind of a Christian consensus will emerge in America. The reason that no Christian consensus emerges from the present moral-ethical debate in our country is simply the fact that the Christian position is declared from the outset to be banned from the discussion. It is this secularistic bias, one that becomes particularly apparent when the discussion takes place under government auspices or in the secular mass media, that makes our pluralism appear so chaotic. Naturally if the majority is proscribed and not allowed to speak, no consensus can emerge from the small groups that make up the minority. Indeed, the groups in the non-Christian minority that are most concerned about moral and ethical issues often share the same ethical position as the orthodox Christians. This is the case, for example, with the Orthodox Jews and Latter-Day Saints (Mormons). Hence their contributions too are disqualified under the guise of pluralism.

A house divided against itself cannot stand, as Jesus told his critics. Abraham Lincoln echoed him in a situation of national crisis. An America that is made up of a variety of self-confident local and voluntary communities, however, need not be a "house divided." Where there is a high degree of unanimity among the various communities, the strength of individual communities can be an element of strength to the national community as a whole. It is the unitary nation, in which there are no longer any vital intermediate institutions, no small communities, no viable voluntary associations, that is totally fragmented. This is the "atomistic mass." Individuals are related to each other only *through the state*. This is the breeding ground of totalitarianism. Only vital intermediate communities can secure the individual from total state supervision and control.

A Program for Churches

The suggestion that America's Christian communities, rather than individual Americans, can begin a reconstruction of the Republic will appeal only to those Christian churches—denominations or individual congregations—who already know who they are, what they believe, and what authority they recognize. To such churches, the challenge is really to be what Christ expects of them. If they fulfil his appeal by becoming a true *body* in which the members care for and sustain one another, they will also become vital elements in the recovery of the nation. To those groups that have no higher goal than to blend into a secularized anonymity, this challenge will be meaningless. To others, who still care about the commission Christ gave them, the program is plain: reconstitute yourselves into true communities, and out of these communities will come a renewed nation. It will not come *only* out of them, for there will be other groups that gain in vigor too. America cannot exist as a community of individuals. Two hundred-odd million are too many for that. But it can exist as a fellowship of communities, if the communities know their calling and measure up to it.

Even the vicious and cruel atheist Stalin, despite all that had been done in thirty years of Communism to create "new Socialist man," found it expedient to make a truce with the churches when Hitler attacked the Soviet Union. He instinctively recognized that despite persecution and repression, the communities of Christian believers in the Soviet Union constituted a tremendous reservoir of strength and of the virtues needed to resist the Germans. American Christians should not expect, and certainly not wait for secular leaders, the news media, and the opinion-makers to come to them as Stalin did to the Orthodox bishops of Russia. If the United States ever faces a crisis like that faced by Russia in 1941, *then* such people will begin appealing to the ordinary Christians they now largely ignore or disdain as behind the times, parochial, and reactionary. But when such a crisis is on us, it will be too late to do the things we have been discussing.

Christians in America should not hesitate to seek the reinforcement and invigoration of their own confessional and even congregation unity, cohesiveness, and community sense, as though this in some way would detract from national unity in a secular society. A secular society with no world view *has* no unity unless it be the unity of the atomistic mass established by totalitarian state control. A nation of vital communities will not be a monolithic unity, but it will have the vitality it needs to face the challenges of our closing century. Without such communities, there can be no spontaneous national vitality. The only alternative to them is state-enforced conformity and a state attempt to propagandize the people into a massive national effort.

It is often said that a free society cannot exist unless free individuals exist in it. This is true: it is a necessary condition of freedom, but not a sufficient one. Between the strong, free society we seek and the free individual that each of us would like to be—and that each Christian is in Christ—there must be intermediate institutions. Strengthening and supporting them, despite their variety and plurality, is not harmful to a free society. It is a barrier to totalitarianism and a condition for freedom. Christians cannot expect the militant secularists who seek to reduce all social and educational expressions to their own spiritually indifferent humanism to agree and to seek actively to promote the vitality of churches. But we can recognize that this is the fact, and we can promote our own fellowship, cohesiveness, and distinctives without any qualms that thereby we harm the nation. In fact, we strengthen it. If even such a man as Stalin, under pressure, could recognize this truth in the USSR, we ought not to be unable to see it ourselves.

18

Applications

For, as things are, you have fewer enemies because of the multitude of the Christians, when nearly all the citizens you have in nearly all the cities are Christian.

Tertullian
Apology

Writing to the magistrates of the Roman Empire, the African Christian Tertullian argued that both they and the Empire were progressively safer and more secure because of the large number of God-fearing, law-abiding Christians under Roman jurisdiction. The Christians of Tertullian's day were successfully doing what only a few church fellowships are doing in America today: they were giving their members a sense of identity, a set of values, and a feeling of security that enabled them to be upright, peaceable, and industrious inhabitants of the Empire, even of a pagan Empire. Nevertheless, what he wrote in the year 197 holds true even today, in 1981. Society and its magistrates have fewer enemies as the number of Christians increases. This has been found to be true in the Soviet Union and Eastern Europe, where the industry and productivity of Christians is recognized even as efforts are made to limit their numbers and restrict their influence.

At the time of the Supreme Court decisions on school prayer and Bible-reading, many people commented that our American government was adopting an attitude that paralleled that of the Soviet Union and the Communist nations of Eastern Europe. In fact, the "separation of church and state" goes *farther* in the United States than in Eastern Europe, where the salary of the offically recognized clergy is paid by the state. (The reason, of course, is not to aid the churches, but because the Communist governments desire, first, to keep the clergy under close observation, so that they will not get out of hand, and second, to limit excuses for any kind of fundraising not organized by the state.) Thus in both the United States and the Union of Soviet Socialist Republics—but not in most of Western Europe—the "separation of church and state" is interpreted to mean that religion, religious acts and concepts, is barred from admission to premises controlled by the state. The state does not permit recognition of religion in schools, except for purely "objective" study. In the USSR such "objective" study is uniformly hostile; in the United States this is frequently the case. There is to be no consideration of religious ideas, or even of social and ethical teachings with their origins in the religious heritage, in public policy deliberation. Because the USSR is officially atheistic, while the United States remains deeply aware of its Christian heritage, it may be *more* difficult to honor an ethical or moral principle of Christian origin in America than in Russia.

The United States is currently going through a period of discrimination against the majority. In practice, of course, it is difficult for any society not ruled by massive coercion and police power to discriminate against the majority of its citizens for a long period of time. Thus much of the American antidiscrimination legislation that actually amounts to reverse discrimination against the white majority, or against males, has more rhetorical impact than real effect. In the realm of ideas, however, this antimajority discrimination is strong and perniciously effective.

It is taken for granted as a fact of American political life that members of a minority have the right to assert the special interests of their group and to demand special consideration for it. Thus every black elected to public office, whether in a district where the majority is black, or where it is white, is automatically expected to be a spokesman for black special interests. This is not necessarily wrong. However, it is also assumed that no whites will speak openly for white special interests. Those that do so usually have to camouflage their intent in vague generalizations, and when their opponents and the media penetrate the disguise, accusations of "racism" and "bigotry" will soon be raised. A Jew elected to public office is expected to defend the interests of Jews in America, and more so, of Jews abroad, and even of a sovereign state with which we have no formal national ties, Israel. Many Americans of Irish ancestry are quick to defend the Republican cause in British-ruled Northern Ireland itself. It is rare for them to be critized as though such international taking of sides were wrong—which is a matter of opinion —or on the grounds that it interferes with American foreign policy,

206

which it certainly does. Christians, by contrast, are virtually pledged *not* to speak for Christian interests and concerns in America. And with a few honorable exceptions, they have little or nothing to say of the plight of Christians in other lands.

It is absolutely essential for the Christians of America first of all to think enough and understand themselves and their responsibility to God, to the church, and to their fellow Christians, and second, to think through and understand their duty to society and their responsibilities as citizens in the light of their calling as Christians. Such a reflective stock-taking would certainly tend to reduce the number of Americans who claim strong and serious ties with historic Christianity and with a distinct Christian fellowship. But those who concluded that their commitment and loyalties really do belong to Christ and his church would then be so much clearer about the implications of their faith that they would begin to have that health-giving influence in American society that early Christians claimed for their church in the Roman Empire.

An End to the Wall of Silence

Ever since Thomas Jefferson wrote to a delegation of Connecticut Baptists concerning the "wall of separation" between church and state, various influences have been at work to make it as high and as thick as possible. The result is that where the ethical precepts of biblical law or the moral teachings of Christ are involved, a wall of silence now reigns in Congress, the state legislatures, the courts, and the schools—in short, everywhere the state rules. Biblical sayings and the teachings of Christ are frequently used for rhetorical effect, particularly by politicians of a particular ethnic and sociological background. But to cite a biblical commandment or a word of Christ as a reason for passing a law? Outrageous! Yet by common consent of all Americans, the Mosaic Law is the foundation not merely of religious justice, but of human justice per se. And Jesus Christ is widely acknowledged to be the greatest, or one of the greatest, teachers of all time. Arthur S. Flemming, former president of the National Council of Churches and Secretary of Health and Human Services under Eisenhower, then chairman of the United States Commission on Civil Rights, maintained in a major report that government may enact no laws for which it cannot give a "wholly secular" reason.[1] What

---

[1] *Constitutional Aspects of the Right to Limit Childbearing*, United States Commission on Civil Rights, Washington, 1975, p. 27. Dr. Flemming personally endorsed this commission view in House hearings in March 1976.

this means is that the "wall of separation" has become a _wall of silence_. Christians outside of the legislatures are not permitted to put forward any principles or ideas of Christian origin, or if they do, they must seek to cloak them in generalities and humanistic slogans. Christians presently in the legislatures must refrain from putting forward any view for which they have an even partly religious reason, or, if they do—as some through conviction or passion actually do from time to time—they will be derided by their opponents or in the national media for an attempt to "impose" their morality on others. Jimmy Carter's son, during his father's campaign for the Democratic nomination for the presidency, stated that the governor did not wish to "inflict" his morality on others. It is always dangerous to read too much into a choice of words that may be inadvertent, but it is certainly true that many Christians in public life are made to feel that to speak out as Christians is to "inflict" something on the rest of society—even when the majority of that rest shares the same general sentiments.

Christians in political life and out of it should adopt a deliberate policy of breaching the "wall of silence" that has been erected around the church to keep it from admonishing the state. Can anyone reasonably object if a political leader says: "I have learned from Jesus Christ and from the Bible to think of every human life as valuable. Hence I cannot endorse legislation that finds no 'compelling state interest'[2] in the protection of unwanted lives and therefore treats them as totally expendable. I would like to share this insight with you, my colleagues, and with my constituents." One may argue, reject the insight, or even fail to re-elect a person holding such views, but one cannot reasonably charge him with "inflicting" his religious views. When someone clearly states that he believes something to be morally wrong, but that because this is a religiously motivated view, he will nevertheless endorse its continuation at public expense, he deserves not praise for his clear separation of politics and morality, but criticism for his apparent hypocrisy.[3] If Christians are unwilling to break down this wall of silence they have no one but themselves to blame for the fact that a society that in its great majority professes a measure of allegiance to Christ now reflects his ethical teachings less than other societies that are officially atheistic. What is needed is not more Congressional prayer breakfasts before

[2]The terminology is that of Associate Supreme Court Justice Harry A. Blackmun in _Roe v. Wade_.

[3]Senator Lowell P. Weicker of Connecticut has repeatedly given such reasons, in public as well as in personal correspondence with the author, for his endorsement of _Roe v. Wade_ despite his "personal" condemnation of abortion as the taking of human life. More recently Weicker has stated that Congress should have "nothing to do" with Judeo-Christian morality.

Congress opens for the day, but a readiness on the part of the Congressmen returning from those breakfasts to share with their colleagues and constituents the insights they claim to receive. We would not think it strange or unacceptable for a Congressman to quote something from Karl Marx in explaining a particular view. Why should it be unacceptable to quote Moses or Jesus Christ?

Since it is clearly unreasonable to expect those already in office and accustomed to respecting the traditional "wall of silence" to begin to break it down, individual Christians in a position to make themselves heard have a responsibility to begin to assert their right to share their insights with fellow Americans in public debate. Thought control may prevail and Christian concepts be proscribed in totalitarian dictatorships, but this is not yet the case in the United States and should and need not be.

Justice, Not Formalism

Both lawyers and theologians are famous for their ability to take refuge in formal concepts and overlook reality. Many American legislators and judges, in dealing with the Constitution and lesser laws, take refuge in formal concepts in such a way as to avoid examining the substantial matter at hand. Slogans such as "freedom of choice," "the right to privacy," and "individual decision" are solemnly intoned to justify the denial of human rights in certain areas, the oft-cited case of abortion on demand being only the most flagrant. But such slogans would carry no weight where other concerns of government are involved. We do not expect such formal concepts to supersede fundamental principles of justice, such as the laws against murder. Neither "freedom of choice" nor "the right to privacy" could successfully be argued as defense against a murder charge. Even where secondary principles of justice are concerned, such as the obligation to contribute by paying of taxes to the support of community expenses, neither "freedom of choice" nor "the right to privacy" can be argued. In fact, in mid-1976 decisions the United States Supreme Court further expanded the already considerable rights of the government to invade the privacy of an individual's financial transactions to assure itself that it is not being cheated of any taxes due.

It is hard to discover a common thread to explain why our courts and legislatures sometimes allow formalistic concepts to prevail, and at others are genuinely concerned with the question of justice rather than mere legal form. The legal formalities were certainly all on the side of states' rights in the original civil rights (school segregation cases, and frequently have been since then. But both the Supreme Court and the lower courts, as well as Congress, tend to inquire not into what the law actually says (formality) but into what it ought to say (justice). The only reasonable principle on which to base a government of laws is the theory that the positive laws enacted by a government correspond to some higher, ultimate law, either a law of God or a law of nature. Only if the Constitution is supposed to reflect certain ultimate values that in effect transcend it does it make sense to inquire so carefully into what is "constitutional." If the Constitution is merely positive law, namely what the original signers and ratifiers adopted, subsequently amended, then tedious inquiries into what the Constitution says today are rather pointless. It would make more sense to inquire directly into what the people want today. The American people of today are willing to consider themselves bound by a Constitution originally adopted in 1787 because they think of it as reflecting far more than the opinions of selected leaders of a small country of the later eighteenth century. They see in it the distillation and embodiment of some higher wisdom and insight. Because this is the only logical basis for considering the Constitution more important than the regulations we might enact in Congress or by popular vote today, it is more reasonable, when the Constitution is silent or gives no answer, to ask directly what justice requires, rather than to attempt to derive a just course of action by a complicated argument from a document that does not deal with the issue.

This too, like a proposal to revise the Fourteenth Amendment, must appear as an affront to the mythology of the American state. Yet it is high time that these forbidden words were said, and said by precisely those who know that there is a higher law than the Constitution and an ultimate Authority over the Founding Fathers. As Christians in America, we should not undertake to prescribe to our fellow Americans what they must deem just. But we can at least urge upon them the necessity, openly and intelligently, to seek justice rather than formalism in the complex issues of the day.

From Theories to Practices

Americans as a people, and American Christians among them, have a distaste for theory and an eagerness to proceed to practicality. Pragmatism (from Greek *pragma,* deed, fact) is a typically American attitude. One of the principal reasons for some of the problems we experience with our government and its increasing control of our lives is that we do not have a clear vision (theory, from Greek *theoria*, a viewing) of the state, its legitimate role, and its limitations. It is important to make changes in practice, but it is also important to develop an adequate theory of the state, by which we need mean no more than a clear vision of what it is and where it is going. Ideas shape policies. Therefore it *is* crucial to understand the way in which the modern state first devours intermediate structures and local communities and finally proceeds to turn free individuals into an atomistic mass, and to have a concept of what principles will stem and reverse these trends. Having developed such a theory or vision, we will then seek to carry it out by introducing certain practical reforms in law, government, and administration. Applications of the theory are necessary first of all so that it will produce results and not remain merely an interesting way of analyzing reality. Second, applications are necessary as a check on the validity and workability of our theory, and in order to perfect it by observing where it works out adequately and where deficiencies appear.

In a work of this length, it is not possible to suggest a comprehensive program of applications, but a few are in order. These may suggest others, and serve as test cases for the further development of our vision of American government and society.

The Limits of the State

The American constitutional system is one of the few in the modern world that is based on the conviction of the limited competence of the state. The state is not supposed to be able to do everything. For this reason our form of government does not absolutize the state or give it all power. There are so-called "reserved powers" that remain with the people as opposed to government. Theologically speaking, we know that the state is subordinate to God, who alone is fully sovereign. The sovereignty of a secular government is always limited by the absolute sovereignty of God. This concept is recognized implicitly in the United States Constitution when it limits the powers it concedes to government, and explicitly in many traditional American forms, such as pledging allegiance to "one nation, under God." How can it be recognized practically?

If the state is not absolute, there are things within its territory that do not belong to it. If everything that exists or is produced within the borders of the state ultimately belongs to the state, to be disposed of as

211

it sees fit, then the state is in effect claiming absoluteness. The state lays effective claims to goods by taxing them. Until now, the state has refrained from attempting to tax all the wealth that exists or is produced in the country. Thus many types of tax deductions are allowed: among others, interest expense, medical expense, taxes to other jurisdictions, and contributions to carefully defined tax-exempt organizations. The theory behind the personal *exemption* from tax is the idea that a person ought to be able to feed and maintain himself and his dependents *before* being called on to contribute to the general community. The idea behind deductions is a bit different. Either they are considered as subtractions from income (as in the case of interest payments), or payments in support of socially desirable goals that the government might otherwise have to finance independently. Home mortgage interest deductions are an example of both considerations.

It has been argued that *deductibility* of certain expenses from income amounts to a form of government subsidy of the project where they are incurred. These deductions are therefore referred to as "tax expenditures," in that the government refrains from collecting taxes on them, although it could properly do so. There is a measure of plausibility to the argument, but if one follows it through, it can be seen to depend on the theory that all the wealth within the state belongs first of all to the state. Others may make use of it only by the state's leave. The federal budget would then be the equal of the Gross National Product; a portion of this GNP would be collected as taxes and spent directly, and the remainder, not collected, would be spent by its owners as an indirect "tax expenditure" of the government.

Most of us would object to the view that all the wealth that exists within the boundaries of the state is the property of the government and is collected as taxes or left to its owners at the discretion of the state. We all know that government *produces* nothing. It can only collect and distribute the fruits of the production of others. Government does have to reach stewardship decisions concerning all the wealth that exists or is produced within its jurisdiction, but it need not and should not claim that all wealth belongs first to it.

At what point can the government be expected to limit the claim that all that exists within its territory belongs first of all to it? A government that claims everything is economically totalitarian, and will probably not hesitate to become totalitarian in every respect. The United States government does not yet claim title to all the wealth that exists within its boundaries, although there is less and less wealth that it does not claim the right to administer, tax, redistribute, or even confiscate.

212

The Importance of the Tithe

If the nation is to be seen as in any sense "under God," then there must be some practical area in which government does not claim to be absolute. One very important area, both symbolically and practically, is that of what the Bible and Christian tradition calls "the first fruits," better known as the tithe. At the present time, contributions made to churches, as to a variety of other nonprofit institutions, are tax-deductible, up to a figure of approximately one-third of one's gross income. It is frequently argued that the federal government, by not taxing people on the income they so contribute, in effect supports the institutions receiving the contributions. This then would be an example of a "tax expenditure" to support churches. Approached in this way, it would be possible to make a case that the deductibility of church contributions constitutes support of the church by the state, and thus is an "establishment of religion" and unconstitutional. But this argument is valid only on the assumption already noted, namely, that all that exists within the state belongs first of all to the government. This a totalitarian assumption, and it is not one that Americans would readily accept, if it were put to them in such language.

If the state does not own everything, but something less, what is the effective limit of its ownership? Unless there is some external limit, both symbolic and practical, the only check to the acquisitiveness of the state is its self-restraint. And the self-restraint of the state cannot be depended upon in the absence of strong pressures from the people. The biblical tradition, out of which our civilization comes, is very explicit at this point: the earth is the Lord's and the fullness thereof (Psalm 24:1). All things belong to God; the "first fruits" are "unto the Lord." When a wage-earner gives a portion of his wages to the Lord's work *before* taxes, this is not a tax expenditure on the part of the state to support that religious cause. It is simply recognition that the first claim is God's. In our tradition, the standard — although not mandatory — first-fruit offering is the tithe, a tenth. If a person wished to contribute two-tenths or three-tenths of his income before taxes to the church, the government might ask him to pay taxes on the second and third tithes prior to contributing them. But if government were to tax the first tithe, that first fruit that in our whole spiritual tradition is so deeply symbolic of the sovereignty and ownership rights of God over the earth, it would be claiming to be absolute.

It is reasonable and proper for Christians in America to defend the principle that the State must halt before the tithe. It cannot tax an individual's tithe without implicitly laying claim to the totality of all the wealth produced within its borders. This is an absolutist claim that would constitute the end of limited government in America. From the perspective of merely limiting government, we could introduce a principle that would make a certain part of an individual's income immune from taxation—the practice exists already, but it is not a fundamental *principle* of American government. But we are not interested just in limiting government in some arbitrary fashion, but in limiting it vis-à-vis that which is greater than the state, namely over against God.

To assert that the state has no right to the first tithe of an individual's income if it is contributed to a religious cause might of course involve the government in making a distinction between authentic religions and fronts posing as such. It could put the government in the position of recognizing or authenticating a religion as bona fide, which would come closer than desirable to that "establishment of religion" that the First Amendment prohibits. This problem could be avoided by exempting the first tithe if contributed to any benevolent, tax-exempt organization, with the understanding that Christians and members of other religions would be free to make their "first-fruit" offerings to God, while other Americans could contribute it or not, as they saw fit, to nonreligious charities qualifying under the law.

It is important to protect the tithe from the state in order to protect the state from its own tendency to become absolutist. Such a principle should be seen as a guaranteed right (it already is a right, but not yet guaranteed as a principle). Once so understood and recognized, it will then have to be utilized by Christians in large numbers. Systematic tithing by members of America's churches would of course provide most of those bodies with far greater income than they presently have (apart from those exemplary bodies where tithing is already the practice). And this would make it possible for religious communities to take over much more of the practical task of caring for their infirm and handicapped members. Since religious and charitable bodies generally operate far more economically than federal or state welfare, one could also expect that widespread tithing, if it resulted in a higher level of church-related assistance to a substantial portion of those now receiving welfare, would cut the government's welfare burden and thus indirectly reduce taxes. Self-help is frequently preached as an alternative to government assistance. However, there are many citizens who simply cannot help themselves, at least not at first. The intervention of vigorous, competent intermediate structures to assist them would not be self-help, but it would come closer to self-help than welfare; it would have a human, social, and community dimension that government welfare lacks. Certain religious communities already do this rather well. It should be a goal of each Christian congregation that no member of the fellowship should be left without necessary assistance as long as the community is in any sense able to help.

The theory of the tithe will limit government symbolically, and such symbols are important. The practice of tithing will limit government practically, both by removing a portion of the public wealth from its administrative stewardship and also, if properly used by the receiving communities, by removing a substantial portion of burdens such as welfare and education from government's shoulders.

Equal Weights and Equal Measures

The world of biblical times was not sophisticated economically, although it did have amazing resemblances to our own. But there is little in the Bible that relates to banking, credit, or international finance. It might be thought that it would have little guidance to offer in the area of national economics. There is at least one principle that is worthy of attention: the Bible exhorts us to maintain "equal weights and equal measures," and condemns the merchants who make "the ephah [measure of volume for selling] small and the shekel [measure of weight for money] great" (Amos 8:5). The reference is to the merchant who gives short quantity to his buyers but demands an excessive weight of silver in payment. Today we have an elaborate series of controls to make sure that merchants do not give short weight. But the merchant no longer weighs the money to determine its value. Value is set by the government that creates the currency and the elaborate fiscal system that maintains and regulates it. And government itself is engaged, in a very dramatic way, in making the "shekel great." Through inflation, a phenomenon caused in large measure by the manner in which government finances its affairs and manages the currency it requires us to use, the government requires us to pay more and more shekels for the same ephah of merchandise. The continual decline in the value of money, which is nothing but the government's promissory notes, is accompanied by and to some extent causes a continuing decline in the value of promises of all kinds. If we wish to have a biblical vision of justice, certainly one element of it involves a government that keeps its promises as it expects its citizens to keep theirs—and this implies a currency that is far more solid and stable than the U.S. dollar in the 1980s.

215

The Return of Punishment

If the maintenance of justice is one of the fundamental tasks of a lawful government under God, then one of the principal aspects of justice is the punishment of evildoers. Paul's concept that civil authority is instituted by God is predicated on the function of that authority in maintaining justice. Our biblical heritage offers several principles that should be reflected in the punitive aspect of justice: punishment should be suited to the offense, it should be swift, it should not be humiliating, and it should be exemplary. As justice is practiced in America today, all four of these principles are regularly violated. Sentences are more often than not based on anything else but the offense: plea bargaining, previous record, willingness to turn state's evidence, to name but a few considerations. Without saying that such factors ought never to be taken into consideration, it should be evident that a variation in length of sentences from four months to thirty years for similar offenses, as was the case with the Watergate defendants, is hard to reconcile with the biblical principle that the penalty should match the offense. Punishment in America is terribly slow. If it does arrive, it is frequently humiliating: jail can be a very degrading experience, far from a rehabilitation, and it is very hard if not impossible for most ex-convicts to regain their dignity and honor. Finally, the tremendous delays, the capriciousness in sentencing, and the relatively small likelihood that an offender will actually be punished greatly reduce the exemplary or deterrent effect of punishment. Much of the argument against capital punishment is based on the unverified and probably mistaken view that it does not act as a deterrent. Even if it did not, it would still be proper to punish some crimes by execution, "for blood defiles the land, and the land cannot be cleansed of the blood that is shed therein, but by the blood of him that shed it" (Numbers 35:33). The Bible does state that capital punishment has a deterrent effect (Deuteronomy 19:20). A society that takes biblical principles seriously will not hesitate to believe what the ordinary citizen has always known, that capital punishment of a murderer does cause many if not all to refrain from imitating his crime.

Straightforwardness

Police officers, social workers, and even jurists are often amazed at the practicality of biblical precepts in the areas of justice and law enforcement. A willingness to consider biblical principles as a vital and meaningful part of our heritage in public policy debate would bring such debate back into the realm of reality where it can be understood by ordinary people. It would lead to decisions that can be respected; it would be a major step to the recovery of *voluntary* obedience, the recognition of that true authority without which freedom is impossible.

19

Blessings and Curses: The Choice

> When the righteous are in authority, the people rejoice: but when the wicked beareth rule, the people mourn.
>
> *Proverbs 29:2*

The Blessings

As the nation celebrated the two hundredth anniversary of its independence, much that is frightful, shameful, and troublesome in our history was at least temporarily forgotten. The strife and controversies of the Vietnam years, the humiliation and self-righteousness of Watergate, and even the passions of the presidential campaign were momentarily forgotten. Taking stock of their past, even those Americans who are most critical of the status quo, of the Establishment, of middle-class morality and mediocrity, the consumer society, and so many other things, reflected on our accomplishments and admitted—or actually proclaimed—that the United States has much to be proud of in its two-hundred-year history.

America has never been a covenant nation in the sense that this was true of biblical Israel. The United States has never formally established Christianity, either in any of its varieties or in general, as the official creed of the nation, as many other countries have done. But there probably has been no other country in the history of the world that was as conscious of God's providence in its history as the American Colonies and the Republic that grew out of them. And there is no country in the

219

consciousness of the rest of the world that so strongly represents Christianity—that carries so many of the hopes of Christians, or calls down such condemnation on itself when it seems to travesty the ideals that Christians profess.

The Bible frequently speaks of the people or nation *called by the Lord*. Properly speaking, this terminology applies only to Israel in the Old Covenant and to the church as the New Testament people in the Christian era. It does not apply to the United States as a "chosen nation." Yet there is no doubt that the United States, in two hundred years of history, has enjoyed blessings far above anything that we might properly expect as the result of our own labors, or even the natural wealth of our vast land. To what can we attribute this? The Bible also knows the concept of the people that is *called by the name of the Lord*. In many cases the two concepts are identical, yet there is a difference. And there is a real sense in which we must say that, although America and Americans are not called by the Lord, they are called by the name of the Lord. That is, this country and its people are identified in the world's eyes with Christ and his church. Its successes are in no small measure seen as indication of his blessing; its failures as evidence of his displeasure, or weakness; most important, when we fail to live up to the standards we set for ourselves, or the standards that others would expect us to exhibit as a "Christian" nation, we are guilty of the offense with which Paul charged Jews of his day: the name of God is blasphemed, i.e., mocked, scorned, among the peoples of the world because of us (Romans 2:24).

As any impartial reading of our historic documents will quickly show, this nation was founded with a trust in the God of the Bible, the God of Israel and of the Christian church. It was part of our original purpose and vision to obey his laws and to establish his righteousness. The great national convulsion that shook our nation to its foundations, the Civil War, was fought because our secular statement of principles, the Constitution, did not give to all human beings in America that freedom and dignity to which, according to our religious understanding of the laws of Nature and Nature's God, they were entitled. The motto "In God We Trust" was not a mere rhetorical flourish. It was not one of the devoutly biblical Presbyterians or Congregationalists or Epsicopalians present but the Deist Benjamin Franklin who reminded a deadlocked Constitutional Convention of the words of Psalm 127: "Except the Lord build the house, they labor in vain that build it: except the Lord keep the city, the watchman waketh but in vain." For the better part of two centuries, we enjoyed a prosperity, a security, and a success unparalleled in the history of nations. It was as though the Lord were indeed building our house. For a small part of our first two centuries, we are becoming acutely conscious that something is going wrong.

July Fourth, 1976, was a Sunday, and Bicentennial services were held in churches all over this country. There was much thanksgiving, much joy, much nostalgia. And yet in many churches there was an apprehension — rather like that so common in secular circles, although of different origin — concerning the future. There is this feeling that, regardless of who guides the destinies of America in the third century, something is missing, and that without it, we may labor in vain and watch in vain.

The Rebellion

In the United States in mid-1976, it was completely evident that the highest authorities, those who create "the Law of the Land," no longer acknowledge that there is such a thing as a Creator who has endowed men with anything, let alone with unalienable rights. There are countless illustrations of the nationwide turning from God, in institutions and public policies, that threatens to undo all the individual seeking of God, even the public pieties and personal testimonies of those in our highest office. But one incident that occurred on the eve of the Bicentennial celebration typifies more than anything else the official repudiation of God and his law on the part of a nation where the majority still believe in him and fear his judgment.

In what future historians will no doubt see as a macabre prelude to the Fourth of July celebrations, the United States Supreme Court drew the logical conclusions from an earlier decision. In *Danforth* v. *Planned Parenthood* (July 1, 1976), it reinforced the position it took in 1973 in *Roe* v. *Wade*. In effect, it established the right to abortion — the destruction of unborn, developing human life — as the only constitutional privilege that the state cannot infringe or limit for any reason. In addition, it transcends paternal and parental rights. The decision is complex, but three salient features stand out: (1) The father of an unborn child has no voice in whether to prevent its killing by abortion. The criterion of "wantedness" is the only consideration, and it holds only for the mother. (2) Although a minor girl could not have her ears pierced without their written consent, her parents have nothing to say about whether the state provides an abortion — even though after the abortion they will presumably be responsible to care for her in the event of complications. The evi-

221

dent implication of this decision is that the "right" to destroy the unborn is so absolute that even those who for other purposes are not considered to have reached the age of independent judgment must be allowed to exercise it at will. (3) Finally, the highly controverted technique of abortion by saline injection, known to be agonizing to the fetus and to take several hours to kill it, cannot be forbidden, because "it is the most common technique."*

What has the Court done by this? First of all, it has shown its contempt for the sensibilities of at least one half of the people of America, who — as repeated polls have shown — are highly agitated about the moral and ethical aspects of abortion, despite rather concerned efforts on the part of the media and public officials to mislead the public as to the nature and extent of the present situation. Second, it has shown its contempt for all those scholars, from Americans such as John Hart Ely, Archibald Cox, and David Louisell, to foreign jurists such as the members of the West German Federal Constitutional Court, who have pointed to defects in its biological knowledge and legal logic. And finally it has seen fit, in the name of a principle that can be found in the Constitution only with the help of a very vivid imagination, to destroy some of the fundamental relations upon which human society is based. In his earlier decision, *Roe* v. *Wade,* Associate Justice Harry A. Blackmun, author of the majority decision in *Danforth* v. *Planned Parenthood,* appealed to the views of "ancient religion" — Roman paganism — to support his endorsement of abortion on demand. In the present case, he makes no appeal to paganism, because not even paganism would support such an affront to the very order of nature. Parents are to have no authority over their own unborn or immature offspring. The father, who shares his heredity with the child just as does the mother, has no voice in whether the child may live or must die: he has been placed in a position of absolute inferiority and total dependence on the willingness of his wife to protest his — and her — posterity against the blandishments of a consumer society and a government that tells her it is safer, neater, and more economical to abort children than to bear and raise them. In the case of the pregnant minor, the parents, who are expected to be responsible for her, are denied the right to say whether she may or should be submitted to an operation the medical and psychological impact of which is far from negligible.

---

*This decision is too involved to treat in detail here, but it seemed relevant to bring up some of its salient points, because it so clearly indicates the Supreme Court's apparent determination to destroy the laws of Nature and Nature's God and to replace them with its own.

Justice Blackmun will be fortunate indeed if future historians do not characterize him as the Herod of the Bicentennial. For a nation to inaugurate the observance of its bicentennial celebration with a new decree condemning still further millions of its unborn children to death is, to use Calvin's expression, "almost monstrous." It is hard to comprehend what motives may have driven the Justice — a title that becomes almost sardonic in light of the justice done by some who bear it — so to reiterate and reinforce the atrocious errors of his earlier decision. The Herod of history, in his slaughter of the infants of Bethlehem, at least thought that he was doing it to preserve his crown. Can it be that Justice Blackmun felt impelled to do what he has done rather than risk his reputation by admitting even the slightest error or exaggeration in his earlier decision? If so, this is an attitude reminiscent of the man who chose him for his present baleful eminence, former President Nixon, who allowed himself to be driven from office rather than admit, in the least of his official acts, to having behaved contrary to justice or morality.

Danforth v. *Planned Parenthood* is a touchstone of official America's repudiation of the God who has blessed us heretofore, not merely because it goes beyond ancient paganism in contravening the very structures of human nature and society, but because it immediately brings upon our people what God describes as punishment for turning from him: the cursing of the fruit of our bodies, the "begetting of sons and daughters" that we will not enjoy.

The Curses

The Deuteronomic blessing has been greatly fulfilled in two hundred years of American history:

> Blessed shall be the fruit of thy body, and the fruit of thy ground, and the fruit of thy cattle, the increase of thy kine, and the flocks of thy sheep.
>
> Blessed shall be thy basket and thy store. . . .
>
> The Lord shall cause thine enemies that rise up against thee to be smitten before thee seven ways. . . .
>
> And all people of the earth shall see that thou art called by the name of the Lord; and they shall be afraid of thee.
>
> And the Lord shall make thee plenteous in goods, in the fruit of thy body, and in the fruit of thy cattle, and in the fruit of thy ground, in the land which the Lord sware unto thy fathers to give thee.

The Lord shall open unto thee his good treasure, the heaven to give the rain to thy land in his season, and to bless all the work of thine hand: and thou shalt lend unto many nations, and thou shalt not borrow.

And the Lord shall make thee the head, and not the tail; and thou shalt be above only, and thou shalt not be beneath; if that thou hearken unto the commandments of the Lord thy God, which I command thee this day, to observe and to do them.

Deuteronomy 28:4-13

All these things Americans have experienced, almost to the jot and the tittle. World War II offered signal examples of the enemy "coming out one way, and fleeing seven ways." Today we are at the beginning of the curses, which also are beginning to apply with almost word-for-word exactness:

But it shall come to pass, if thou wilt not hearken unto the voice of the Lord thy God, to observe to do all his commandments and his statutes which I command thee this day; that all these curses shall come upon thee, and overtake thee:

Cursed shalt thou be in the city, and cursed shalt thou be in the field.

Cursed shall be thy basket and thy store.

Cursed shall be the fruit of thy body, and the fruit of thy land, the increase of thy kine, and the flocks of thy sheep.

Cursed shalt thou be when thou comest in, and cursed shalt thou be when thou goest out. . . .

The Lord shall cause thee to be smitten before thine enemies: thou shalt go out one way against them, and flee seven ways before them: and shalt be removed into all the kingdoms of the earth. . . .

Thou shalt betroth a wife, and another man shall lie with her: thou shalt build a house, and thou shalt not dwell therein: thou shalt plant a vineyard, and shalt not gather the grapes thereof. . . .

The fruit of thy land, and all thy labours, shall a nation which thou knowest not eat up: and thou shalt be only oppressed and crushed alway:

So that thou shalt be mad for the sight of thine eyes which thou shalt see. . . .

Thou shalt beget sons and daughters, but thou shalt not enjoy them, for they shall go into captivity. . . .

The stranger that is within thee shall get up above thee very high, and thou shalt come down very low.

He shall lend to thee, and thou shalt not lend to him: he shall be the head, and thou shalt be the tail. . . .

Because thou servest not the Lord thy God with joyfulness and with gladness of heart, for the abundance of all things:

Therefore shalt thou serve thine enemies which the Lord shall send against thee, in hunger and in thirst, and in nakedness, and in want of all things: and he shall put a yoke of iron upon thy neck, until he have destroyed thee.

Deuteronomy 28:15-47

These blessings and curses make solemn reading at any time, but particularly so at this point in our nation's history. In a July 5, 1976 address at Thomas Jefferson's home in Monticello, President Ford said that this is not the occasion to lament our shortcomings. When shall we lament them? When "all these curses shall come upon thee, and shall pursue thee, and shall overtake thee, till thou be destroyed" (Deuteronomy 28:45)? In the Vietnam War, concluded by something ironically called "peace with honor," at least for a few months, it is hard to deny that America went out with superior numbers and superior equipment "one way, and fled seven ways." We may praise ourselves in our Bicentennial, and other nations may send congratulations. Indeed, there is much to praise, and there are the niceties of diplomacy. But we cannot obscure the fact that the world over, we have become, as the curses say, "an astonishment, and a byword." We are still admired, at least by some, But we are also ridiculed and held in contempt, and it would be rash to claim that our admirers are more numerous than those who despise us.

The Deuteronomic fates are overtaking us, and replacing the blessings. Of course, divorce in America is "social progress," and "a higher standard for marriage." Adultery is "swinging," "wife-swapping," or "marriage therapy." But the curse still is there. It is happening, just as predicted, even if we think that it is by our choice and is progress. We build a house, but do not dwell in it. This is "mobility," "freedom." But as we observe what the rapid mobility and transience of our way of life does to children, how it prevents us from establishing roots, we are beginning to suspect why it can be seen in Deuteronomy as a curse. When a family manages to keep a house until retirement, economic and tax developments frequently make it impossible for the older couple to retain it, even though it is finally paid for.

America's agricultural production is the wonder of the world. We can feed ourselves many times over. We can sell to those who have money, and generously we give to millions of those who have none. And we also give to those who have money, but are also able to put certain kinds of pressure on us. The now infamous 1972 wheat deal might more properly be called a "grain tribute" than a grain sale. The chief benefit America received from it was a contribution to the size of the majority of Nixon's short-lived election victory. There is truth to the wry joke, cracked when a Russian circus was on tour in America, that this is bread and circuses again — they get the bread, we get the circus. Truly, "The fruit of thy land, and all thy labours, shall a nation which thou knowest not eat up . . ."

For eighteen decades we have experienced, almost word for word, the blessings promised to those who keep the commandments of God. During this period Americans were derided by sophisticated Europeans as a rustic nation of Puritans, concerned with narrow-minded morality and obsessed with respectability. We have finally "outgrown" that image. Now America, if it cannot claim to be in the lead, is at least well towards the front in the decline of the West. And during the past two decades we have begun to experience the curses — again, almost word for word. Are we going to continue "till thou be destroyed"?

The Choice

A standard feature of popular American mythology is the fear of "Puritanism." Whatever else the Puritans stood for, this much is clear: they were committed to the conviction that God is sovereign in human affairs, and that his Law should be the standard for our laws. The charge that the United States was "puritanical" was never really appropriate, to the extent that it meant that as a nation we applied, or pretended to apply, strict Puritan standards of sexual morality in daily life. America may have been Victorian or petit bourgeois, but neither of those phenomena was particularly *Puritan*. But in fact America *was* puritanical in that our public laws reflected, and were intended to reflect, principles of biblical law. Puritanism as a religious movement is a thing of the past, but puritanical designs to legislate morality and to force the whole society into a more biblical pattern are attributed to other religious groups — to the Roman Catholics, to the fundamentalists, to the less strident evangelicals. It is almost a truism of American political orthodoxy that such a thing would not merely be bad, but totally unacceptable, foreign to the whole spirit of American independence. But is that the case? As a matter of fact, it is fundamental to American independence that the laws of mankind, and the regulations of government, *ought* to be conformed to the laws of "Nature and Nature's God."

226

Our constitutional institutions embody safeguards against any real or presumed threats of religious control, in the sense of a theocratic or caesaropapal system. Religion is not a threat to free America, nor is any church or group of churches. The real danger threatening our free institutions is that they will collapse because there is no one left with the values and virtues necessary to sustain them. And those free institutions are being perverted, sometimes consciously, sometimes unwittingly, to destroy the source of those values and virtues.

There are many who fear that organized religion in America might aspire to impose a biblical view on the nation as a whole, in a form of religious orthodoxy, defining the terms of political discourse in America in biblical concepts just as they are defined in Communist societies in Marxist-Leninist ones. That might be a danger; there is no doubt that Christian churches, like other institutions, have frequently been intolerant of dissent when they held sufficient power to enforce conformity to their views. But the tendency to stifle dissent is a temptation to anyone with strong convictions. Should the fact that this possibility exists be a reason for non-Christians to ban biblical concepts from the political scene? And is it any reason for Christians to lay upon themselves a vow of silence?

In a democratic society, those who believe in the value of the biblical vision will recognize and respect the right of others to argue against it and to seek to limit its influence. But they will not acknowledge their right to silence all discussion of it. The real reason for the "silencing of the church" to which we have alluded is not the resistance of those outside the biblical frame of reference. In fact, many of them would prefer Christians to give them a *clearer* word, so that they could know what —if anything—Christians and their churches think and believe. No, it is Christians themselves, smug in the memory of the influence they once held in church and society, and embarrassed by the constant carping of sophisticated media against "puritanism" and "outmoded morality," who themselves play the primary role in keeping Christian values and insights out of government and public policy. Mr. Carter himself has expressed similar intentions. If Christians continue to play their almost traditional role of muzzling themselves, America will continue to have a government and a society with no freely accepted, trusted values. In Francis Schaeffer's words, ethics becomes statistics. The Supreme Court will continue to decide questions of justice on the basis of sociologists' tabulations. The nation will be left with neither the will nor the wit to stand up to those who have a vision, however twisted, of what man and society ought to be.

The real danger to America is not religious tyranny, but the tyranny of statistics and of secular administrative bureaucracy. Will the American republic experience a Tricentennial? Or even a two hundred and twenty-fourth anniversary in A.D. 2000? The reconstruction of the Republic does not depend on the imposition of dogmas, but it does depend on the recovery of the biblical vision. It was shared by the majority of our ancestors, those who fought for freedom or who chose it in preference to the tightly bound structures of Europe. It is the only vision capable of strengthening us without making prisoners of us.

Where there is no vision, the Proverb has it, the people perish. The challenge to America in the third century is to return consciously to the vision that our forefathers took so naturally: the biblical vision of God as sovereign, and of man as his fallen but redeemed creature, responsible to him. Yet the choice is not merely to return, as it were, to "the gods our fathers served." For those, as we have seen, were not always faithful representations of the God of Abraham, but rationalistic, philosophical, or humanistic images and derivations. We must do more than return "to the sources"; we must return to the Source of the sources of our liberty. There can be no more fitting challenge to America at the threshold of our third century than that given by Joshua to Israel during their conquest of the Promised Land:

> Choose you this day whom ye will serve; whether the gods which your fathers served, that were on the other side of the flood, or the gods of the Amorites, in whose land ye dwell, but as for me and my house, we will serve the Lord.
>
> *Joshua 24:15*

228

Index

232

233